READINGS FOR RESEARCH METHODS IN CRIMINOLOGY AND CRIMINAL JUSTICE

READINGS FOR RESEARCH METHODS IN CRIMINOLOGY AND CRIMINAL JUSTICE

Edited by M.L. Dantzker, Ph.D.

University of Texas—Pan American
Department of Criminal Justice

BUTTERWORTH HEINEMANN

Boston • Oxford • Auckland • Johannesburg • Melbourne • New Delhi

A member of the Reed Elsevier group

Recognizing the importance of preserving what has been written, Butterworth-Heinemann prints its books on acid-free paper whenever possible.

Butterworth-Heinemann supports the efforts of American Forests and the Global ReLeaf program in its campaign for the betterment of trees, forests, and our environment.

Library of Congress Cataloging-in-Publication Data
Readings for research methods in criminology and criminal justice / edited by M.L. Dantzker.
p. cm.
Includes bibliographical references and index.
ISBN 0-7506-7000-2 (paperback : alk. paper)
1. Criminology—Research—Methodology. 2. Criminal justice, Administration of—Research—Methodology. I. Dantzker, Mark L., 1958– .
HV6024.5.R43 1999 98-22623
364′.072—DC21 CIP

British Library Cataloguing-in-Publication Data
A catalogue record for this book is available from the British Library.

The publisher offers special discounts on bulk orders of this book.
For information, please contact:
Manager of Special Sales
Butterworth-Heinemann
225 Wildwood Avenue
Woburn, MA 01801-2041
Tel: 781-904-2500
Fax: 781-904-2620

For information on all Butterworth-Heinemann publications available, contact our World Wide Web home page at: http://www.bh.com

10 9 8 7 6 5 4 3 2 1

Printed in the United States of America

Table of Contents

Foreword

From the time we are born to the day that we die, we may experience a process we understand as learning. How we learn may be accidental or intentional. What we learn might be trivial or quite useful to our survival. What drives many of us is a desire to learn about things we are not familiar with or to learn more about what we know something about. This drive is quite evident in academic studies, whether in the natural sciences or the social sciences, in business or professional studies. In each academic discipline there is often a need to further understand how or why something works or responds as it does. In many cases, to pursue this understanding some form of *research* must be conducted.

Research, for the purpose of this text, is viewed as "an act for pursuing further knowledge of some phenomenon." The phenomena of interest here are those related to the fields of criminology and criminal justice. While not all the articles in this collection deal with a topic that may be of interest to both disciplines, how the topics are researched may be of interest to both. These articles represent a variety of methodological techniques that can be employed by students, academics, and researchers of criminology and criminal justice. Yet, they also offer some interesting topics not necessarily given much attention in the research arena.

Beginning with the first article, "Some Impressions from a Qualitative Study of Implementation of Community Policing in North Carolina," Dr. John M. Memory (University of North Carolina—Pembroke) takes a look at community policing from a perspective few researchers have yet tried—firsthand. He employs an "observation-participant" technique to examine community policing in North Carolina. This method's results lead to the offering of a qualitative article.

Dr. Laura J. Moriarty (Virginia Commonwealth University) helps understand the process of conceptualizing and operationalizing a variable in her article, "The Conceptualization and Operationalization of the Intervening Dimensions of Social Disorganization." Exploring the variable Social Disorganization, Dr. Moriarty, using telephone surveys and a random sample, demonstrates the process and means of identifying the dimensions of this variable.

What do students think about policing? Does a class in policing change their perceptions? It is questions of this nature that are explored in the third article by Dr. M.L. Dantzker (University of Texas—Pan American) and Dr. J. Eugene Waters (Georgia Southern University), "Examining Students' Perceptions of Policing—A Pre- and Post-Comparison between Students in Criminal Justice and Noncriminal Justice Courses." In seeking answers to these types of research questions, they use a pre- and post-methodology on a purposive sample.

In "Human/Cultural Diversity Training for Justice Personnel," Dr. Marilyn Chandler Ford (Volusia County Department of Corrections) and Commander Lexie Williams (Daytona Beach Police Department) survey a convenience sample of police and correctional personnel in an effort to obtain perceptions of the human/cultural diversity training required by the State of Florida. A helpful contribution is the actual questionnaire used in the study.

Considering the growing involvement of women in criminality, research examining connections between drugs and crime among women is extremely relevant. To study this growing phenomenon, Dr. Dennis J. Stevens (Mount Olive College), in "Women Offenders, Drug Addiction, and Crime," conducted survey research among a convenience sample of women inmates. Of noted interest is that the study is conducted within the confines of the prison setting.

Although a common area of study, because of its continued existence and growth in some areas, violent crime continues to be a popular topic for research. In "Measuring Violent Crime in North Carolina," Drs. Laura J. Moriarty and William V. Pelfrey (Virginia Commonwealth University) and Michael L. Vasu (North Carolina State University), look at violent crime in North Carolina using both telephone and mail surveys of a random sample of citizens. Furthermore, this article also provides a good example of the operationalization of variables.

It is common to see a plethora of research on the various aspects of police officers. However, despite their important role in the criminal justice system, the research on correctional officers is not as plentiful. Dr. Jill Gordon (Virginia Commonwealth University) adds interesting information to the literature regarding correctional officers' attitudes in "Correctional Officers' Attitudes toward Delinquents and Delinquency: Does the Type of Institution Make a Difference?" To accomplish this she employed a cross-sectional design and a purposive sample. Particularly useful is Dr. Gordon's clarity regarding the difference between the independent and dependent variables and readily recognized hypotheses.

Dr. Colleen Fitzpatrick (University of Northern Colorado) demonstrates the use of a quasi-experimetal design in "A Survey of Citizen Perceptions of Treatment and Satisfaction with a Telephone Service Option in a Rural Sheriff's Department." This case study includes questionnaire construction and research questions revolving around an option to police agencies that could very well be a future trend for providing service to citizens.

As noted previously, the research into women and criminality is still in its infancy. In "Women as Organized Criminals: An Examination of the Numbers Gambling Industry in New York City," Dr. Donald R. Liddick, Jr. (University of Pittsburgh—Greensburg) uses secondary data to examine one area of criminality that women are seldom connected with but in which they apparently have had larger roles than previously perceived.

The use of secondary data to research a subject is supported in the study of federal asset forfeiture in "A Cross-sectional Quantitative Analysis of Federal Asset Forfeiture" by Drs. Greg L. Warchol (Bureau of Justice Studies) and Brian R. Johnson (Grand Valley State University). This article looks at an area of criminal justice that may be well-known, but its results are not. The large N and cross-sectional sampling are highlights of this research.

Finally, conducting any research regardless of the methodology can be extremely difficult. Ms. Chrisann M. Flanyak (University of Illinois, Chicago), in "Accessing Data: Procedures, Practices, and Problems of Academic Researchers," accomplishes two useful feats: (1) she provides a good example of how to conduct qualitative research using interviewing and snowball and convenience sampling, and (2) she offers insights into the difficulty of conducting any kind of research.

In conclusion, while this text was prepared primarily as a companion to a research methods textbook, its articles present a diverse and interesting array of topics that should be found useful in more than one context. The reality is that there is a lot of research underway in this country with respect to criminology and criminal justice, and any vehicle that helps highlight it should be welcomed and used in whatever manner possible. I trust you'll agree.

M.L. Dantzker, Ph.D.

Acknowledgments

"No man is an island" and no book can be written and published without assistance. I'd like to begin by thanking all the contributors who believed that the book was worth taking the time and effort to provide an article. Your assistance and support are greatly appreciated. As always, my appreciation and gratitude to my acquisitions editor, Laurel DeWolf, who continues to believe in and support me; Rita Lombard, assistant editor, for all her efforts to help complete this work; and to my production editor, Maura Kelly, whose devotion led to the completion of this book as a readable, understandable text. Finally, my continued gratitude to my wife Gail Dantzker for her undying support and devotion. I thank you all.

1

Some Impressions from a Qualitative Study of Implementation of Community Policing in North Carolina

John M. Memory, University of North Carolina—Pembroke

Methodological Focus. Although quantitative is a more widely used method of conducting research, **qualitative** methods can be useful, too. This article is a good example of how qualitative research can be used. Of particular interest is the researcher's use of **observer-participant** data collection conducted through ride-alongs with a variety of police officers where observations and informal interviews could be completed.

Abstract

As community policing continues to grow so will the research exploring its efficiency, efficacy, and feasibility. Although a great deal of research has already taken place, a majority of it is quantitative. This article is a result of a major study of the implementation of community policing in five North Carolina cities and one county. The study's goal was to provide a qualitative dimension to the research. The following is just one aspect of this research.

As part of a 1995–1996 study of implementation of community policing in five cities (Asheville, Greensboro, Morehead City, Whiteville, and Lumberton) and one county (Forsyth) in North Carolina (Rohe, Adams, Arcury, Memory & Klopovic, 1996), I rode along with community policing and patrol officers in each jurisdiction to provide a qualitative dimension to the research. This article reports one conclusive, descriptive finding and several impressions in the nature of description or explanation relating to community policing. In several instances, I make tentative recommendations concerning implementation of community policing, like Guarino-Ghezzi (1994). The findings and impressions are based solely on my ride-alongs.

Because an in-depth literature review supporting the full initial research design, including the qualitative aspect, is provided in the report of the full research project (Rohe, Adams, Arcury, Memory & Klopovic, 1996), only the research literature relevant to the findings and impressions presented in this article is included.

Conducting qualitative research requires in-depth knowledge of the culture, social group, or other type of group studied, including the relevant theory, research, and vernacular. As a researcher who has a J.D. degree and extensive experience as a lawyer, I believe that conduct of participant-observation research with police requires knowledge of applicable law. My knowledge of policing comes from practical experience as a military police commander; doctoral studies in criminology, with emphasis on policing; extensive teaching of relevant law and social science; relevant work as a lawyer; and relevant research, writing, and consulting for more than twenty years. My knowledge concerning community policing has come from teaching eleven courses concerned with community policing, reading much of the literature on community policing, and attending about twenty conference sessions concerned with community policing, all since the fall of 1993. I have lived in North Carolina for a total of thirty-three years since early childhood and have traveled extensively in the state, including significant exposure to the five cities and one county included in the research. Therefore, the jurisdictions did not present unfamiliar cultures.

METHODOLOGY

The initial qualitative research design, developed in conjunction with the director of the full research project, called for full process evaluation (Patton, 1980, p. 60) of the implementation of community policing in the five cities and one county. The participant-observation research was to fit the category of "observer as participant" (Maxfield & Babbie, 1995, p. 246). Soon after undertaking the ride-alongs, I realized that, because of the many different aspects and forms of community policing (Rosenbaum & Lurigio, 1994) being implemented in the six jurisdictions, and because of the limited number of hours—no more than 180—available for ride-along observation (cf. Vinzant & Crothers, 1994; Klinger, 1995; Mastrofski, Worden & Snipes, 1995; Giacomazzi & Thurman, 1994), completing the qualitative research aspect according to the original design was impossible.

The important issue then was whether meaningful qualitative research could be conducted through ride-alongs. I remained confident concerning the feasibility of gaining an understanding of officers' attitudes and behaviors in their natural setting (Maxfield & Babbie, 1995, p. 245) as they relate to the implementation of community policing. Therefore, the research took on a primarily "*verstehen*" aspect (Weber, 1949, 1978; Ferrell, 1997), consistent with Ferrell's argument that the *verstehen* method allows a researcher, "through attentiveness and participation," to "begin to apprehend and appreciate the specific roles and experiences of . . . crime control agents . . . caught up in the day-to-day reality of crime" (Ferrell, 1997, p. 10). I decided to identify subjects for special attention as the ride-alongs progressed.

Data Collection

The ride-alongs were arranged ahead of time by departmental contact persons. Because the heads of the six law enforcement agencies had agreed to involve their agencies in the overall research project, I did not need to "gain access" (Maxfield & Babbie, 1995, pp. 249–51). Still, I had to behave during agency visits in ways that would maintain access, such as fully complying with agency and officer directions.

The city departments were well-selected by the principal investigator to represent a wide spectrum of types of cities and a wide variety in approaches to implementation of community policing. I rode some during daylight and darkness in each jurisdiction, but rode nearly none between 1:00 A.M. and 1:00 P.M.

As an "observer as participant," dressed in slacks, a dress shirt, and sport coat, I observed everything that occurred concerning the officers I rode with. While I began the ride-alongs with the expectation to carry out neatly structured interviews of the officers using a list of issues developed by the principal investigator, it soon became obvious that only unstructured interviewing was feasible. As I identified subjects to address, I included those subjects in an informal list of areas for questions. Asking follow-up questions was usually workable. To facilitate remembering individual officers, I recorded each officer's department, name, age, race, and sex.

Especially given the largely exploratory and qualitative nature of the research and consistent with *verstehen* methodology (Weber, 1949, 1978), I attempted to stay as alert as possible to be able to notice when something significant happened or was said. The discovery of new information and the development of new insights concerning community policing were central goals of the research. For example, during a ride-along in Morehead City that involved no dispatches of the officer, I was alert enough, fortunately, to realize it was significant when the officer said, "During slow shifts, getting out of my vehicle, walking, and meeting people helps with boredom." Also, by observing community policing in six different jurisdictions while riding with many different police officers, I sought to grasp the qualitative essence of community policing.

Data collection involved taking notes on the front and back of data-collection forms developed with the principal investigator of the research project. I recorded observations, the words of officers and citizens, and my own impressions and ideas. I collected no analyzable quantitative data during the ride-alongs. During darkness, officers usually allowed a light to be turned on for note-taking. Occasionally, so many significant things happened quickly that I got behind in note-taking, but I would eventually have time to catch up. Though I have foregone note-taking during previous ride-alongs to avoid inhibiting an officer during particularly significant actions, that never occurred during these ride-alongs.

Each ride-along was begun with an assurance to the officer that, unless the officer committed a crime in my presence, nothing the officer would do or say would result in me "getting the officer in trouble with his police superiors." Most of the officers seemed to be responsive and candid in answering questions. This candor was exemplified by an experience during a ride-along with an African American officer, who initially seemed very hesitant to provide significant information. After more than two hours of riding, he asked me, "Well, what do you think?" I said, "I think you don't trust me." That "broke the ice," and, for the next hour, he was obviously very candid concerning the subjects of the research. I believe that, during many ride-alongs in Lumberton, I gained the trust of the officers in that department. Fortunately, I was never put in the position of thinking that I was ethically bound to make an adverse report regarding a Lumberton officer to the chief or other superior officer. I have the entirely subjective impression that my presence usually didn't influence an officer's actions or his handling of situations.

If possible, I rode with each officer for at least three hours. This appeared to allow officers to become comfortable with my presence, and it made it unnecessary to broach sensitive issues within the first hour of exposure. In several instances, I completed three hours by riding with an officer during two different visits to his or her city.

To gain officers' confidence, I usually disclosed early in the ride-along that I was a military police company commander in the early 1970s, was later a military prosecutor, and, later still, a civilian prosecutor. Since a significant number of the officers had served in the armed forces, the mentioning of military-police command duty fairly often prompted helpful sharing of tales of experiences in uniform. To gain the confidence of an officer, I occasionally said something I didn't want the officer to repeat to a departmental administrator. After preliminary conversations, I generally tried to have the officer do most of the talking. Because the officers were usually genuinely interesting to me, I usually didn't have to try to make an officer feel that what he or she was saying or doing was interesting.

Though I nearly always told officers about my previous work as a prosecutor, I was voluntarily unlicensed to practice law during the research and was careful never to express a legal opinion, though a few officers asked for legal advice. I believe that, since I was studying community policing and related behaviors and attitudes and not line officers' unethical or illegal behaviors, knowledge of my legal background probably didn't influence officers' actions or words.

I first carried out police ride-alongs in the middle 1970s as a criminology graduate student. Since that time, I have benefited from a personal freedom from both the tendency to "go native" (Maxfield & Babbie, 1995, p. 247) by becoming a police officer or a hanger-on to the police subcultural group and the tendency to be morally revolted by their behaviors or attitudes. I maintained this attitude during this research. I carefully avoided expressing negative judgments concerning the actions or statements of officers. I did very occasionally compliment an officer concerning clearly appropriate behavior to bolster his trust of me.

Occasionally during the research, citizens apparently assumed I was a police officer. Still, deception was never consciously used with citizens or officers. Citizens' often thinking that I was a police officer may have reduced the tendency of my presence to influence the behavior of citizens.

As part of the ride-along data collection, I rode in police vehicles with community policing and beat officers on duty in the six jurisdictions. Specifically for this project, I rode along thirty-four times for a total of about 105 hours. Also, from July of 1994 through the start of this project, I rode with Lumberton Police Department beat and community policing officers (CPOs) for about 60 hours as part of an evaluation of community policing in the Lumberton Police Department, which was not completed because of the commencement of this project. This length and depth of exposure to the Lumberton Police Department allowed me to witness turnover of personnel, changes of assignments, changes in the departmental structure, and changes in the nature of community policing in Lumberton.

While I did not develop "key informants," as generally conceived of in the literature (Maxfield & Babbie, 1995, p. 251), in each department I had at least one officer who provided especially important information and insights.

Data Analysis

This research is in the Weberian *verstehen* tradition of participant observation, which does not involve analysis of quantitative data (Weber, 1949, 1978). After completing all of the ride-alongs, I reread my notes several times, marking what seemed to be significant materials. Then, I responded to the principal investigator's request that I provide information and insights for inclusion in the full project research report. This required that I read my notes several additional times. While there was no quantitative data analysis in the conventional sense, the coding and review of the notes allowed for the detection of patterns.

I tried to avoid reaching premature conclusions, even tentative ones. For example, during the first night of riding with a Lumberton Police Department officer, I was with a beat officer in the predominantly Black south side of the city. The officer answered three calls, each of which involved a Black, female single parent asking the officer, who was Native American, to serve, in effect, as a substitute father by lecturing a teenager. I saw those calls as indicating a remarkable acceptance of the Lumberton police officers by the Black community. During the remainder of the ride-alongs, I witnessed only one more call of that type, in Morehead City. Therefore, situations of that sort are not made the subject of even a tentative conclusion or suggestion of future research.

RESULTS

Relations of Officers with Black Children

Research has consistently found that Blacks have more negative attitudes concerning police than Whites do and that, among research respondents, age is directly related to the positivity of citizen attitudes concerning police (McGarrell & Flanagan, 1985). While that research has generally not involved subjects younger than 15 or 16, some research has been done on pro-White and pro-Black biases of younger children. Morland and Suthers (1980) documented a shift from pro-White bias among preschool Black children to pro-Black bias among older Black children.

Two of the most consistent and interesting observations in this research were that (1) in practically every city and every city neighborhood, nearly all Black children younger than 11 were friendly with nearly every police officer; and (2) in practically every city and every city neighborhood, virtually all Black juveniles older than 11 were less than friendly with nearly every police officer. Because there were virtually no exceptions to these observations in about 165 hours of ride-alongs, these generalizations are presented with confidence as findings of this research. None of the later observations or impressions are reported with equal confidence as the bases for generalization.

Nearly all of the officers agreed with this distinction based on age. Most of the officers attributed the friendliness of young Black children to D.A.R.E. (Drug Abuse Resistance Education) and similar police programs, and the lack of friendliness of older children, to the peer culture of Black children in middle school. While D.A.R.E. programs appear to be ineffective in preventing drug use (Wysong & Wright, 1995; Dukes, Ullman & Stein, 1996), they may promote positive attitudes of young Black children concerning police officers.

IMPRESSIONS

Receptivity of Residents of City Areas to Community Policing

Several researchers have recently studied citizen receptivity to community policing (Bennett, 1995; Capowich & Roehl, 1994; Friedmen, 1994; Grinc, 1994; Murphy, 1988; Sadd & Grinc, 1994). Trojanowicz and Bucqueroux

(1994, pp. 40–41) have provided a detailed discussion of factors that "influence the attitudes of the citizens and the acceptability of various problem-solving techniques."

I often talked to community policing officers about what types of city areas can be expected to be receptive or unreceptive to community policing. Based on extensive observation, conversations, and subjective analysis, I have the impression that there are four factors related to the receptivity of citizens to community policing:

1. Degree of community/cohesiveness/affiliation within the city area. The more community there is, the greater potential there is for receptivity to community policing. When there is an absence of community/cohesiveness/affiliation, as can be the case in public housing developments and in upper middle class suburban developments, officers have no community leaders or organizations to work with.
2. Extent of informal social control within the area. Lack of informal social control can be seen in conditions with "broken windows" (Wilson & Kelling, 1982) and in troublesome minor misbehavior, such as loud noise late at night and loitering of juveniles. I believe that there is often little potential for community policing when there is effective informal social control. Interestingly, informal social control is often accomplished in North Carolina through the operation of real estate law, as through restrictive covenants in real estate deeds.
3. Extent of internal or external crime threat. Shared crime threat tends to bring a community together and increase the prospects for community policing. When young Black males living in the area with their mothers or grandmothers constitute the crime threat, their mothers, grandmothers, and neighbors may feel inhibited or intimidated concerning cooperation with community policing.
4. Whether the area has almost exclusively Black residents. I rode through many city areas with almost exclusively Black residents and was told that the residents had not supported community/neighborhood watch or other aspects of community policing. There were notable exceptions. In several cases, Black area residents had gotten fed up with crime and drug dealing and cooperated with the police in trying to "win back" their neighborhoods.

Some city areas have low community, ineffective informal social control, high crime threat, and proportionately large Black populations. I believe, with DiIulio (1992–1993), that police departments have a duty to persist with community policing efforts in these areas, even when the residents are not initially cooperative.

Other city areas have low community, highly effective informal social control, low crime threat, and exclusively White populations. There is no pressing need for community policing. Given limited police budgets and personnel, I believe that police departments shouldn't persist in community policing activities if residents of this type of community, as predicted, are unreceptive.

Feasibility of Community Policing in Conjunction with Types of Community Organizations

As suggested by some of the research literature on community/neighborhood watch (Cordner, Gaines & Kappeler, 1996, p. 405), all participating departments were having problems keeping citizens, especially those not perceiving a major crime threat, interested in community/neighborhood watch. In Asheville and Greensboro, there was greater success in keeping neighborhood residents interested in neighborhood associations. There is an extensive research literature on the general efficacy of neighborhood associations (Olsen, Perlstadt, Fonseca & Hogan, 1989; Logan & Rabrenovic, 1990; Austin, 1991; Mesch & Schwirian, 1996).

Neighborhood associations differ from community/neighborhood watch groups in the number and nature of aspects and activities. A neighborhood association can be, in effect, a genuine grassroots community group concerned with, in addition to crime and disorder, the physical environment, availability of good outlets and activities for juveniles, community beautification, charitable activities, arts and crafts, local history, promotion of friendships and mutual assistance among community residents, local political issues of important to the neighborhood, and other topics. Maintaining interest in such a group appears to be easier than maintaining interest in a unifaceted community/neighborhood watch group.

Receptivity of Citizens to Return Home Visits by Officers

Trojanowicz and Bucqueroux (1994) have argued that community policing officers should "maintain daily, direct, face-to-face contact with the people they serve" (p. 5; cf. Eig, 1996), partly through visits to residents' homes (Trojanowicz & Bucqueroux, 1994, p. 77 and p. 85).

Most of the officers reported to me that they generally got positive receptions when they, as officers with community policing duties, made initial visits to homes. Several beat officers or CPOs told me, however, that the residents' responses were often much less positive when the officer visited for a second or third time. One White beat officer told me that, in the officer's predominantly Black community policing area, nine out of ten community residents would go inside if he came on a resident's porch. Making repeated visits to the homes of residents in a CPO's area may, in many cases, be counterproductive.

Race of Community Policing Officers and Populations Served

While all of the departments reject a policy of assigning White officers in White areas and Black officers in Black areas, I believe, consistent with Trojanowicz and Bucqueroux (1994, p. 70), that having a Black officer involved in implementing community policing, including organizing a community association, in a predominantly Black area of a city should increase the prospects for at least initial success.

Activities of Teams or Groups of Community Policing Officers

In their important description of the ways a police department should implement community policing, Trojanowicz and Bucqueroux (1994) mention only the community policing activities of individual community policing officers (pp. 78–79).

One of my major impressions is that there is especially great positive potential for police activities of teams or groups of community policing officers. I observed and received descriptions of this type of activity in Asheville, Greensboro, and, to a lesser extent, Whiteville and Lumberton. Group action by community policing officers can accomplish many things individual officers can't accomplish. Also, acting as part of a community policing team, such as the PACT (Police and Community Together) team in Asheville, may shield officers from the stress and burnout that may result from working alone and interacting primarily with beat officers, who often belittle community policing. Team/group activities that I observed or that were described to me included the following:

1. Antidrug operations, usually in cooperation with departmental drug officers. These include dealer busts, buyer busts, surveillance, and "knock-and-talks," which involve asking suspected drug dealers for permission to search their homes. Amazingly, they often consent.
2. Antiprostitution operations, usually in cooperation with departmental vice officers. Prostitutes or their customers can be targeted.
3. Operations against semipublic sexual acts by homosexuals. Responding to citizen complaints, community policing officers arranged for such an operation in a Greensboro park.
4. Development of basis for a nuisance-abatement action. This can involve surveillance, arrests, citations, and documentation of complaints.
5. Surveillance of businesses that have been targeted by criminals for break-ins.
6. Maintenance of order in city parks that have gotten somewhat out of control.
7. Concerted efforts to gain city code enforcement.

Time of Day When Community Policing Activities Occur

Trojanowicz and Bucqueroux (1994) point out that most community policing activities occur during daylight hours but suggest that community policing officers should work some weekends and night shifts (p. 18). In most of the research-site cities, community policing activities occur primarily during the day shift. Greensboro beat officers working nights and answering many important calls have little opportunity to do walk patrol in city communities and introduce themselves to residents, except possibly during the late daylight hours of the summer. Attention should be given in research and training to identification of community policing activities that community policing and patrol officers can perform at night.

Frequency of Call Answering and Backup by Community Policing Officers

Trojanowicz and Bucqueroux (1994) seem to contradict themselves on whether community policing officers should be dispatched on ordinary calls for service as primary or backup officers. They argue that community policing officers should be "freed from . . . demands of the police radio" (p. 5). Later, they opine that CPOs "should handle all kinds of calls . . . and continue to perform traditional activities, like making arrests" (p. 18).

I observed and was told of much variation to which community policing officers are dispatched to answer calls for service or go, with or without dispatch, as a backup on a call. My strong impression is that it promotes the success of community policing and helps to overcome beat officer opposition to community policing for CPOs to volunteer over the radio to take or act as backup on calls that relate to their community policing activities.

Cross-Benefits of Community Policing Activities and Ordinary Patrol Activities

Information obtained in community policing activities can assist officers when they carry out law enforcement and order-maintenance activities. Conversely, information obtained in law enforcement and order-maintenance activities can assist officers in their community policing activities. When CPOs do little law enforcement or order maintenance work, or when patrol officers do no community policing or POP activities, this crossover effect is lost.

Resistance of Some Officers to Community Policing

Numerous researchers have studied line and community policing officer attitudes concerning community policing, and some have documented line police officer reservations about and even opposition to community policing (Greene, 1989; Lurigio & Skogan, 1994; Pate & Shtull, 1994; Sadd & Grinc, 1994; Wilkinson & Rosenbaum, 1994; cf. Wilson & Bennett, 1994; Yates & Pillai, 1996). I became aware of resistance to community policing by a significant percentage of beat officers, especially officers with more than two years in police work, in the site jurisdictions. This appears to be a very complex phenomenon that may involve the operation of officer subcultural norms; race relations and race-related attitudes of officers and citizens; reflexive resistance to change; reaction of officers to excessive claims regarding the efficacy of community policing; resistance of many officers to assignment of new work-requiring duties; and resistance of officers to citizens gaining control over their activities. Overcoming this resistance is obviously a major challenge.

Implications of Line-Officer Opposition to Community Policing for Participative Management

Trojanowicz and Bucqueroux (1994) urge, consistent with participative management, "transferring decision making from top to the bottom of the police pyramid" (p. 98). Participatory management was implemented in Madison, Wisconsin in conjunction with community policing (Wycoff & Skogan, 1994).

Unfortunately, the pervasive opposition of line officers to community policing undoubtedly can have the significant secondary effect of making it difficult for the departmental implementation of participative management within the department relating to community policing. I believe that, in some of the five city departments, if the rank-and-file officers could democratically influence community policing in their departments, it would be eliminated or reduced. Because researchers have found support for participative management among line police officers (Witte, Travis & Langworthy, 1989), and because it may have generally positive effects on police morale (Gaines, Southerland & Angell, 1991), it is unfortunate that participative management may in some departments have limited utility relating to community policing.

Police Experience and Support for Community Policing among Beat Officers

Trojanowicz and Bucqueroux (1994) discuss the pros and cons of rookie officers and veterans as CPOs. Several CPOs mentioned to me that the most effective beat officers in community policing and problem-oriented policing have less than three years in police work. If that is true, and I have the impression that it is, it will be important for departments to develop ways to increase the interest in and the productivity of the community policing and problem-oriented policing of experienced officers.

Use of Force by Officers

I asked most of the officers, "About how many times have you had to wrestle somebody on duty in the last two years?" There was a great variety of responses. Two calm, persuasive, six-foot, muscular Black male officers reported not having to wrestle anyone. Two very assertive White officers had to wrestle between twenty and forty times apiece. These White officers may be quite courageously and proactively seeking to perform their jobs fully. They may have been justified in every use of force. Still, I agree with Trojanowicz and Bucqueroux (1994, p. 14; cf. McCoy, 1986; Klinger, 1995) that this dimension, use of force, is important concerning officers' adaptability to community policing. Obviously, it is better for officers with community policing duties to rely, if possible, on persuasion and cooperation rather than force.

SUMMARY AND IMPLICATIONS

Based on a total of 165 hours of ride-alongs with patrol and community policing officers in six research-site jurisdictions in North Carolina, I reported one descriptive finding and numerous descriptive, explanatory, and evaluative impressions. This finding and the impressions can be used in the development of focused quantitative research relating to community policing. It may also be of value to administrators in departments that are implementing community policing.

REFERENCES

Austin, D.M. (1991). Community context and complexity of organizational structure in neighborhood associations. *Administration and Society, 22*, 516–531.

Bennett, S.F. (1995). Community organizations and crime. *Annals of the American Academy of Political and Social Sciences, 539*, 72–84.

Capowich, G., & Roehl, J. (1994). Problem-oriented policing: Actions and effectiveness in San Diego. In D. Rosenbaum (Ed.), *The challenge of community policing: Testing the promises*, pp. 127–146. Thousand Oaks, CA: Sage.

Cordner, G.W., Gaines, L.K., & Kappeler, V.E. (1996). *Police operations: Analysis and evaluation*. Cincinnati: Anderson.

DiIulio, J.J., Jr. (1992–93). Inner-city crime: What the federal government should do. *Responsive Community, 3*, 15–25.

Dukes, R.L., Ullman, J.B., & Stein, J.A. (1996). Three-year follow-up of drug abuse resistance education (D.A.R.E.). *Evaluation Review, 20*(1), 49–66.

Eig, J. (1996). Eyes on the street: Community policing in Chicago. *American Prospect, 29*, 60–68.

Ferrell, J. (1997). Criminological *verstehen*: Inside the immediacy of crime. *Justice Quarterly, 14*, 3–23.

Friedman, W. (1994). The community role in community policing. In D. Rosenbaum (Ed.), *The Challenge of Community Policing: Testing the Promises*, pp. 263–269. Thousand Oaks, CA: Sage.

Gaines, L.K., Southerland, M.D., & Angell, J.E. (1991). *Police administration.* New York: McGraw-Hill.

Giacomazzi, A., & Thurman, Q.C. (1994). Cops and kids revisited: A second-year assessment of a community policing and delinquency prevention innovation. *Police Studies, 17*, 1–20.

Greene, J.R. (1989). Police officer job satisfaction and community perceptions: Implications for community-oriented policing. *Journal of Research in Crime and Delinquency, 26*, 168–183.

Grinc, R.M. (1994). "Angels in Marble": Problems in stimulating community involvement in community policing. *Crime and Delinquency, 40*, 437–468.

Guarino-Ghezzi, S. (1994). Reintegrative police surveillance of juvenile offenders: Forging an urban model. *Crime and Delinquency, 40*, 131–151.

Klinger, D.A. (1995). The micro-structure of nonlethal force: Baseline data from an observational study. *Criminal Justice Review, 20*, 169–186.

Logan, J.R., & Rabrenovic, G. (1990). Neighborhood associations: Their issues, their allies, and their opponents. *Urban Affairs Quarterly, 26*, 68–94.

Lurigio, A.J., & Skogan, W.G. (1994). Winning the hearts and minds of police officers: An assessment of staff perceptions of community policing in Chicago. *Crime and Delinquency, 40*, 315–330.

Mastrofski, S.D., Worden, R.E., & Snipes, J.B. (1995). Law enforcement in a time of community policing. *Criminology, 33*, 539–563.

Maxfield, M.G., & Babbie, E. (1995). *Research methods for criminal justice and criminology*. Belmont, CA: Wadsworth.

McCoy, C. (1986). The cop's world: Modern policing and the difficulty of legitimizing the use of force. *Human Rights Quarterly, 8*, 270–293.

McGarrell, E.F., & Flanagan, T.J. (1985). *Sourcebook of criminal justice statistics—1984*. Washington, DC: U.S. Department of Justice.

Mesch, G.S., & Schwirian, K.P. (1996). The effectiveness of neighborhood collective action. *Social Problems, 43*, 467–483.

Morland, J.K., & Suthers, E. (1980). Racial attitudes of children: Perspectives on the structural-normative theory of prejudice. *Phylon, 41*, 267–275.

Murphy, C. (1988). Community problems, problem communities and community policing in Toronto. *Journal of Research in Crime and Delinquency, 25*, 392–410.

Olsen, M., Perlstadt, H., Fonseca, V., & Hogan, J. (1989). Participation in neighborhood associations. *Sociological Focus, 22*, 1–17.

Pate, A.M., & Shtull, P. (1994) Community policing grows in Brooklyn: An inside view of the New York City Police Department's model precinct. *Crime and Delinquency, 40*, 384–410.

Patton, M.Q. (1980). *Qualitative Evaluation Methods.* Beverly Hills: Sage.

Rohe, W.M., Adams, R.E., Arcury, T.A., Memory, J., & Klopovic, J. (1996). *Community oriented policing: The North Carolina experience.* Raleigh, NC: Division of the Governor's Crime Commission.

Rosenbaum, D.P., & Lurigio, A.J. (1994). An inside look at community policing reform: Definitions, organizational changes, and evaluation findings. *Crime and Delinquency, 40*, 299–314.

Sadd, S., & Grinc, R. (1994). Innovative neighborhood oriented policing: An evaluation of community policing programs in eight cities. In D. Rosenbaum (Ed.), *The challenge of community policing: testing the promises*, pp. 27–52. Thousand Oaks, CA: Sage.

Trojanowicz, R., & Bucqueroux, B. (1994). *Community policing: How to get started.* Cincinnati: Anderson.

Vinzant, J., & Crothers, L. (1994). Street-level leadership: The role of patrol officers in community policing. *Criminal Justice Review, 19*, 189–211.

Weber, M. (1949). *The methodology of the social sciences.* New York: Free Press.

———. (1978). *Economy and society*. Berkeley: University of California Press.

Wilkinson, D., & Rosenbaum, D. (1994). The effects of organizational structure on community policing: A comparison of two cities. In D. Rosenbaum (Ed.), *The challenge of community policing: Testing the promises*, pp. 110–126. Thousand Oaks, CA: Sage.

Wilson, D.G., & Bennett, S.F. (1994). Officers' response to community policing: Variations on a theme. *Crime and Delinquency, 40*, 354–370.

Wilson, J.Q., & Kelling, G.L. (1982). Broken windows: The police and neighborhood safety. *The Atlantic Monthly*, March, 29–38.

Witte, J.H., Travis, L.F., & Langworthy, R.H. (1989). *Participatory management in law enforcement.* Paper presented at the annual meeting of the Academy of Criminal Justice Sciences, Washington.

Wycoff, M.A., & Skogan, W.G. (1994). The effect of a community policing management style on officers' attitudes. *Crime and Delinquency, 40*, 371–383.

Wysong, E., & Wright, D.W. (1995). A decode of DARE: Efficacy, politics and drug education. *Sociological Focus, 28*, 283–311.

Yates, D.L., & Pillai, V.K. (1996). Attitudes toward community policing: A casual analysis. *Social Science Journal, 33*(2), 193–209.

2

The Conceptualization and Operationalization of the Intervening Dimensions of Social Disorganization*

Laura J. Moriarty, Virginia Commonwealth University

Methodological Focus. Probably one of the more difficult tasks for the new researcher is being able to **conceptualize** and **operationalize** variables. This article shows how the process can be done through an exploration of the main variable Social Disorganization. In addition, attention should be given to identification of **variables**, use of telephone **surveys**, and **random sampling**.

Abstract

Social disorganization has been conceptualized and operationalized in many ways. The process of conceptualization results in indicators and dimensions of the concepts or variables under study. Operationalization is the process where actual questions or measurements of the concept(s) are identified. The purpose of this research is to expand on the measurement of social disorganization using data collected to evaluate an alcohol and other drug (AOD) coalition. The population studied was one rural county in Western North Carolina, with the units of analysis being the residents. The mode of observation is survey research, specifically a telephone survey.

Social disorganization has been conceptualized and operationalized in many ways. "Conceptualization is the process through which we specify precisely what we will mean when we use particular terms" (Babbie, 1995, p. 114). Sometimes, conceptualization is referred to as the definition of the concepts or variables under study. The process of conceptualization results in indicators and dimensions of the concepts or variables under study. Operationalization is

*An earlier version of this paper was presented at the American Society of Criminology Annual Meeting, Chicago, IL, November, 1996.

the process where actual questions or measurements of the concept(s) are identified. Sometimes this is referred to as the operational definition(s). Both of these processes together are referred to as measurement.

The purpose of this research is to expand on the measurement of social disorganization using data collected to evaluate an alcohol and other drug (AOD) coalition. Two prominent researchers, who have previously tested social disorganization, Robert Sampson and Byron Groves, argue that social disorganization must be measured more accurately. This paper attempts to expand the measurement of social disorganization by exploring the role community empowerment variables play in measuring social disorganization.

OVERVIEW OF SOCIAL DISORGANIZATION

Social disorganization is a term applied to communities with certain structural characteristics. Chief among them is the community's inability to realize the common values of its residents. A by-product of this is the lack of effective social controls in the community (Bursik, 1984; Kornhauser, 1978; Sampson & Groves, 1989). Researchers studying social disorganization often examine the "structural barriers" that block the formal and informal bonds (or ties) to a community, a situation which results in an inability to solve common community problems (Sampson & Groves, 1989).

Shaw and McKay (1942; 1969) identified three structural factors of social disorganization: low economic status, ethnic heterogeneity, and residential mobility. They believed these factors interfered with a community's social organization. The bonds or ties to the community are not formed, resulting in informal social controls being less effective. Shaw and McKay argued that when these social conditions are present, crime and delinquency are more likely to occur. Sampson and Groves (1989) further develop Shaw and McKay's model, explaining that the external factors are only one component of social disorganization and that intervening variables, including unsupervised teenage gangs, informal friendship bonds, and low organizational participation, also measure social disorganization. These external sources and intervening dimensions of social disorganization will explain rates of crime. The authors tested their model and found support for the theory (Sampson & Groves, 1989).

A great deal of research has focused on social disorganization; Bursik (1988), however, argues that these researchers misunderstood Shaw and McKay. He states that Shaw and McKay did not regard social disorganization variables (urban ecology, economic conditions, rapid social change) as direct causes of crime and delinquency. In his view, these variables weaken "informal social controls found within the community and neighborhood, thus allowing for high rates of crime to occur" (Akers, 1994, p. 144). Sampson and Groves (1989) similarly assert that social disorganization variables such as social class and racial composition are not direct causes of crime and delinquency.

OVERVIEW OF COMMUNITY EMPOWERMENT

Community empowerment is a concept used to describe a group of individuals living in close proximity who, as a group, unite to form a force to combat a common problem. The focus of the group is the common problem. If a community is to be empowered, the residents must first be aware that a problem exists (community awareness), to such an extent that it is disturbing or troubling (community concern), which results in the organization of the community (community mobilization) to fight against it (community action). Researchers who evaluate coalitions have equated community empowerment with community mobilization (McConnell, 1994, p. 1). The more empowered a community feels, the more active the community, hence a stronger degree of community mobilization results. Community mobilization is the overall category embracing community concern, community awareness, and community action. Goodman and Wandersman (1994) have evaluated several community coalitions using measures of community awareness, community concern, and community action. These variables, although not entitled "intervening dimensions of social disorganization," are thought to be extensions of social disorganization. The purpose of this research is to examine further these variables to determine if they are really intervening dimensions of social disorganization. It seems logical that the community empowerment variables are just different examples of controls (or lack thereof) within a community. As a result, these variables should be highly intercorrelated with the established measures of social disorganization.

Community empowerment and social disorganization are two concepts that previously have not been tied together (see Moriarty, 1991). This research will determine through factor analysis whether both are really measuring the same phenomenon. In other words, are community empowerment variables measuring additional "structural barriers" that block the formal and informal ties (bonds) to a community?

MEASUREMENTS IN THE CURRENT RESEARCH

Sampson and Groves (1989) provide exogenous sources and intervening dimensions of social disorganization theory and clearly articulate how to measure them. The five exogenous sources are low economic status, ethnic heterogeneity, residential mobility, family disruption, and urbanization. The three intervening dimensions are sparse local friendship networks, unsupervised teenage peer groups, and low organizational participation.

The present study includes questions measuring all of the exogenous sources; only two of the intervening dimensions are measured, however. Further, these measurements are limited because only one aspect of each is measured. At best, the present research has adequate measures of the exogenous sources but is somewhat limited when capturing the intervening dimensions.

The variables used in this study to measure community awareness, community concern, and community action are attitudinal and behavioral measures. Community awareness was conceptualized as the level of knowledge about the use of alcohol and other drugs in the community. Four variables reflected community awareness: drug usage in the neighborhood; drug dealing in the neighborhood; alcohol/drug prevention messages; and availability of certain drugs (eight different drugs in all). The following are the actual questions used to establish each variable.

Drug Usage in the Neighborhood. Respondents were asked, "How many people in this neighborhood use drugs?" The responses included: many, some, not many, or no residents use drugs.

Drug Dealing in the Neighborhood. Respondents were asked, "How often do you see drug dealing in this neighborhood?" The responses included: very often, sometimes, rarely, never.

Alcohol/Drug Prevention Message. Respondents were asked if they had heard or seen any drug or alcohol prevention messages in the past six months.

Availability of Certain Drugs. Respondents were asked about the difficulty or ease of obtaining specific drugs in the county. The list of drugs included: marijuana, crack cocaine, other forms of cocaine, heroin, other narcotics (methadone, opium, codeine, paregoric), tranquilizers, barbiturates, amphetamines, and LSD. Each drug availability represents one variable. Community Concern was conceptualized as anxiety or uneasiness about alcohol and other drug usage in the neighborhood. Four variables measured community concern. Below are the questions used to establish these variables.

Assessment of Drug Problem in Neighborhood. Respondents were asked, "How much of a problem are drugs in your neighborhood?" Responses included: a major problem, a minor problem, no problem.

Control over Drug Usage in Neighborhood. Respondents were asked whether they felt they had control over the use of drugs in their neighborhood.

Drug Dealing in Your Neighborhood This Year Compared to Last Year. Respondents were asked, "Compared to one year ago, would you say drug dealing in your neighborhood has become . . . much worse than before, a little worse than before, about the same as before, a little better than before, or much better than before?"

Drug Usage in Your Neighborhood This Year Compared to Last Year. Respondents were asked, "Compared to one year ago, in your neighborhood, is drug usage . . . much worse than before, a little worse than before, about the same as before, a little better than before, or much better than before?"

Community action was conceptualized as involvement in reducing AOD usage. Two variables measured community action and are explained below.

Participation in Prevention Activities at Neighborhood Level to Prevent or Stop Drug Use. Respondents were asked, "How actively involved are the people in your neighborhood in preventing drug usage?" Responses included: very active, somewhat active, a little active, not at all active.

Awareness and Participation in Drug Prevention Coalition. Respondents were asked if they were aware that the county has a drug coalition.

There are 24 variables listed above measuring both social disorganization and community empowerment. In the next section, the research methodology is described. Included are the population and sample, units of analysis, and the mode of observation. In order to determine if the community empowerment variables are intervening dimensions of social disorganization, data must be collected and analyzed. The data used here are from a larger community coalition evaluation project (see Moriarty, 1995).

METHODOLOGY

The population studied is one rural county in Western North Carolina. The units of analysis are the residents. The county was selected because it has a community AOD coalition[1] that is evaluated yearly (see Moriarty, 1994, 1995, 1996).

The mode of observation is survey research, specifically a telephone survey. The telephone survey was administered in the Spring of 1994 by Virginia Commonwealth University's Survey Research Lab. A random sample of telephone numbers was purchased from Survey Sampling, Inc. of Fairfield, Connecticut. A total of 809 telephone interviews were completed. Given the size of the population under study, this sample size represents a +/−5 point margin of error with a 95% confidence interval.

The sample contains more females than males and the majority are white. There are more married respondents than single, divorced, separated, or widowed persons. The educational level of the sample reflects a fairly well-educated group: one-third of the respondents have some college background, almost 20% received a bachelor's degree, and almost 10% have professional degrees. Fewer than 10% of the sample have less than a high school education, and 29% are high school graduates.

The sample is representative of the county population, except that females are slightly overrepresented. The other variables—race, marital status, and education—are representative of the county, with a slight bias toward more highly educated persons completing the surveys. Table 2.1 compares the sample statistics with the population statistics for the county.

Table 2.1 Comparison of Demographic Data

Demographic Variable	1994 Survey *f*	percent	Population Statistics *f*	percent
Gender				
Male	315	39%	82,894	47.0%
Female	494	61%	91,927	53.0%
Race				
White	725	91%	159,005	91.0%
Black	46	6%	14,108	8.1%
Other	29	3%	1,708	.9%
Marital Status				
Single	154	19%	30,671	21.0%
Married	469	58%	82,773	58.0%
Divorced	83	10%	12,012	8.0%
Separated	29	4%	3,948	3.0%
Widowed	69	9%	13,333	9.0%
Education				
Less than high school	81	10%	30,551	25.0%
High school graduate	206	25%	35,723	29.0%
Some college	268	33%	30,632	26.0%
BA degree	155	19%	14,934	12.0%
Professional	97	12%	7,975	7.0%

Factor Analysis

Factor analysis is a way of measuring a general variable, or factor, underlying a large set of variables. The 24 variables identified above are thought to measure the intervening dimensions and exogenous factors of social disorganization. The factor analysis technique will allow those variables measuring the same basic factor to aggregate. The set of variables will form a factor. There may be a range of factors associated with the variables. Here, we expect at least two factors because we know there are two categories of social disorganization: intervening dimensions and exogenous factors. Factor analysis is performed on all the variables to determine where the variables fall in terms of the factors identified.

Before doing a factor analysis, a correlation matrix should be conducted on all the variables under study. In order to include the variables in the factor analysis, the correlation coefficient must be at least .4 in absolute value (Hedderson, 1987).

As described above, the 24 variables explained are thought to be dimensions of social disorganization, although other researchers have not labeled them as such. These 24 variables were entered into a correlation matrix, because if they truly are measuring the same concept, then all should be intercorrelated. Only 13 of the variables were found to be correlated with coefficients of .4 or better.

The variables measuring the exogenous factors and intervening dimensions of social disorganization were not correlated with any of the community empowerment variables. Further, the group of variables measuring community action were not correlated either. The 13 variables that were correlated with each other were entered into a factor analysis. The procedure revealed that the variables produced two factors. Factor 1 consisted of 8 variables. These variables measure how easy it is to obtain certain drugs in the community. The drugs identified in Factor 1 include crack cocaine, other forms of cocaine, heroin, other narcotics, tranquilizers, barbiturates, amphetamines, and LSD.

Factor 2 consisted of five variables:

1. "How many people in this neighborhood use drugs?"
2. "Would you say that you see drug dealing . . . daily, weekly, monthly, or yearly?"
3. "How much of a problem are drugs in your neighborhood?"
4. "Compared to one year ago, would you say drug dealing in your neighborhood has become . . . much worse, a little worse, about the same as before, a little better, or much better than before?"
5. "Compared to one year ago, in your neighborhood, is drug usage . . . much worse, a little worse, about the same as before, a little better, or much better than before?"

Factor 1, containing the drug availability variables, has an Eigenvalue[2] of 6.66, explaining 51.3% of the factor variance. Factor 2, containing some measures of community awareness and community concern, has an Eigenvalue of 2.35, explaining 18.1% of the factor variance (see Table 2.2).

While Factor 1 makes intuitive sense and is a measure of community awareness, Factor 2 is a little bit troublesome. The variables that should have loaded on Factor 2 should have all been measures of community concern. The analysis revealed that those variables with high loadings on Factor 2 are a mixture of community concern and community awareness.

While this might be troublesome from a health education model, it is less problematic from a social disorganization perspective. The two factors, community awareness and community concern, and availability of drugs, may be separate elements of social disorganization.

DISCUSSION AND CONCLUSIONS

The community empowerment variables were not intercorrelated with any of the social disorganization variables. This lack of intercorrelation is a necessary

Table 2.2 Factor Analysis Final Statistics

Variable	Communality	Factor	Eigenvalue	Percent of Variable
Q1	.64620	1	6.66376	51.3
Q2A	.49839	2	2.35171	18.1
Q5	.38402			
Q9	.73722			
Q8	.48996			
Q22B	.72230			
Q22C	.70497			
Q22D	.81480			
Q22E	.81210			
Q22F	.67405			
Q22G	.88101			
Q22H	.85357			
Q22I	.79688			

Q1—"How common is it for groups of teenagers to hang out in public and make nuisances of themselves?"
Q2a—"How often do you see drug dealing in this neighborhood?"
Q5—"How much of a problem are drugs in your neighborhood?"
Q9—"Compared to one year ago, in your neighborhood, has drug dealing become . . . ?"
Q8—"Compared to one year ago, how has drug dealing in your neighborhood become?"
Q22B–Q22I—"How easy or difficult would it be for you to get crack cocaine (Q22b), other forms of cocaine (Q22c), heroin (Q22d), other narcotics (Q22e), tranquilizers (Q22f), barbiturates (Q22g), amphetamines (Q22h), LSD (Q22i)?"

first step before one can assess if the variables are measuring the same dimension of a concept. One can maintain, however, that these factors are intervening dimensions of social disorganization.

A concept may have many levels or dimensions to it (Babbie, 1995). As Sampson and Groves assert, social disorganization is measured utilizing exogenous sources and intervening dimensions, all measuring the structural barriers to forming ties or bonds to a community. From this analysis, one can add the variables of community concern and community awareness, or lack thereof, as additional measures of structural barriers to forming ties to a community. Intuitively, this makes sense. How can one form a bond to a community when he or she is riddled with concern for neighborhood drug usage?

Additionally, one can add the variables measuring drug availability in a community as intervening dimensions of social disorganization. The perception that drugs are readily available in a community weakens the community bonds as well.

These two factors can easily be seen as impeding participation in other activities that increase the bonds to a community. For example, participation in organizations or group meetings may be restricted because of the concern regarding drug usage and the availability of drugs in a community. It is logical to surmise that those who feel drugs are readily available in the community may also feel more threatened because of such activity and its by-product—crime. This proposed model of social disorganization, adding to Sampson and Groves' previous model, must be tested empirically. While the data analyzed support the present analysis, it cannot be used further to test social disorganization and crime because criminal activity is not measured. However, with the reliance on coalitions as a way to combat community health problems, which often includes crime, it seems quite probable that in the future researchers can begin to test these additional intervening dimensions of social disorganization.

REFERENCES

Akers, Ronald L. (1994). *Criminological theories: Introduction and evaluation.* Los Angeles: Roxbury Publishing Company.

Babbie, E. (1995). *The practice of social research* (7th ed.). Belmont, CA: Wadsworth.

Bursik, R.J. (1988). Social disorganization and theories of crime and delinquency: Problems and perspectives. *Criminology, 26*(4), 519–551.

Butterfoss, F.D., Goodman, R.M., & Wandersman, A. (1993). Community coalitions for prevention and health promotion. *Heath Education Research, 8*(3), 315–330.

———. (1996). Community coalitions for prevention and health promotion: Factors predicting satisfaction, participation, and planning. *Heath Education Quarterly, 23*(1), 65–79.

Florin, P., Mitchell, R., & Stevenson, J. (1993). Identifying training and technical assistance needs in community coalitions: A developmental approach. *Health Education Research, 8*(3), 417–432.

Goodman, R.M., Burdine, J.N., Meehan, E., & McLeroy, K. (1993). Introduction: Coalitions. *Health Education Research, 8*(3), 313–314.

Goodman, R.M., & Wandersman, A. (1994). *Using multiple methods to evaluate community partnerships.* Presentation at the Eastern Regional Workshop, Baltimore, MD.

Goodman, R.M., Wandersman, A., Chinman, M., Imm, P., & Morrissey, E. (1996). An ecological assessment of community-based interventions for prevention and health promotion: Approaches to measuring community coalitions. *American Journal of Community Psychology, 24*(1), 33–61.

Hedderson, J. (1987). *SPSS Made Simple.* Belmont, CA: Wadsworth.

Herman, K.A., Wolfson, M., & Forster, J.L. (1993). The evolution, operation and future of Minnesota SAFEPLAN: A coalition for family planning. *Health Education Research, 8*(3), 331–344.

Kornhauser, R.R. (1978). *Social sources of delinquency.* Chicago: University of Chicago Press.

McConnell, E.H. (1994). An evaluation of community mobilization training: Youth gang intervention and prevention in Texas—Bringing communities together for positive action. Paper presented at the Academy of Criminal Justice Sciences annual meeting, Chicago, IL.

McLeroy, K.R., Steckler, A.B., Simons-Morton, B., Goodman, R.M., Gottlieb, N., & Burdine, J.N. (1993). Social science theory in health education: Time for a new model? *Health Education Research, 8*(3), 305–312.

McMillan, B., Florin, P., Stevenson, J., Kerman, B., & Mitchell, R.E. (1995). Empowerment praxis in community coalitions. *American Journal of Community Psychology, 23*(5), 699–727.

Moriarty, L.J. (1991). Social disorganization theory, community empowerment, and coalition building: Exploring the linkages. *Criminal Justice Policy Review, 6*(3), 229–240.

———. (1994). 1993 community survey evaluation report. Technical report prepared for Vaughn Ownbey, Executive Director, Buncombe United, Asheville, North Carolina.

———. (1995). 1994 community survey evaluation report. Technical report prepared for Vaughn Ownbey, Executive Director, Buncombe United, Asheville, North Carolina.

———. (1996). 1995 community survey evaluation report. Technical report prepared for Vaughn Ownbey, Executive Director, Buncombe United, Asheville, North Carolina.

Nezlek, J.B., & Galano, J. (1993). Developing and maintaining state-wide adolescent pregnancy prevention coalitions: A preliminary investigation. *Health Education Research, 8*(3), 433–447.

Rogers, T., Howard-Pitney, B., Feighery, E.C., Altman, D.G., Endres, J.M., & Roeseler, A.G. (1993). Characteristics and participant perceptions of tobacco control coalitions in California. *Health Education Research, 8*(3), 345–357.

Sampson, R.J., & Groves, W.B. (1989). Community structure and crime: Testing social disorganization theory. *American Journal of Sociology, 94*, 774–802.

Shaw, C., & McKay, H. (1942). *Juvenile delinquency and urban areas.* Chicago: University of Chicago Press.

———. (1969). *Juvenile delinquency and urban areas* (Rev. Ed.). Chicago: University of Chicago Press.

Wandersman, A., Valois, R., Ochs, L., de la Cruz, D.S., Adkins, E., & Goodman, R.M. (1993). Toward a social ecology of community coalitions. *American Journal of Health Promotion, 10*(4), 299–307.

ENDNOTES

1. Coalitions are formed to improve health status (McLeroy et al., 1993). Examples include family planning coalitions (Herman, Wolfson & Forster, 1993), adolescent pregnancy coalitions (Nezlek & Galano, 1993), tobacco control coalitions (Rogers et al., 1993), and alcohol and other drug (AOD) coalitions (Goodman et al., 1993; Goodman et al., 1996; Florin, Mitchell & Stevenson, 1993; McMillan et al., 1995; Wandersman et al., 1996).

   There are over 250 federally funded alcohol and other drug (AOD) coalitions in the United States (Butterfoss, Goodman & Wandersman, 1993). The primary purpose of these coalitions is to reduce AOD usage in the communities through active citizen participation and community change.

   Until recently, coalitions had not been "studied in an organized and systematic way, and relatively little empirical evidence existed to support their effectiveness" (Butterfoss et al., 1993, p. 315). Many coalitions have been evaluated primarily because federally funded projects required it. One of the best measures of success is participation in the various coalitions. Regardless of what type of coalition it is, as community residents' and key leaders' participation increases, so does the effectiveness of the coalition (Butterfoss, Goodman & Wandersman, 1996).

Coalitions are built on the theoretical underpinnings of ecology theory. This approach combines many theories and "suggests ecological approaches for understanding the psychological and social factors that contribute to the production of health problems" (McLeroy et al., 1993, p. 306). These authors maintain that regardless of the health issue, such as "smoking, nutrition, exercise, stress or participation in screening programs . . . there are clearly important intrapersonal, interpersonal, organizational, community and public policy factors affecting these behaviors" (McLeroy et al., 1993, p. 306).

These authors are attempting to lay the theoretical foundation for coalitions. Their reliance on ecological theory and the factors affecting participation in coalitions mirror social disorganization, although this term is never identified. It can be argued that the factors affecting participation in coalitions are really measures of weakened social bonds.

2. Eigenvalue statistics pertain to the factors, not the individual variables loading on the factors. The Eigenvalue statistics are used to show the proportion of variance explained by the factor. For example, the Eigenvalue of 6.66 in an analysis of 13 variables (the current amount of variables under review) shows that the proportion of the variance explained by factor 1 is 6.66 divided by 13, or 51.3%. This is the value found in Table 2.2 under the "percent of variance" column. For a more detailed explanation of factor analysis see Hedderson, 1987.

3

Examining Students' Perceptions of Policing: A Pre- and Post-Comparison between Students in Criminal Justice and Non-Criminal Justice Courses

M.L. Dantzker, University of Texas—Pan American, and
J. Eugene Waters, Georgia Southern University

Methodological Focus. In most cases, the goal of research is to answer a question related to a particular subject. Developing the research question is among the first steps of conducting research. This article offers the **research questions** addressed along with the **hypotheses**. Other issues of interest include **questionnaire design**, **purposive** sampling, and a **pre-** and **post-test** methodology.

Abstract

The influence on our perceptions about issues, activities, and people by a variety of external sources, including TV, newspapers, movies, and other print mediums, is well-documented. The role of the police appears with great frequency in each of these sources; thus, a reasonable assumption is that the depictions of the police in print or in media impact one's view of police officers' roles and behavior. Similarly, college courses are oriented toward improving knowledge—and attitudes—about specific subjects. Since criminal justice is a popular area in which students take courses, a reasonable question is, What influence, if any, do these courses have on a student's perceptions about aspects of the criminal justice system? Here, our interest is in whether criminal justice courses influence students' perceptions about police officers. This article examines what, if any, changes occur in students' perceptions about police officers after completing a criminal justice course and how they compare with perceptions of students in a non-criminal justice course. These data were obtained using a survey instrument designed specifically for studying this issue both pre- and post-course.

Various societal elements and socialization agents influence our attitudes and perceptions, such as family members, peers, or the various visual media (news, television, movies, etc.) and print media (newspapers, magazines, etc.). One of the most influential sources on attitudes and perceptions has been the various forms of media; this is particularly true with respect to criminal justice and its related topics (Bailey & Hale, 1998; Kappeler, Blumberg & Potter, 1996; Surrette, 1992). One facet of criminal justice that appears to be a major recipient of media attention, and its influence, is the police.

Previous research suggests that citizens have various perceptions about policing (Carte, 1973; Dantzker & Ali-Jackson, 1998; Decker, 1981, 1985; Glauser & Tullar, 1985; O'Brien, 1978; Walklate, 1992). Personal experiences and media representations are variables believed to influence these perceptions. These beliefs of what the police should or should not do, often drawn from perceptions of the police role, can affect how citizens respond to police officers, and vice versa. This is particularly true when the perceptions are negative. For example, incidents in which police officers are indicted and arrested on various drug charges or accused of brutally assaulting an arrested suspect, can cause the public to develop adverse perceptions of police officers.

Because of such incidents and other similar controversies that effect perceptions of the officer's role, police departments continue to search for ways to counteract negative perceptions. These attempts often arise in some form of community-outreach programs (Alpert & Dunham, 1986; Meagher, 1985). Most recently, community policing has been advocated as a method of improving community relations. Furthermore, television shows such as *COPS* and *LAPD* have added a new, more positive perspective on policing. Yet, despite these efforts, perceptions of policing are still rather negative. Since American college students also observe these public images, their perceptions can easily be said to be reflective of society. With a continuously growing number of students entering college to study criminal justice and related fields, interest in the variables that influence students' perceptions of criminal justice and its various components have become a research interest. Many of these students will either work as police officers or work directly with police officers. Thus, perceptions of policing has become an important area of interest. Furthermore, colleges and universities have done little to study the impact of criminal justice courses on students' perceptions of policing. Such a study raises an interesting question, are educators helping to create a better image of our police system?

This article continues the reporting of research that first began in 1995, when it was hypothesized that students completing a course on policing would have improved perceptions of the police. It was for this research that the scale was developed and validated. The results allowed for acceptance of the hypothesis by showing that there was a positive change in perceptions of policing from the beginning of the semester (pre-course) to the end of the semester (post-course) (Dantzker & Ali-Jackson, 1998). However, these findings lead to several new research questions that obviously required examination:

1. Was it the course that influenced the change, or simply the passing of time?
2. Would students in non-police classes (other criminal justice topics or non-criminal justice) have a different perception of policing than those in police classes?
3. How would completion of these courses affect students' perceptions?

This article explores these questions. Two hypotheses were examined:

1. Students in criminal justice courses would have a more positive perception of policing than students in a non-criminal justice course.
2. There will be a change in students' perceptions at the end of such courses where criminal justice students' perceptions will remain more positive than the non-criminal justice students' perceptions.

Students from several universities and colleges across the country who attended various criminal justice and non-criminal justice courses, and students attending police academies in Massachusetts and Tennessee, were surveyed using the 14-item questionnaire previously developed (Dantzker & Ali-Jackson, 1998). The data were analyzed using SPSS/PC+.

METHODOLOGY

When this research first began, a 20-item questionnaire was designed specifically to tap students' perceptions of policing. For each statement about policing, respondents indicated their level of agreement to the statement. A 5-point Likert scale ranging from −2 (extremely disagree) to +2 (extremely agree) was used. Each statement's content was based on anecdotal and observational experiences of the scale's designer. Twelve statements were written so that a positive perception required disagreement with the statement, while the remaining eight were written where a positive response suggested a positive perception. Overall, the more negative the combined mean values of each statement, the stronger the indications of a positive perception of policing.

The questionnaire was first pretested during the 1995 spring semester. Results showed that it measured what the researchers were interested in measuring. Employing face validity, responses were what was expected. An internal consistency analysis was conducted to learn if the twenty statements could be used as a scale. The findings showed that fourteen of the twenty statements had high internal consistency providing a scale called Perception (Chronbach's Alpha = .80). Select demographic information was requested as well (see Appendix A). This 14-item questionnaire was then distributed to a purposive sample of students attending police-related courses at two Chicago-area Universities in the fall of 1995 ($n = 96$). The results were consistent with the pretest, requiring no additional changes and allowing continued use with the belief that the questionnaire was reliable.

To examine whether there was a difference in perceptions among students in classes other than those in police-related courses, the questionnaire was distributed to students in criminal justice courses at two Missouri universities (Missouri Western State and Truman State), one Massachusetts college (Quincy College), and one Georgia university (Georgia Southern University). The classes at the Georgia university were Introduction to Criminal Justice, while at the other institutions, the classes were various upper level courses. Students in two sections of an American Government course at Georgia Southern University were also surveyed. Finally, to add to the mix, individuals attending local and regional academies in Massachusetts and Tennessee were also surveyed. To date, fourteen courses, sections, or classes have been surveyed. Class sizes ranged from 12 to 106. The survey was distributed and collected by the instructor of each course: (1) during the first week of class—in most cases it was accomplished on the first day; and (2) during the last week of the course, prior to the final exam. Only completed questionnaires were returned to the researchers. The data were coded and analyzed using SPSS/PC+.

RESULTS

Among the fourteen sections surveyed, more than 700 usable surveys were returned. However, since this article examined whether a change in perceptions occurred, pre- and post-course surveys had to be matched. Due to many factors, the post-course survey was not completed in several sections. Therefore, the data reported here are from 259 respondents of both pre- and post-surveys. Furthermore, since the main interest of this study is the comparison of perceptions held by students in criminal justice versus non-criminal justice courses, the data are reported for this comparison.

The gender distribution for the whole sample only slightly favored males (131 to 123, 51% to 49%), which appears consistent with the general composition of college students nationally. Ethnically, Caucasians comprised 68% ($n = 175$); in terms of age, 28% ($n = 70$) of the sample were twenty-one years of age or older. By course type, 154 students (61%) were criminal justice students and 98 (39%) were non-criminal justice students. Among the criminal justice students: 85 were males, 98 were Caucasian, and 81 were eighteen years old or under. For the non-criminal justice students, 74 were male, 77 were white, and 34 were eighteen or under (see Table 3.1).

Because the goal was to examine differences in perceptions and whether these perceptions changed after completing the course, only the overall scale value is reported. The first analysis examined the pre-course perceptions with the post-course perceptions of the complete sample. The post-course perceptions were more positive ($m = -.314$ to $m = -.308$), but the difference was not statistically significant. The next analyses were by the two major types of classes: criminal justice versus non-criminal justice (American Government). For the pre-course results, students in the criminal justice classes were more positive in their perceptions than were the students in the political science classes ($m = -.463$ to $m = -.064$), and the difference was significant at $p \leq .01$. Perceptions were then compared for the post-course perceptions. Again, the criminal justice students were much more positive than the non-criminal justice students ($m = -.498$ to $m = -.023$, $p \leq .01$) (see Table 3.2). The end result was that both hypotheses were accepted.

Table 3.1 Sample Demographics ($n = 257$)

Variable	*n*/percent (CJ students)	*n*/percent (Non-CJ students)	Total *n*/percent
Gender			
Males	85 (53a/65b)	46 (47/35)	131 (51/100)
Females	74 (47/59)	52 (53/41)	126 (49/100)
Totals	159 (100/62)	98 (100/38)	257 (100)
Ethnicity			
Caucasian	98 (62/56)	77 (79/44)	175 (68/100)
African American	24 (15/60)	16 (18/40)	40 (16/100)
Hispanic	29 (18/97)	1 (01/03)	30 (12/100)
Other	8 (05/67)	4 (02/33)	12 (05/100)
Totals	159 (100/62)	98 (100/38)	257 (100)
Age			
18 and under	81 (53/70)	34 (35/30)	115 (46/100)
19	06 (04/14)	36 (37/86)	42 (17/100)
20	08 (05/32)	17 (17/68)	25 (10/100)
21+	59 (38/84)	11 (11/16)	70 (28/100)
Totals	154 (100/62)	98 (100/38)	252 (100)

a = column percentage
b = row percentage
Note: Rounding or missing data account for some totals not equaling the *n* of 257 or 100%.

Table 3.2 T-tests, Scale-Perception

	Mean	Standard Deviation	t-Value
For complete sample			
Perception 1 (Pre)	−.308	.573	
			.21
Perception 2 (Post)	−.314	.558	
By Type of Student			
Perception 1 (Pre)			
Non-CJ Students	−.064	.520	
			5.56*
CJ Students	−.463	.554	
Perception 2 (Post)			
Non-CJ Students	−.023	.506	
			7.21*
CJ Students	−.498	.505	

*$P \leq .01$

DISCUSSION

Whether a student or not, an individual's perception affects how he or she thinks or views something. When perceptions are negative, it can obviously have adverse effects. An obvious area in which negative perceptions held by the public can have a tremendous impact on human interaction is policing. Additionally, such perceptions might influence students' choice of a major or approach to a major, that is, attitudes and values brought to courses. Furthermore, these perceptions might affect how a student approaches a college major. For example, what are the chances that someone with strong negative perceptions of police officers will major in criminal justice? Because there are growing numbers of students who are majoring in criminal justice, it is interesting to examine their perceptions of policing. Additionally, it is interesting to compare these perceptions with those of students not interested in criminal justice. This article examined this phenomenon.

The results found that students' perceptions of policing, overall, were not very positive when comparing pre- ($m = -.308$) to post- ($m = -.314$) course perceptions, essentially indicating no change in perception over the life of the course. (Extremely positive equals −2.0, and the means here were around −.3). However, when students' perceptions by course type were compared, we found significant differences at both test administrations, the pre- and post-course assessments. There was a significant difference in perceptions by the nature of the classes (CJ versus non-CJ). Students in criminal justice courses had a significantly higher positive perception of police than their non-CJ peers prior to the course, and those differences increased over the life of the course. Furthermore, the post-course perception of policing was more positive for CJ students but less positive for non-CJ students. Yet, the differences between the pre- and post-course perceptions by course type were not statistically significant (CJ Students = −.463 to −.498, Non-CJ students = −.064 to −.023, respectively).

Initially, these results tend to indicate that CJ courses (despite the emphasis) can have a positive effect on perceptions where a non-CJ course might cause a more negative perception. The results provide a very interesting question for debate: Are non-CJ courses, in this case American Government, detrimental to perceptions of policing? Obviously, further exploration is required before this question can be properly answered.

APPENDIX A

Questionnaire: Student's Perceptions of Policing

This survey was designed to examine students' perceptions of policing prior to taking and after completing an introductory level police course. Please read statement and without spending too much time "analyzing" the statement, indicate your level of agreement/disagreement using the scale provided. Thank you for your cooperation.

Strongly Disagree	Disagree	Not Sure	Agree	Strongly Agree
−2	−1	0	1	2

(1) Although police officers are often called upon to do a variety of tasks, their primary role is crimefighter. −2 −1 0 1 2
(2) Most police officers do not solve more crimes because they are incompetent. −2 −1 0 1 2
(3) The motto "to Protect and Serve" is merely a public relations concept and has nothing to do with what police officers actually do. −2 −1 0 1 2
(4) At some point in their careers, all police officers commit a corrupt act. −2 −1 0 1 2
(5) Police officers are quicker to physically strike a minority group member than a white person. −2 −1 0 1 2
(6) Ignoring the needs of citizens is a common action of police officers. −2 −1 0 1 2
(7) Preventing crimes for rich, white people is more important to police officers than solving crimes for or assisting any ethnic or cultural group member. −2 −1 0 1 2
(8) Police officers are only out to hurt or harass people instead of being out to help them. −2 −1 0 1 2

(9) A problem people have with police officers is that they know police are always out there, but they never know what to expect from them. −2 −1 0 1 2

(10) Many individuals who become police officers want to help society. −2 −1 0 1 2

(11) Any time you see a police officer you should try to avoid having contact with him or her. −2 −1 0 1 2

(12) The reason police officers are still primarily white males is because of politics, discrimination, and the "good old boy" system of recruitment. −2 −1 0 1 2

(13) Police officers who take drugs or drink on duty should be immediately fired instead of being offered counseling or other assistance. −2 −1 0 1 2

(14) No matter what the circumstances, if a police officer violates an individual's constitutional rights, s/he should be held accountable. −2 −1 0 1 2

Please provide the following information:

Gender: Male ______ Female ______
Race/Ethnicity: White ______ African American ______ Hispanic ______
Other ______
Age: ______
Year in College: Freshman ______ Sophomore ______ Junior ______
Senior ______ Other ______
Major: ____________________ Minor: ____________________
Last four digits of social security number (for analysis purposes only) ______

FOR CRIMINAL JUSTICE STUDENTS ONLY
Other than Intro to Criminal Justice, have you taken any other courses with a police component? Yes ______ No ______
If Yes, how many? ______
Employment Goal: Law Enforcement ______ Probation ______
Courts ______ Corrections ______ Law ______ Other ______
Are you related to a police officer? Yes ______ No ______
If Yes, what is the relationship? ____________

REFERENCES

Alpert, G.P., & Dunham, R.G. (1986). Community policing. *Journal of Police Science and Administration, 14*(3), 212–222.

Bailey, F., & Hale, D. (1998). *Popular culture, crime, and justice*. Belmont, CA: West/Wadsworth.

Carte, G.E. (1973). Changes in public attitudes toward the police: A comparison of 1938 and 1971 surveys. *Journal of Police Science and Administration, 1*(2), 182–200.

Dantzker, M.L., & Ali-Jackson, N. (1998). Examining students' perceptions of policing and the affect of completing a police-related course. In M.L. Dantzker, A. Lurigio, M. Seng, and J. Sinacore (Eds.), *Practical applications for criminal justice statistics*, pp. 195–205. Boston, MA: Butterworth-Heinemann.

Decker, S.H. (1981) Citizens attitudes toward the police: A review of past findings and suggestions for future policy. *Journal of Police Science and Administration, 9*(1), 80–87.

———. (1985). The Police and the public: Perceptions and policy recommendations. In R.J. Homant & D.B. Kennedy (Eds), *Police and law enforcement,* vol.3, pp. 89–105. New York: AMS Press.

Glauser, M.J., & Tullar, W.L. (1985) Communicator style of police officers and citizen satisfaction with officer/citizen telephone conversations. *Journal of Police Science and Administration, 13*(1), 70–77.

Kappeler, V.E., Blumberg, M., & Potter, G.W. (1996). *The mythology of crime and criminal justice* (2nd Ed.). Prospect Heights, IL: Waveland Press.

Meagher, S. (1985) Police patrol styles: How pervasive is community variation. *Journal of Police_Science and Administration, 13*, 36–45.

O'Brien, J.T. (1978) Public attitudes toward police. *Journal of Police Science and Administration, 6*(3), 303–310.

Surette, R. (1992). *Media, crime, and criminal justice: Images and realities.* Belmont, CA: Wadsworth.

Walklate, S. (1992). Jack and Jill join up at Sunhill: Public images of police officers. *Policing and Society, 2*, 219–232.

4

Human/Cultural Diversity Training for Justice Personnel*

Marilyn Chandler Ford, Volusia County Department of Corrections
Lexie Williams, Daytona Beach, Florida, Police Department

Methodological Focus. One of the most popular means of conducting research is through surveys. This article discusses the challenges in conducting survey research. In addition, it provides the method for administering and results of a self-administered **survey**. Furthermore, questionnaire development, **face validity**, **convenience** sampling, and the question of generalizing results are represented.

Abstract

Many jurisdictions require some form of human diversity training for law enforcement officers. The State of Florida has required a standardized curriculum for all law enforcement and correctional officers since 1993. This study evaluated the effectiveness of Florida's human/cultural diversity curriculum in one jurisdiction in 1996. Certified law enforcement and correctional personnel were surveyed about the course's effectiveness in influencing postgraduate attitudes and behaviors. The survey of 260 officers indicates that while attitudinal change was reported by many, altered on-the-job conduct was less likely to occur. The overall consensus was that the human diversity curriculum was important, although there were a number of recommendations for making the course more effective. These findings are particularly timely as they relate to community policing initiatives.

Since the late 1960s, media commentators, social critics, academics, and the average citizen's attention increasingly has focused on one of the more salient

*This article is an adaptation of a paper presented at the annual meeting of the Academy of Criminal Justice Sciences, Las Vegas, March 12–17, 1996. Errors of fact or omissions are the sole responsibility of the authors, as well as a reflection of the individual views of the authors, and not that of their employers.

issues in the war on crime in America: the impact of race on judgment and action. The message is not new—or newly-inserted—in the public's conscious. The gulf between the races has been center stage since the Civil Rights Movement and, more recently, since the Rodney King arrest and trial in 1992 and the O.J. Simpson trial in 1995.

One reason for this gulf between the races is the demographic change experienced in the past decade and a half in America (increases in minority group members and a decreasing percentage in the "White" majority). Writers have described this phenomenon as the greatest in U.S. history, and it is virtually unparalleled in any other nation in the world. These demographic changes, although affecting the nation as a whole, have created almost insurmountable challenges for law enforcement personnel. With the increased emphasis on community-oriented policing, there has been an increased awareness of the critical need for a vehicle to teach, enhance, and reinforce the skills and knowledge relating to multicultural communities if there is to be a partnership for changing crime control efforts.

One mechanism for change has been to provide information about different races and cultures to those who work in the criminal justice system. Most notably, this material has been introduced through training classes, often termed human/cultural diversity training. In 1990, the State of Florida mandated human/cultural diversity training for all certified law enforcement officers, that is, police and corrections officers. The curriculum was developed by training center staff, members of the Criminal Justice Standards and Training Commission, regional council chairs, law enforcement and correctional administrators, state university research staffs, and local citizens. The first classes were incorporated in the Basic Recruit Training curriculum on January 1, 1993. Because Florida requires continuing retraining for police and correctional officers to maintain their certifications, human/cultural diversity training was also included in the mandatory retraining programs beginning July 1, 1993. Officers must complete 40 hours of retraining every four years (or an average of 10 hours per year). The human/cultural diversity segment is 16 hours of the 40 hours required.[1]

The human/cultural diversity curriculum has been deemed an integral part of the State's certification training for law enforcement and correctional personnel. Yet the curriculum has not been significantly revised since its inception. At the same time, Training Center instructors, and even some agency supervisors, report negative feedback about the course from graduates and from officers completing the recertification component. While course and instructor evaluations are routinely administered after course completion, there has been no effort to gather assessments from officers once they are on the job. A subsequent evaluation may provide important information about course relevancy and its potency or carryover effects. When placed in the context of the current national agenda, to encourage multicultural education, along with the renewed interest and discourse about cultural diversity initiatives, such an investigation becomes even more compelling.

This study reviews the history of Florida's effort and describes the state-mandated training curriculum. It provides a descriptive analysis of officers' reactions to human diversity training in one county in Florida. The article concludes with a discussion of the relevancy and design of this type of educational program for other justice personnel and for students of criminal justice.

HISTORY

The need to provide information about different races and cultures to law enforcement and correctional officers was never more evident than in the State of Florida in the 1970s. Because of Florida's proximity to the Caribbean Basin and to Latin and South America, the state became a destination of choice for both legal and illegal immigrants coming to the United States. During the period 1950–1975 the population of the state more than doubled, from approximately four million to nine million permanent residents. Although a majority of these residents had emigrated from large Eastern Atlantic states, many also immigrated from Mexico, Cuba, Haiti, Columbia, and other Caribbean/Latin and South American nations. While the new arrivals concentrated in southeastern Florida, the cultural impact on the rest of the state was evident: both in the media coverage of racial/cultural conflict that resulted in civil disorders, and in the flight of the indigenous population to less populated and less diverse areas of the state.

America is no stranger to immigration. However, the population of immigrants entering Florida during this period brought with them different (and usually adverse) attitudes about the justice system. Many of the immigrants were seeking asylum from political regimes that did not ascribe to the rights of individuals. These regimes often sanctioned violence and brutality as a means to control the populace. In turn, the use of violence against government officials was an accepted way of life in the countries of origin of many immigrants. It was in this context that law enforcement officers answered calls for service. Many of Florida's law enforcement officers found it increasingly difficult to cope with the attitudes and behavior that impeded the effective administration of the criminal justice system.

Aside from the challenges presented by the immigrant population, there were different perceptions and expectations of the emigrant population relocating from major U.S. cities along the North Atlantic states. Many of these new residents had relocated in reaction to the rising crime problems in their states, which they attributed to minority and other immigrant populations. Not surprisingly, their attitudes about the effectiveness of law enforcement were based on their experiences from the areas of the country from which they came. Many had observed the gradual administrative and operational decay of large law enforcement agencies; they had learned to accept widespread corruption and abusive use of force as elemental to their operations. These attitudes of the emigrant population were personified as the ranks of the local law enforcement agencies swelled with the children of these newcomers.

National attention surrounding the issues of culture and race was focused on Florida during the summer of 1980 after a Black insurance salesman, Arthur McDuffie, was killed by Miami police officers during a motorcycle chase. After a cover-up and acquittal of the officers by an all-White jury, the city of Miami experienced its worst riots in history. Not only was the city of Miami affected, but many major cities in Florida, including Orlando, Tampa, Ft. Lauderdale, West Palm Beach, and Tallahassee, saw widespread civil disorders as a result of this incident.

Officers policing the more volatile riot-impacted areas reported many arrests and injuries resulted from their inability to communicate effectively with the population. This inability to communicate, coupled with past complaints from minority populations concerned with police practices and attitudes, was now perceived by criminal justice officials as a message for change. There was agreement that something had to be done to reduce crosscultural conflict when policing diverse populations. The greatest amount of conflict occurred in five areas: cultural values, spiritual beliefs, family behavior patterns/roles, thinking patterns, and communication styles. Based on a report to the Governor concerning the origins of the civil disturbances in Florida following the McDuffie incident, the Criminal Justice Standards and Training Commission (formerly the Police Standards and Training Commission) was assigned the task of developing a mechanism to incorporate such material into the new recruit and in-service training curriculum.

HUMAN DIVERSITY TRAINING

The concept of diversity applies not only to persons of different races or cultures, but also to those of different genders, those of different ages, and those with disabling conditions. However, Florida's human diversity training course focuses on the issues of gender, race, and ethnicity to the exclusion of other issues. Human diversity training is aimed at the large "gray area" where an individual's culture is likely to intrude and condition the exercise of discretion (i.e., judgment).

The course recognizes that many of the values about culture are "hard wired." That is, many of these issues are emotionally laden and resistant to challenge. They are the accumulation of a lifetime of messages and experiences that affect the officer's view of those who are different from himself or herself.

As noted earlier, there are two forms of the curriculum. One is designed as a segment of the Basic Recruit Curriculum and consists of 24 hours of instruction. Since all police and correctional officers in the State of Florida must be certified prior to or within one year of hire, the Basic Recruit Curriculum is presented to all individuals going through the Academy for initial certification. The second curriculum is designed for officers who already hold certification and who must take courses within a four-year cycle to maintain their certification. The 16-hour retraining curriculum presents most of the objectives from the 24-hour basic curriculum, but in abbreviated form. Table 4.1 displays the curriculum components.

The instructional method emphasizes experiential learning. Activities designed to promote thought and class discussion are the preferred means for transmitting course material. The core of the course is designed to force participants to assess and reassess their values. The instructor's training manual also states that the course "models behaviors it wants/suggests for understanding and resolving differences between people of different races/cultures." The course provides this modeling through exercises and discussions to identify one's own background, to develop the individual's self-awareness about these issues, and then, to consider how the viewpoint of another may differ. Key objectives of the exercises are to have class participants listen effectively, resist judgmental reactions, monitor perceptions, seek feedback, and take risks. This process is designed to have the participant acknowledge the legitimacy of racial/cultural differences.

The expected outcomes of the training include: to understand and recognize the importance of individual and organizational cultures; to celebrate individual cultural heritage and contributions; to understand prejudice

Table 4.1 Human Diversity Training Curriculum

	Basic Recruit (*24 total hours*)		Mandatory Retraining (*16 hours*)	
		Hours		Hours
Session 1	Introduction	1.5	Introduction	1.5
Session 2	Understanding Cultural Influence	2.5	Understanding Cultural Influence	1
Session 3	Multicultural Communications	7	Multicultural Communications	7
Session 4	Empowerment	6	Empowerment	3.5
Session 5	The Law	3	The Law	2
Session 6	Cultural Effectiveness	2.5	Cultural Effectiveness	1
Session 7	Reducing Stress through Cultural Awareness (*optional*)	.75	N/A	

and stereotyping; to consider how mindsets are related to language; to understand the changing demographics of the American workforce and the advantages of organizations that value all its members.

The architects of the course did not focus on producing attitudinal change, since the brief instruction could not be hoped to alter messages about other races and cultures that were the product of a lifetime of experiences. Rather, course training goals are more modest: to enhance the officer's *understanding* of human diversity issues. The hope is that officers will become more effective in their interactions with increasingly diverse populations through broader awareness and understanding of other cultures, resulting in greater safety for all officers and the public they serve (Training Manual, 1992). In a nutshell, the model training is aimed at increasing the officer's skills to effectively interact with people of diverse cultural backgrounds (Barrett, 1993, pp. i–iii).

Approximately seven jurisdictions pretested the curriculum prior to its adoption statewide. According to state officials, officers' evaluations of the curriculum were "overwhelmingly favorable" (Barrett, 1993, p. 3). Many of the trial participants suggested the training segment could be longer, while some believed there was a slant to the materials, favoring one ethnic group over another. The first generation of trainers were schooled together by project staff who helped draft the program. The inaugural class bonded around the objective that human diversity classes would translate into differences in police interactions with people of other races and cultures.

As noted earlier, the purpose of this study was to gauge officer assessments about the human/cultural diversity curriculum well after Academy graduation or course completion. A key area of interest was the relevancy and saliency of course materials and, most importantly, the application of course principles in the field.

METHODOLOGY

Design

A self-administered survey was used to collect data during early 1996. The survey was distributed and collected at the officers' work sites during a two-week period. The self-administered survey was selected for a number of reasons, most of which adhere in the method itself. It was inexpensive in terms of money; the survey instrument was developed with relative ease; and the duration of the research project (at least at the data collection stage) was relatively brief.

The time factor was important for reasons that may not be apparent to the uninitiated, and it merits additional discussion. Real world operations typically pose barriers to conducting research. In our case, there were four challenges to overcome: (1) obtaining the cooperation of the agency head, (2) obtaining the cooperation of the supervisor in disseminating the questionnaire to all officers, (3) obtaining the cooperation of line staff in completing the survey, and (4) trying to ensure that those who answered did so fully, freely, and honestly. In short, it was imperative that we convince all involved that our project was not a significant disruption to their operation or a significant inconvenience for the officers. To the extent that our research method could be conducted simply, without undue instruction, and that the survey instrument was straightforward and short, these objectives were more likely to be accomplished.

These objectives might also have been achieved using an interview format, but only if the interview was brief and the researchers' efforts did not tax agency staff. Yet there was another reason for selecting the self-administered survey. As indicated earlier, there was reported discontent with the human/cultural diversity course. The researchers held upper management positions within their respective agencies, and one of them also taught the human diversity course at the Training Academy. The researchers' statuses would make it difficult for respondents to answer candidly, and/or for the researchers' to determine respondents' degree of candor.

Survey Instrument

The survey attempted to elicit information about the influence of the state-mandated human diversity curriculum on officers' postgraduation attitudes and behavior. Our survey contrasts substantially from the typical course evaluation conducted at the Training Academy. Course evaluations typically focus on instructor competencies: knowledge of subject, and instructor techniques and effectiveness. Academy evaluations make little attempt to link instruction in a particular topic to subsequent job performance. However, this was a prime objective in our study.

Additionally, since we were aware of discontent with the course, an effort was made to tap this issue, albeit in a general way. Informal feedback about the human diversity class centered on the course material and instructors. Yet there could be a biasing effect if we emphasized this issue to the exclusion of others. For example, if the survey asked specifically about course material and/or instructors, a self-fulfilling prophecy may have been fostered: a finding resulting from the survey's design rather than gauged from officers' unprompted responses. Thus, the questionnaire contained a more general question about the best and the worst feature of the human/cultural diversity training. The unstructured answers permitted by this question and its open-ended format presumably captured that which was remembered by officers, or what remained salient about the human/cultural diversity instruction.

Both close-ended and open-ended questions were used in the self-administered survey; demographic information was also requested (see Appendix A). The demographic information was positioned at the end of the survey instrument. This was done to address two considerations that arise with the survey method. First, by asking "meaty" questions at the outset we hoped to garner respondent interest and, hence, improve completion rates. Second, we hoped that the early questions would produce a response mode and lessen whatever concerns officers had about being identified from the demographic information. In other words, we hoped to desensitize respondents to personal information that might be viewed as locating them within their organization.[2] While we were careful in our instructions to let respondents know their surveys were anonymous and that completed forms would be kept confidential, many respondents have concerns about subsequent identification, which can influence their completion of and candor about personal information in addition to the more substantive survey questions.

A separate concern was how to gain officer interest and participation in the project when the researchers were not administering the surveys. Many employees approach questionnaires in the workplace with suspicion (at worst) or mild misgivings (at best). Other studies suggest that law enforcement officers tend to have a cynical world view. To address this, a statement was included at the beginning of the survey about the researchers' affiliations with police and corrections agencies, and the purpose of the survey. The reference to the cooperation of the department head in disseminating the survey was also made in the hopes that it would promote greater response.[3] Care was taken, however, to indicate that the chief/director had no direct investment in the research outcomes, and that their participation was limited to the access they had provided in permitting distribution and collection of the surveys from their staffs.[4]

Study Population and Sample

The survey was distributed to two area law enforcement agencies and to the local department of corrections. The two police departments were from the first and second largest cities in the county; the departments ranked second and third among law enforcement agencies in sworn officers, with 265 and 70 officers respectively.[5] One corrections agency serves the 13 municipalities and the county, state, and federal law enforcement agents within the jurisdiction. The corrections department has a fluctuating sworn staff of 250.

The actual study population was limited to those who had completed the human diversity recruit training or recertification training. Since our study was conducted in early 1996 and officers are given four years within which to complete retraining requirements, and in light of the fact that the curriculum was not implemented until 1993, a large number of officers had not yet taken the course. This applied to about half of the officers in the largest police agency and two-thirds of the correctional officers; response rates (reported infra) were adjusted for this fact.

Survey Respondents

As much as we would have liked to utilize agency training records to precisely identify officers who had taken the human/cultural diversity course, and then to select a sample using random procedures, this was not feasible. Agency training records are often imperfect and lacked sufficient detail. Officers hired directly from the Academy within the prior three years were sure to have had the human/cultural diversity course, but experienced officers were not uniformly required to report retraining courses taken to their departments. The State's governing body for officer certification maintains the official records and notifies departments when officer certifications lapse for failure to meet retraining requirements. Therefore, all officers were to receive surveys, and returned surveys were then sorted based on whether or not the officer had completed the human diversity course.

Agency staff were asked to distribute surveys to officers at shift briefings (or lineup) or to place in officer mailboxes, where provided. Realistically, however, the researchers did not control the actual manner of distribution, and there may well have been deviation from this procedure by agency staff.

The resulting sample was a nonrandom one and would best be termed a convenience sample. With the exception of one shift in one police department, where we could tell that the shift supervisor recorded survey distribution to all those under his command and then ensured a return survey or provided an explanation for the nonrespondent (e.g, on medical leave),[6] all officers controlled whether or not they actually returned the survey.

Completed surveys totaled 260 (*n*), with 165 from police and 95 from corrections officers. The survey response rate for the police officers was 85% for one of the police departments and approximately 90% for the other. It was 95% for correctional personnel. A majority of the nonrespondents in both groups were individuals who were on vacation, ill, or not at the work site for other reasons during the week the survey was administered.

Unfortunately, it is not clear how closely our respondents differed from all employed officers in the study jurisdiction because a composite officer profile does not exist. However, based on our knowledge of the local law enforcement personnel pool, we believe the respondent group is a fair approximation of employed, sworn officers (see Table 4.2 for sample's demographics). Law enforcement officers in the jurisdiction tend to be predominantly White and male; this was also true in the study sample. Over 60% of the sample was under 40 years of age, 71% were line officers (nonsupervisors), and 56% were high school graduates or had a GED. Officer age and years in policing/corrections closely corresponded, and was to be expected given the minimum age for certification in the state (18 years of age). The only deviation in the study group appears to be that it slightly overrepresents younger officers (and hence those with less time in the profession). This was expected, since the criteria for sample inclusion was completion of the human/cultural diversity curriculum, which was relatively new.

The lack of baseline data from which to measure the adequacy of the resulting sample is not unusual. One way researchers may assess a sample is to analyze subgroups in an effort to ferret out the ways in which a different sample would show different results. Of course, such analyses provide only a

Table 4.2 Police and Correctional Officer Demographics—Survey Respondents

Characteristic	Percent[a] (*n* = *260*)
Race	
White	84.9
Non-White[b]	15.1
Gender	
Male	80.1
Female	19.9
Age of Officer	
18–29	29.7
30–39	34.4
40–49	26.6
50 and older	9.4
Years in Policing	
1–4	31.8
5–9	32.6
10 or more years	35.7
(x = 8.7; *median* = 7; *mode* = 1,3,7)	
Rank	
Line Officer	70.7
Supervisor	29.3
Education	
High School/GED	56.1
2-year degree	25.5
4-year degree	13.3
Graduate school degree	5.1

[a] Percents may not sum to 100 due to rounding.
[b] 2.8% Asian or Hispanic.

crude indication of how subpopulations may differ on the variables of interest. As discussed later, the subgroup analysis revealed only minor differences. This suggests that our results may apply across other officer groupings in the study site.

RESULTS

The descriptive analysis was designed to explore the racial/cultural awareness and behavior of officers who completed a state-mandated human diversity course. Key variables were officers' reported understanding prior to and after

Table 4.3 Police and Correctional Officers' Responses about State-Mandated Human/Cultural Diversity Class

	Percent[a] (*n* = 260)	
Understanding of Diversity		
	Before class	After class
Fair[b]	43.1	30.0
Good[b]	56.9	70.0
Difference after Class		
	On-the-job behaviors	Off-duty behaviors
No	75.4	86.5
Yes	24.6	13.5
Recommend class to others?		
No	49.2	
Yes	50.8	
Why not recommend?		
Class can't change attitudes	22	
Class as presented, not effective	78	
Why recommend?		
Need to understand other cultures	100	

[a] Percents may not sum to 100 due to rounding.
[b] Includes 4 individuals who rated their understanding as "poor" prior to taking the course, and 5 individuals who rated their understanding as "poor" after the course.

the course, and reported changes in their conduct as a result of the training. In addition to on-the-job behaviors, one question probed for possible changes in off-duty conduct. Off-duty conduct was investigated because it is possible that an officer might react to suspects/inmates in an undifferentiated manner, that is, to treat or label those encountered at work in a singular fashion, such as "a criminal is a criminal is a criminal" or "they are all the same—no good." At the same time, officers might employ a broader view away from the work site, acknowledging that people are not all the same and that they do vary (see Table 4.3).

Understanding Human Diversity and Behavior Changes

Overall, the officers responding to the survey reported increased understanding of human/cultural diversity following the course. Slightly over half rated their understanding as "good" prior to the course; this rating was given by nearly three-quarters of the respondent group upon course completion. Of course, of greater interest to us was the reported impact of the human diversity course in the officers' lives. Did the reportedly greater understanding translate into behavioral differences?

Interestingly, while officers reported increased understanding, they were not so quick to report a difference in their conduct. Only one-quarter reported a change in their on-the-job behaviors, and only 13.5% reported differences in their off-duty behaviors. Follow-up questions asked respondents to supply an example of the altered behavior. This probing was done so that we might understand the respondent's frame of reference. Unfortunately, half of those who indicated a change in their behavior failed to provide an example.

Yet those who provided examples added to our understanding. For example, one officer reported:

> I believe I know how people of different ethnic backgrounds can feel upset about how their [sic] treated by other ethnic backgrounds. I also understand different cultures act and behave in different ways, and that does not make them bad or wrong.

Admittedly, it was difficult to assess the actual meaning of some responses, given the open-ended questions and the imprecision of language skills.[7] A few officers appeared to refer to a change in knowledge (awareness), while others related ways in which their conduct had actually changed (action). Whether increased understanding is a precursor for altered behavior (which it undoubtedly is in some instances), there was no way to gauge the extent to which increased understanding facilitated altered conduct. For example, the two statements below may or may not reflect actual behavioral differences:

> I stay away from the words that I now know offend those of other races or cultures. I also know now that the majority of blacks . . . take every word apart—and relate it to race.

and,

> Certain actions and vocal expressions of some minorities are now more easily understood and less threatening to me. I perceive some behavior differently now.

A number of officers reported that the human/cultural diversity course did not affect their behavior because they already treated everyone as individuals. In the words of one officer:

> My relationships with those of different cultures both personally and professionally have always been the same: I treat people as individuals rather than dwelling on their differences from me. I have always found this evokes a positive response.

One of the most poignant examples of change—and certainly an affirmation of the purpose of the course—was delivered in two short sentences:

> I am no longer afraid to say hello or talk to someone of a different ethnic background. Now it is very much of an interest of mine.

Examples provided by the officers who reported changes in their conduct after the course were similar, regardless of whether they were discussing job-related or off-duty behavior.

Course Evaluations

Independent of the issue of whether class participants believed that their understanding of human diversity improved and had an effect on their conduct was their rating of the course. Evaluations of the course were particularly revealing.

Nineteen percent reported satisfaction with the course as it was presented (i.e., responded that "nothing" was bad about the class). Yet an overwhelming 81% mentioned some way that they considered the class deficient. Over three-quarters reporting a deficiency related a problem with the class presentation, the course material, or the instructional method, and another 12% described factors that might also fit those descriptions (see Table 4.4). These deficiencies may be categorized as "correctable" since instructional materials can be revised, instructors can be retrained, and instructional methods can be altered.

Table 4.4 Worst Features of Human/Cultural Diversity Course

[Listed in rank order within category]

"Correctable"
Instructors
Dry, boring, repetitive, waste of time
Focus too much on Black/White and not on other cultures
Instructional method
Length
Instructional materials
Individuals took things too personally
Too much racism
Scheduling of class
Too much theory, not enough practicalities
Slanted towards one's opinion
"Hard Wired"
Course will not change others' feelings about race/culture
Not enough diversity in class

Alternately, 10% reported dissatisfaction about something that might be considered "not correctable" or "hard wired."

Of the reported deficiencies, those that seem at crosspurposes with the goals of human diversity training are the most disturbing. For example, there were a number of comments echoing this officer's opinion:

> I have always looked at the individual and not the color of skin. However, after this class I felt that the other ethnic groups are very prejudiced.

Other officers cited "too much racism" or "some officers took the comments too personally" as the worst features of the course. Comments in this vein seemed to refer to the highly charged, volatile, and often blunt comments made by officers about other races and cultures during the class. Placed in context, the class format relied on exercises that tapped emotions and attitudes. Thus, it is not surprising that participants may have had strong (and negative) reactions to the plain talk by other class members. This is a point that we will return to later.

Survey respondents were evenly divided about whether they would recommend the course to someone else (refer to Table 4.3). Yet the degree of similarity in reasons for recommending/not recommending the course were remarkable. As Table 4.3 indicates, among those who would recommend the course there was unanimous agreement of the need to understand other cultures. Among those who would not recommend the course, 78% reported that the course's current presentation was not effective for communicating cultural diversity issues, while 22% indicated they didn't believe a single class could change attitudes. In their words: "Sixteen hours of classroom training is not sufficient time to re-educate someone," and "Adults already have fixed ideas on this; they have made up their minds." Respondents who believed the course to be ineffective in promoting cultural understanding cited many of the same themes already discussed and shown in Table 4.4.

Of particular interest was the distinction made by officers away from the generalized, "this is important information for everyone," to "*others* need this knowledge." The former statement appeared to indicate "I need to understand and be aware of cultural differences," while the latter seemed clearly to reference "officers other than myself [need to understand . . .]." This finding is probably not surprising to those who work or teach in this area. It is not unusual for persons exposed to this type of material to claim their own lack of bias, but to attribute prejudice to others.

The Subgroup Analyses

Subgroup analyses were conducted to determine whether officer attitudes and behaviors varied by race/ethnicity, length of time in the profession, rank, or career path (police/corrections).[8] Characteristically, the patterns evidenced in the full group analyses held for the subgroups. Notable differences in responses occurred for the subgroup analyses comparing career path (police/corrections) and, to some extent, the White/non-White officers. A greater proportion of corrections officers rated their knowledge of human/cultural diversity as "poor or fair" prior to taking the course when compared to police officers. The reported lag in their cultural knowledge continued when officers were asked to rate their understanding of human diversity after class. A smaller proportion of corrections officers reported "good" understanding following the course (see Table 4.5).

These findings might be explained by the fact that a majority of the correctional officers took the class as part of the State's mandatory retraining. Several officers complained about having to take the class on their own time. Yet perhaps a more telling reason for dissatisfaction is that the COs who took the course as part of their mandatory retraining had to pay. All the other courses for re-certification are free, but Correctional Officers (COs) were required to pay $12 for the human diversity course. This created a triple imposition on the corrections officer: not only was the course mandated for recertification, not only did the officer have to take it in his/her free time, but the officer also was forced to pay for the requirement! While several police officers expressed similar concerns, they did not have to pay for the course.

An alternate explanation is that correctional officers were less receptive because of the potency of their attitudes about inmates. Specifically, by virtue of the status of the inmate, the COs saw no need to differentiate or to understand them. If inmates are "here to be punished," or "they are all the same [bad] and should be treated that way," there is no need for any training about how to handle cultural differences. This latter explanation comes from personal observation, which suggests that there has been a greater resiliency of status-based and/or intolerant attitudes that have been transmitted from the prior generation of guards and that, coupled with less attrition in the CO ranks, this creates a less than hospitable climate among COs about the need for accepting cultural diversity initiatives.

Several differences were noted in the subgroup analysis performed for White/non-White officers. While the very small *n* in the non-White officer group limits confidence in the results, the trends are nonetheless interesting. A greater proportion of these officers—32%—reported satisfaction with the human/cultural diversity course than for any other officer subgroup. Also, a substantially greater proportion of non-White officers than White officers indicated they would recommend the human diversity course to others. Among those who would not recommend the course, every non-White officer suggested that the course could be made effective through revisions, while only three-quarters of the White officers believed the course could be corrected.

Although many survey questions were open-ended, there appeared to be a high degree of correspondence in the subgroup analyses, and between the subgroups and the full study population. This suggests the commonality of

Table 4.5 Analyses by Police and Correctional Officer Subgroups

Characteristic	Race/Ethnicity		Police/ Corrections		Rank		Education Level		Years on the Job		
	Non-White	White	Police	CO	Line	Supervisor	H.S.	College	1–4	5–9	10+
	n = 38	*n* = 214	*n* = 165	*n* = 95	*n* = 174	*n* = 72	*n* = 143	*n* = 112	*n* = 82	*n* = 84	*n* = 92
Knowledge of HD before class											
Fair	42.1	43.0	38.8	50.4	43.1	44.4	46.9	37.5	46.3	42.9	40.2
Good	57.9	57.0	61.2	49.5	56.9	55.6	53.1	62.5	53.7	57.1	59.8
Knowledge of HD after class											
Fair	31.6	30.3	23.6	41.1	27.0	37.5	32.9	25.9	25.6	34.5	29.3
Good	68.4	69.6	76.4	58.9	73.0	62.5	67.1	74.1	74.4	65.5	70.7
Change on-the-job behaviors											
No	78.9	74.8	70.9	83.2	73.6	79.2	77.6	72.3	65.9	84.5	75.0
Yes	21.1	25.2	29.1	16.8	26.4	20.8	22.4	27.7	34.1	15.5	25.0
Change in conduct											
More understanding	11.4	14.4	15.8	11.2	14.7	12.3	13.3	15.6	20.6	6.6	15.9
Already dealt with people as individuals	14.3	7.5	9.4	6.7	9.3	7.7	10.2	6.3	7.4	7.9	9.8

Change off-duty behaviors											
No	89.5	86.0	84.8	89.5	84.5	90.3	86.7	85.7	79.3	90.5	89.1
Yes	10.5	14.0	15.2	10.5	15.5	9.7	13.3	14.3	20.7	9.5	10.9
Worst thing about course											
Correctable	42.8	67.3	56.9	75.0	59.7	69.6	71.6	52.4	63.5	60.3	65.8
Hard wired	25.0	16.7	20.3	12.5	18.6	16.1	13.8	22.0	17.5	25.9	20.5
Nothing	32.1	16.0	22.8	12.5	21.7	14.3	14.7	25.6	19.0	13.8	13.7
Recommend course to others?											
No	37.1	52.1	36.8	71.0	48.0	49.3	56.1	40.2	41.3	53.7	51.1
Yes	62.9	47.9	63.2	29.0	52.0	50.7	43.9	59.8	58.8	46.3	48.9
Why not recommend?											
Correctable	100.0	74.4	63.0	95.7	77.4	77.8	75.0	85.7	66.7	91.7	76.0
Hard wired	0.0	25.6	37.0	4.3	22.6	22.2	25.0	14.3	33.3	8.3	24.0
Why recommend?											
Others need to know	43.8	25.0	28.0	31.3	28.6	31.8	32.0	27.5	21.7	35.0	30.4

[a] Percents may not sum to 100 due to rounding.

experience and of officer interpretation of the state-mandated human/cultural diversity course.

DISCUSSION

These data are the product of a self-administered survey to police and corrections officers. As noted above, there was a fair degree of consistency in the officer responses, irrespective of factors such as race/ethnicity, years on the job, or education, which might well condition attitudes or conduct. Several important talking points emerge from these data.

First, is there a link between increased awareness and modification of conduct? A course objective was to improve officer awareness of cultural diversity so that officers might more effectively interact with people from other racial and cultural backgrounds. Our findings are that officers reported increased understanding of human diversity issues. However, it does not appear that increased knowledge translated into altered behavior. By their own admission, significantly fewer officers reported differences in their on- and off-duty conduct. It is difficult to judge whether our findings reflect actual realities for several reasons.

The format of the survey may have led to nonconfirming responses (i.e., no change in conduct). The follow-up question to "Did your on/off-duty conduct change?" was worded to have the respondent supply an example regardless of a "yes/no" to the screening question. It is not unusual for individuals to have trouble when asked to provide an example. Where the individual could not recollect an example, he/she may have provided a nonconfirming response to the screening question. A different type of limitation relates to whether (1) the officer defined for himself or herself that behavioral changes had occurred, and (2) that any such changes were the result of the human diversity class. Another factor to consider is the limitation explicitly acknowledged by course architects: that the course was not designed to change attitudes, but only to create an awareness that might improve their interactions. It may be that without real attitudinal change behavioral change is unlikely. Our analysis is not dispositive of this issue. Nonetheless, to the extent that the course was designed to improve officer reactions to individuals of other races and cultures, our findings are sure to disappoint.

Second, the data suggest that those who have completed the state-mandated human diversity training may be a more sophisticated audience than the architects of the course anticipated. For example, a number of officers remarked:

> I felt the course was being taught from a 1950s point of view and not the present culture.
>
> It is patronizing to think that college-educated, rational people have to be told that cultures differ.

> Didn't learn anything new—it was the same information most people pick up in the fifth grade. There was no challenge.

Some of these reactions were due to the officers' prior experiences. A number of officers cited the fact that they had been in the military and had been exposed to this material previously. The nature of the law enforcement job also is likely to sensitize officers. Police and correctional officers interact with individuals of other cultures on a daily basis. Officers learn fairly quickly that racial and cultural variations exist. The successful officer must utilize good interpersonal relations; this means, in many respects, treating everyone as individuals and seeing beyond superficial traits (i.e., race).

Additionally, police and corrections officers are not immune to the messages in the broader society. Messages about racial/cultural tolerance are perhaps more dominant than at any time in the past 15 years. The vocabulary of cultural diversity—of celebrating cultural diversity—is high on the current national agenda.

At the other extreme were comments that suggest the class was a *negative* learning experience. This leads to the question whether course goals were unwittingly sabotaged by the instructional method. Some survey respondents suggested that there was a hardening of intolerant attitudes, or that the course supplied fresh evidence that fellow officers were indeed biased. To some extent this (mis)perception may relate to the tone set by the instructor. More than one class graduate believed the instructor was biased.

Quality control in instructors is difficult. Yet it was obvious that the instructor's actions were critical to valuations of the class, which has been recognized by others engaged in human diversity training (Kelly, 1996). Among the first generation trainers there was a sense that human diversity training was important, needed, and that it could enhance officers' awareness. Training Centers in Florida are now staffed by second and third generation trainers. It is not clear that these individuals are communicating the same message about the vitality of human/cultural diversity as did the first group. Alternately, the composition of the current workforce is an important consideration. If law enforcement staff does not truly reflect the diversity of the population it serves, who is likely to be teaching the cultural diversity class? Those with the greatest stake in maintaining the status quo may communicate in subtle ways less-than-positive messages about cultural diversity. It is also difficult to separate valuations about a particular component from an overall assessment of an entire training program. If a training academy is poorly regarded overall, what is the likelihood that graduates will not generalize such attitudes to specific classes?

Evaluations of the course also may have been influenced by the interplay between course format and class composition. The course promotes a free exchange of ideas from participants, supposedly in a neutral and judgment-free setting. The issues are emotional and value-laden. Also operative is the fact that minority representation remains relatively low in police and correctional agencies in the county. The lack of diversity within the classes did not go unnoticed by some officers. Specifically, negative reactions about the human diversity classes might be fueled when non-White officers (who are in the minority) speak out about their perceptions of racial/cultural intolerance in the human diversity class. Similarly, officers from departments where the workforce is not diverse may feel little need to change or see nothing wrong with cultural homogeneity.

While we believe that human diversity training is an important component of the mandated training for police and corrections officers, this study clearly suggests the need to revisit the curriculum. A majority of class graduates reporting dissatisfaction with the course cited factors that appear to be correctable. The curriculum should be reviewed with an eye to: updating references and exercises, broadening the scope of the material, and providing more insights into how the materials translate to situations the officers will encounter in their jobs. It also seems clear that instructor competencies need to be improved.

One of the more perplexing questions about course revision concerns the comment made by officers that the material was too focused on Black/White issues and not on other cultures. On the one hand, this may indicate the sophistication of the officer population and their desire for a more global perspective. On the other hand, why teach officers about races/cultures that they are not likely to encounter in their daily activities?[9]

The bottom line to this study is the acknowledgment from the officers involved that their understanding of other races and cultures was improved by human/cultural diversity training. Justice system personnel do not act within a vacuum. It is important that police and correctional officers understand cultural differences, for understanding increases the possibility that their interactions may be more positively resolved.

Methodology and Study Limitations

A final word is merited about the study's methodology. The constraints of conducting research in the real world of policing and corrections shaped this study. In turn, those real world constraints limit the generalizability of study findings. Of particular note are two factors: the validity of the survey instrument and the representativeness of the study sample.

The survey instrument was not formally pretested. While the researchers believe the survey had face validity, its internal validity is less clear. The survey findings resonated with both of the researchers, who are knowledgeable about the Florida's human/cultural diversity curriculum and officer on-the-job conduct. This reverberation suggests that, at least to the researchers, the survey tapped the issues of interest. In addition, as noted earlier, there was a high degree of correspondence in the subgroup analyses. This suggests the commonality of officer interpretation of the State's human/cultural diversity curriculum and its outcomes.

A Non-Probability Sample Was Used

While not the ideal, the most problematic aspect of the sample is that no baseline data on officer characteristics existed for the researchers to make comparisons against, and it also was impossible to evaluate sample error. We don't know whether our sample mirrored officer demographics or actual attitudes and experiences in the study jurisdiction. Aside from the usual problems in generalizing the results of a study in one jurisdiction to another, this further served to limit the study's generalizability.

Having acknowledged these two limitations then, how is it possible to accept the study findings? From the purist's perspective, it may be difficult. However, from the realist's perspective, this is but one example of how real world processes constrain research endeavors. It is further evidence of why researchers seek to replicate studies and research findings. This raises another aspect of the dilemmas faced by researchers when they study current criminal justice processes.

When the justice system decision maker is interested in the research outcome, it is more likely that the research methods used will approach the ideals of the research craft (or textbook). This is to say that where there is commitment from a justice system CEO about the research endeavor, there is greater support for the researcher and for following research tenets. However, if the interests of the researcher lay outside agency agendas, then it will be more difficult for the researcher to enlist the cooperation of the staff.

The researcher is then faced with a dilemma: not to conduct the test or to do so under less than ideal circumstances. How much latitude should there be in conducting research in the pursuit of increasing the body of knowledge? Certainly the integrity of research principles should not be significantly compromised. However, interpretations about how serious a compromise of research principles is involved in any particular study is surely a matter of debate—and it often rests in the eye of the beholder.

Unyielding adherence to rigid methodological principles may foreclose research into topics of great importance and interest. Yet boundaries that are too flexible pervert the scientific method that is integral to social science research. At a minimum, the threshold for methodological compromise should be governed by the study's purpose. For example, if the study's purpose is to examine juror deliberations, the study typically will involve experimental design—and all that it entails to address that method's shortcomings—because other avenues of research are legally foreclosed to studying American juries (see, for example, Ford, 1986). In addition, we suggest that research compromises should be made with regard to some notion of face and construct validity, with adequate application of the research technique chosen, and when using a large enough sample.

Turning attention to the specific study at hand, we believe that these criteria were met. There are limitations to these data to be sure. Yet until there are studies with higher order methodologies, our findings provide information that is woefully lacking in the literature about the impact of human/cultural diversity training. These findings should be of interest to those who wish to impart and improve officer sensitivity about different races and cultures through human diversity curricula; our findings also should be of particular interest in light of community policing initiatives.

APPENDIX A

Survey Instrument

Survey on Human Diversity Training—Certified Law Enforcement Officers

Introduction: This study is being conducted by two professionals who work in the law enforcement and correctional fields. We are conducting the survey to understand your reactions to the Human Diversity Training course that was required in the Academy for initial certification or in later retraining. While this survey is being distributed at your worksite through the courtesy of your Chief/Director, it is not intended to be shown/used there. We would appreciate your help—and your honesty—about this course. You do not have to put your name on the survey; it is anonymous. The personal questions at the end of the survey may help us interpret differences in survey responses. Thank you for your time!

1. When did you take the human diversity course? Year ____________
2. How would you rate your understanding of other cultures prior to taking the course?

   ( ) Good ( ) Fair ( ) Poor
3. How would you rate your understanding of other cultures after taking the course?

   ( ) Good ( ) Fair ( ) Poor
4. Has there been a difference in your on-the-job behaviors (beliefs, the way you think about others, or your actions) since you took the course?

   ( ) Yes ( ) No

   Can you give an example? [Use the reverse side if you need more room]
5. Has there been a difference in your off-duty behavior or your personal life since you took the course?

   ( ) Yes ( ) No

   Can you give an example? [Use the reverse side if you need more room]

6. What do you feel is the single most important thing you learned from the course? [Use the reverse side if you need more room]
7. What, if anything, was the worst thing about the course? [Use the reverse side if you need more room]
8. Would you recommend/have you recommended the course to others?

   ( ) Yes ( ) No

   Why/why not? [Use the reverse side if you need more room]

Personal Information		
Sex: ( ) M ( ) F	Race: ( ) American Indian ( ) Hispanic ( ) Asian ( ) White ( ) Black ( ) Other _________	Age: ( ) 18–21 ( ) 35–39 ( ) 22–24 ( ) 40–44 ( ) 25–29 ( ) 45–49 ( ) 30–34 ( ) 50+
Number of years in policing/corrections: _______________	Rank: Patrol OR ___________ Supervisor	Ed: ( ) High school/GED ( ) 2 yr AA degree ( ) 4 yr BS/BA degree ( ) Grad school or degree

REFERENCES

Barrett, M.E. (1993). *Training manual-update.* Tallahassee, FL: Florida Commission of Standards and Training.

Ford, M.C. (1986). The role of extralegal factors in jury verdicts. *The Justice System Journal 11*, 1 (Spring), 16–39.

Kelly, P.M. (1996). Conducting human diversity training. *The Florida Police Chief* (February) 11, 13.

State of Florida. (1992). *Training manual.* Tallahassee, FL: Florida Commission of Standards and Training.

ENDNOTES

1. In mid-1997 the Florida Criminal Justice Standards and Training Commission, which sets standards for officer certification and training, reduced the number of hours required for the retraining component from 16 to 8. Minor revisions in course materials also occurred. These changes did not become effective until 1998.
2. It was apparent this was a concern for a number of respondents. There was more missing data on race, gender, and officer rank than for other demographic items. Given the preponderance of White, male officers (a situation common in other jurisdictions), it was surmised that it was the minority officers (as judged by race/ethnicity and gender) who were less likely to report personal characteristics that would tend to locate them within their agency and which could be linked to their responses.

3. It was recognized that mention of an agency's chief executive support for the project in the survey instructions may have a subtle, biasing effect. The potential effect of this linkage is interesting but unknown, since alternate versions of the survey (one with this instruction and one without it) were not tested. However, the researchers judged there was greater benefit in mentioning the CEO to gain cooperation for survey completion than to an unknown bias effect that might be produced.
4. The survey instrument was not formally pretested but reviewed by the researchers and one police chief for face validity. This same chief provided input for determining how the study sample could be collected and the method of survey distribution.
5. In the case of at least one of the police departments, the chief is an opinion leader in the local police culture. The initial plan was to begin data collection at two police agencies and the corrections department, and then involve the other law enforcement agencies. Several factors altered this plan: leadership changes in some of the other police departments; nonresponsiveness on the part of the head of the remaining large police organization; and the small number of officers in the remaining police agencies.
6. These surveys were returned with a shift roster, notated for every completed survey, and the accompanying survey had each officer's name written at the top for distribution. The roster also provided notations where a completed survey was not attached (e.g., on vacation leave, jury duty). It is not clear if this procedure had a biasing effect on officers' responses. Inspection of the surveys did not reveal any major differences (they were not uniformly positive or negative); the number was too small to statistically analyze.
7. This illustrates one of the drawbacks with open-ended and/or self-administered surveys that is better addressed when close-ended and/or interviews are performed. Specifically, the researcher must categorize the narratives from open-ended questions in order to analyze them, and the researcher is unable to probe for exact meanings. The resulting categorizations involve the researcher interpreting remarks provided, and thus introduces another element of error. The article's subsequent discussion of the worst features of the human diversity curriculum further elucidates this concern.
8. Another subgroup analysis for those who had taken the course prior to 1995 and those who had taken the course during or after 1995 was conducted. Findings mirrored those of the full study population and the subgroups reported in Table 4.5.
9. The dominant racial/cultural groups are Black/White and, to a much smaller extent and only in one area of the county, Hispanic. It cannot be said that the officers' reactions may signal a defensiveness on the part of White officers, since Black officers were as likely to comment about the narrow focus of the course.

5

Women Offenders, Drug Addiction, and Crime

Dennis J. Stevens, Mount Olive College

Methodological Focus. This article continues with the concepts of convenience sampling and survey research, showing how both can be used within the confines of a prison setting.

Abstract

This exploratory study examines the relationship between drug addiction and criminal activity among incarcerated women who were in a prison drug rehabilitation program. It has been believed that drug addiction gives rise to criminality among females, but, this notion was largely unsupported by the data. One implication of this finding is that drug addiction in itself is not necessarily a causal factor producing crimes of violence, especially among women. Since the respondents committed crimes such as shoplifting, prostitution, assault, armed robbery, and property crimes at ages as early as 12, and many were apprehended yet not prosecuted, it is recommended that a zero-tolerance toward justice intervention of juveniles be considered as one method of future drug control. A longitudinal study should be conducted examining the relationship between early prosecution and future criminal activities of females.

A major contributor of criminal lifestyles is illicit drug use (Bureau of Justice Statistics [BJS], 1996). Many writers claim that violence, including homicide, is perpetrated under the influence of substances such as psychoactive medications and illegal drugs such as cocaine, amphetamine, inhalants, LSD, and a host of designer drugs (Jackson, 1995; Nurco, Hanlon, Kinlock & Slaght, 1996). Many studies show that high rates of criminal activities including death by homicide are attributed to an increased involvement with both drug trafficking and drug use (BJS, 1996; Klein & Maxson, 1994). Other writers, such as Akers (1984), add that the risk factors most closely associated with delinquency are drug use followed by family dysfunction. These advocates of a drug-violence association postulate that a significant causal link exits between addiction and violence. Certainly, illicit drug activity impacts individuals and society-at-large, yet it disproportionately affects poor minority communities more often and differently than other communities.

On the other hand, some writers suggest that the use of deadly force by law-abiding individuals in poor minority communities is seen as an appropriate response to environmental conditions created in part by dysfunctional justice agencies and organizations, suggesting that drug use in and by itself is hardly causal in nature but merely a characteristic of some members of society (Stevens, 1997a, 1997c, 1996). Other writers add that the presence of patrol time and zero-tolerance policies of arrest and prosecution significantly affect criminal activities, including drug use (Green, 1995; Karmen, 1996; Sherman & Rogan, 1995; Sherman & Weisburd, 1995).[1] Then, too, a few writers add to the debate, pointing out that the war on drugs is far too expensive for the few results it has produced relative to drug control, due in part, they argue, because drugs are largely by products of crime (Benson & Rasmussen, 1996).

It is plausible that the relationship of substance abuse to violence in poor and underserved communities is complex. But, Kristal (1991) argues that most drug-violence studies use young poor minority males as subjects. I ask how closely linked is drug addiction to violent crimes among women? In light of Boyum and Kleiman (1995), who argue that the relationship between drug addiction and violent crime has not been proven among women, one mission of this study is to show that drug addiction gives rise to female criminal careers.

It is hoped that this study will fill the literature gap regarding drug addiction and female criminality, despite the belief that women are more likely to use drugs to cope with life than men, who tend to use drugs for pleasure (Moon, Thompson & Bennett, 1993). Miller (1990) adds that female substance abuse can be described as an attempt to control the perceived invasion of physical or psychological boundaries, since females are victimized more often than males, a fact supported by government statistics (BJS, 1996). In addition, substance abuse among females appears to be both supported and encouraged by society-at-large (Moon, Thompson, & Bennett, 1993).[2] But is it a primary contributor[3] to factors leading women into criminal careers? Criminal careers are characterized as ongoing high-risk lifestyles centered on criminal activities and victimization. Both events seem determined by convenience and opportunity, a thought consistent with Gottfredson and Hirschi (1990) and Friday (Wright, 1994).[4]

Drug use, as it relates to a physical (and probably psychological) addiction, suggests a drug-induced change in an individual such that she or he requires continued use of the drug to function "normally" and to prevent the occurrence of a withdrawal syndrome (Liska, 1997). This definition is consistent with the American Psychological Association's (APA, 1996) perspective on drugs. The APA adds that the criterion for substance abuse is a pattern of substance use leading to clinically significant impairment or distress.[5] The

APA says that drug addiction includes tolerance, withdrawal, and a pattern of compulsive use of drugs. Therefore, for the purposes of this paper, drug addiction is defined as illicit, compulsive drug use with salient experiences of drug tolerance and fear of withdrawal.

METHODOLOGY

This paper examines the relationship between drug addiction and crime among 68 women incarcerated at a high custody penitentiary in North Carolina where I was a prison teacher during the spring of 1997. Women who had received treatment from DART (drug and alcohol recovery treatment), a prison recovery unit for substance-dependent inmates regardless of their conviction, were surveyed with the aid of correctional officers, DART counselors, and student-inmates.[6] The survey distributed to the respondents included demographic questions about the participants and inquired about early criminal activities; frequency of criminal activities (choices included: always, very often, often, sometimes, seldom, and never); and age of the participants at the time of those activities. It inquired about early drug experiences, frequency of drug use, as well as ages at the time of those experiences. Data collection was followed by keyed-in computer grid entries and numerous statistical tests to determine the relationship of the variables. Many tests (i.e., frequency tests, Chi Square, and T tests) were used to help understand the data.

Sample

The average respondent (66%, 45) surveyed was 30 years old and completed either a GED or a high school diploma (see Table 5.1) before confinement. Thirty-seven percent (25) of them were married; all but 10% (7) had at least one child. Sixty percent (41) were Black, 37% (25) were White, and 4% (2) were Hispanic. The average respondent served 34 months and had been arrested three times before confinement. Fifty-eight percent (40) were incarcerated at the average age of 26, with a range from 17 to 45. Forty percent (27) were convicted of a crime of violence including assault[7]; 27% (18) were convicted of a property crime; 22% (15) were convicted of public order violations, including driving while intoxicated and nontrafficking drug crimes; 12% (8) were probation or parole violators. All of the participants reported that they were former or current clients of DART and were drug dependent (but not necessarily convicted of drug violations). The statistics of the North Carolina Division of Prison show that the sample in this study and the demographics of the general female prison population in North Carolina were similar at the time this study was conducted.

Table 5.1 Characteristics of Sample ($n = 68$)

Characteristic	Average/Percent	Range/Age
Age	30	19–47
Education	12	8–15
Married	37%	
Divorced/Widowed	24%	
Single	36%	
Children	1	0–7
Black	60%	
White	37%	
Hispanic	4%	
Months served	34	7–96
Arrests	3	1–6
Age at incarceration	26	17–45
Conviction		
Violence	40%	27
Property	27%	18
Public Order	22%	15
Technical	12%	8

FINDINGS

First Crime, Age, and Frequency

When the participants reported on their early criminal activities, the frequency of those events, and their age at the time of those events, shoplifting, prostitution, and assault were the first crimes committed by the respondents at an average age of 14 (see Table 5.2).[8]

More specifically, 65% (44) of the respondents reported that their first crime was shoplifting at 14, although some of the participants reported that they committed that crime for the first time at age 10. The shoplifting respondents indicated that they "very often" continued to commit that crime well into their early 20s. Sixteen percent (11) of the participants first committed the crime of prostitution at the average age of 15, but many of those offenders first committed this crime as early as 12. The prostitution respondents "sometimes" continued that crime well up to the time of their incarceration, as well as other crimes. Then, too, 4% (3) of the respondents reported that they first committed the crime of assault at 15, while some of the assault respondents reported that they first committed assault at age 13. Three percent (2) of the participants reported that their first crime was armed robbery at 14 and 15 years of age. Also, 6% (4) reported that crimes against property were the first crimes they committed at 13, but two of the participants started at age 12, and 6% (4) participants reported to committing "other" types of crimes at the age of 12.

Table 5.2 Criminal Activities of Sample ($N = 68$)

Criminal Activities	Percent*	Frequency	Age	Range
Shoplifting	65%	Very often	14	10–25
Prostitution	16%	Sometimes	15	12–23
Assault	4%	Seldom	15	13–21
Armed Robbery	3%	Seldom	16	14–15
Property Crimes	3%	Sometimes	13	12–15
Other	6%	Seldom	12	12–14
Murder	3%	Once	25	23–27

* percents rounded

Table 5.3 Drug of Choice, Percentile, Frequency, and Age of First Use ($n = 68$)

Drug of Choice	Percentile*	Frequency	Age	Range
Marijuana	59%	Often	14	13–22
Crack/Cocaine	19%	Seldom	13	12–21
Heroin	12%	Seldom	14	13–21
Other/unknown	10%	None	14	12–23

* percents rounded

Lastly, 3% (3) of the respondents were first-time offenders who were convicted of murder at 23 and 27 years of age.

First Drug Experience, Age, and Frequency

When the participants were asked about their first illicit drug experience, their age at the time of that first experience, and the frequency of use afterwards, 59% (40) of them reported using marijuana as their first drug at the average age of 14, but some of the respondents said they used this drug as early as 13 years of age (see Table 5.3). The average marijuana respondent reported using this drug often throughout their teenage years, but it appears that those respondents who first used it at a younger age reported an increased frequency rate greater than those respondents who first used it later than 16 years of age. Also, 19% (13) tried crack cocaine as their first drug, but they seldom used it until they graduated from high school or received their GED. Twelve percent (8) tried heroin at 13 or 14 as their first drug, and they, too, seldom used it until their late teens. Lastly, 10% (7) of the sample used "other" drugs or were not sure which drugs or at what age they were when they first used drugs.

Getting Caught But Not Arrested or Prosecuted

When the sample were asked about their early criminal activities and getting caught or being discovered, data show that the average participant had been caught (apprehended and/or discovered) an average of 3 times, largely, prior to their first arrest and prosecution (see Table 5.4). That is, 6% (4) were first apprehended by a social worker; 7% (4) by teachers; 18% (12) by store security; 10% (7) by their parents; 42% (28) by the police, but not arrested or prosecuted; 7% (5) were arrested and prosecuted; and 10% (7) were never apprehended while they were teenagers.

Specifically, of those 44 participants who first committed and continued with the crime of shoplifting, 5% (2) of them were first discovered as shoplifters by family welfare or social workers examining the family of the offender; 9% (4) were first discovered by their teachers; 27% (12) were first apprehended by retail staff or security; 14% (6) were first discovered by their parent(s) or caretaker(s); 36% (16) were first apprehended by the police as a teenager, but not arrested; none were ever prosecuted while a teenager; and 9% (4) were never apprehended or discovered. On the average, shoplifters were apprehended or discovered as shoplifters an average of 4 times each with a range of from zero to six, and not one of them, at any time were prosecuted for these crimes.

The prostitutes reported similar findings. That is, of the 11 who first committed the crime of prostitution and engaged in this crime until they were incarcerated, 9% (1) of them was first discovered by a social worker; 9% (1) was discovered by a parent; 55% (6) were first stopped by the police but not arrested; 9% (1) was arrested but not prosecuted; and 18% (2) were never apprehended. The average prostitute was apprehended or discovered 6 times, with a range from 0 to 12 times, but none were ever prosecuted.

Of those three participants who first committed the crime of assault, one was first discovered by a social worker, one by a teacher, and one by the police.

Table 5.4 Getting Caught* (N = 68)

Discovery Method	*N*/Per %	1	2	3	4	5	6	7
Totals	68/100%	44	11	3	2	2	4	2
Social Workers	4/5%	7%	9%	33%				
School	5/9%	9%		33%				
Store	12/27%	27%						
Parent(s)	7/14%	14%	9%					
Police/No arrest	28/36%	36%	55%	33%	50%	100%	100%	
Prosecution	5/7%		9%				100%	100%
Never Caught	7/10%	9%	18%		50%			

**N* = number, P = percent, 1 = Shoplifters, 2 = Prostitution, 3 = Assault, 4 = Armed Robbery, 5 = Property, 6 = Other, 7 = Murder

*percents rounded and includes missing cases

None were ever prosecuted. The average discovery or apprehension for those individuals who committed this crime was two each. A similar finding was found among the armed robbers, property offenders, and "other" offenders. The two murderers in category 7 on Table 5.4 were both first-time offenders who were arrested, prosecuted, and sentenced to life.

Getting Arrested, Prosecuted, and Committing Felony Crimes

In the above findings, many of the participants were discovered, stopped, and sometimes arrested, yet none were prosecuted. This category shows that the average respondent was 21 when first arrested and prosecuted. When the data were examined concerning career criminal lifestyles, 76% (52) of the participants were engaged in high-risk characteristics, as previously defined in a criminal lifestyle, prior to a 21st birthday (see Table 5.5); that is, three-quarters of the participants reported that they "always" or "very often" committed felony crimes against others (assault, larceny, fraud, robbery).[9] This latter finding leads me to suspect that many of the participants in this sample lived a life of crime prior to criminal prosecution.

Career Criminal Lifestyles

In addition to reporting that they committed felony crimes against others prior to a 21st birthday, the participants also reported high degrees of smoking, drinking, sexual relationships, unwanted pregnancies, everyday living expenses from illegal sources, household accidents, and criminal friends.[10] More specifically, when the respondents were asked, how often did you experience the following things before your 21st birthday, the average response to most of

Table 5.5 Career Criminal Lifestyles Before 21 ($N = 68$)

Indicators	always	very often	sometimes	seldom	never*
Committed felony crimes against others	46%	30%	22%	2%	0%
Smoking	84%	11%	3%	1%	1%
Drinking	63%	30%	3%	3%	3%
Sex	23%	45%	27%	3%	0%
Unwanted pregnancy	28%	24%	13%	13%	22%
Everyday living expenses from illegal sources	43%	23%	25%	3%	3%
Household accidents	28%	25%	23%	9%	16%
Criminal friends	60%	25%	10%	3%	3%
Beaten, robbed, raped	33%	33%	23%	9%	3%

*percents rounded and includes missing cases

these indicators was that these activities happened either always or very often before they turned 21. For example, over half of the respondents experienced an unwanted pregnancy and 66% (45) of the respondents received their everyday living expenses from illegal sources (see Table 5.5). As far as victimization, the participants reported that 66% (45) of them were beaten up, robbed, and/or raped either all of the time or most of the time, while only one offender reported that she never was attacked.

These findings are somewhat consistent with Fletcher, Rolison, and Moon (1993) and Friday (Wright, 1994), who add that many incarcerated females ran away from home many times as minors due to feelings of insecurity, were easily manipulated by others, and were more likely to become victims of violent crimes than others.

Frequency and Addiction

While ages 12 through 14 were some of the ages the participants first tried drugs, 41% (28) of the offenders had not used drugs more than twice a week until their 18th birthday, and 56% (38) reported that drugs were used about once a week at age 20.[11] Furthermore, the indicators of addiction, as implied by experiences of drug tolerance, withdrawal avoidance, and compulsive use of drugs, were reported by the participants as occurring at an average age of 23, with a range of 16 to 36.

Of particular interest is the finding that the average age of the first arrest followed by prosecution for this sample occurred around an average age of 21. The implication that arrests and prosecution can lead to addiction might be considered here. That is, when the ages of first arrest and prosecution are computed with addiction ages, it appears that there is a significant relationship between these two variables.[12] Thus, addiction seems to have followed the first arrest and prosecution of the participants by a spread of 15 months.

Additionally, 10% (7) of the respondents reported that they had not tried drugs prior to their 18th birthday. Of the five, three first tried crack cocaine and/or heroin and experienced indicators of addiction with its first use. The same was reported by the other two respondents, but their first experience and addiction happened while incarcerated.

In summary, the findings show that the average respondent reported experiences suggesting drug addiction an average of 15 months after her first arrest followed by prosecution, but two reported drug addiction experiences after incarceration.

CONCLUSION

The hypothesis that drug addiction gives rise to criminality among women was unsupported by the data. Results show that female offenders lived lifestyles comparable to that of career criminals prior to drug addiction experiences and prior to their first arrest followed by prosecution. That is, female criminal careers lead to drug addiction. But what becomes clear in this study is that most female offenders are discovered or apprehended early in their criminal careers, but are rarely arrested; and if they are arrested, they are rarely prosecuted. It is not clear if male offenders experienced similar events in their younger life. Perhaps the relationship between crime and addiction should be studied among male offenders, too.

One implication arising from society's failure to prosecute these offenders early in their careers is a weakening of a societal "collective conscience," as Emile Durkheim (1933, 1984) would argue, lending itself to a rise in criminally violent behavior. Thus, more individuals might feel that violent crime is either a right or an appropriate response to the conditions in their environment due in part to inadequate police protection and in part to justice agencies that produce violent offenders—as I argue in my work of Black on Black homicide, women who kill, juvenile homes, and prisons (Stevens, 1998b, 1997b, 1997d, 1994). For example, it is clear that the presence of law enforcement patrols in "Hot Spots" represents modest reductions in crime and disorder (Sherman & Weisburd, 1995; Sherman & Rogan, 1995). Simply put, when law enforcement agencies do not control crime, law-abiding individuals defend themselves and violators commit more crimes (Stevens, 1998a). To lend support to this perspective are official reports from New York City, where "murders are plummeting, slayings in visible locations are declining, and deaths from gunfire are dropping. Clearance rates [are] recovering, police strength is up and misdemeanor arrests are soaring" (Karmen, 1996).

Although there are many explanations that could possibly affect crime rates, a clear one for the New York Police Department is that an increase in misdemeanor arrests leads to fewer gun-related crimes (Karmen, 1996). Thus, more arrests or a zero-tolerance policy can translate to greater police presence and, perhaps, greater community protection. On the other hand, arrests by the Los Angeles Police Department have dropped precipitously in the past five years, plunging from 290,000 to 189,000, a trend that has far exceeded a modest dip in reported crimes and appears at odds with the growth of the LAPD over the same period (Newton, 1996). Police officials say they are alarmed with the lower arrest rates, fearing that the decline is evidence that police officers are no longer pursuing their jobs with the same vigor as they had prior to the Rodney G. King beating (Newton, 1996).

Now, more than at any other time in American history, society calls on law enforcement to cope with the debris of social and institutional collapse, such as a deterioration of the traditional family structure and an increase in individual rights lending itself to more self-centered individuals (Brown, 1992; Stevens, 1997b). Therefore, based on the findings of this study, the following policies should be considered regarding repeat juvenile offenders, especially female offenders:

- law enforcement agencies given more local control over juvenile enforcement procedures to limit personal liabilities;
- substantial increases in police patrol presence in "Hot Spot" areas;
- law enforcement agencies pursue a zero-tolerance (make arrests) policy;
- prosecutors pursue justice (bring charges);
- courts administer justice (render judgment);
- youth service agencies provide custody and mandatory work, producing life's daily necessities.

It is further recommended that the above be executed in a professional, objective, and "caring manner"—a return to *Parens patriae*. Law and order should follow a swift and consistent philosophy, but in so doing, should provide appropriate protection against personal liabilities for the enforcers themselves in order for professionals to fulfill their tasks. That is, zero tolerance toward repeat offenders conducted by agencies with more rights than the individuals they detain. Perhaps, consistent with Durkheim (1933, 1984), juvenile intervention might strengthen societal "collective conscience" and lend itself to a general rise in law-abiding behavior.

The assumption by some experts is that drug control is centered in juvenile crime prevention, which means more than scaring children with inconsistent threats. That is, it is a known fact that serious criminals are rarely deterred by the threat of prison sentences or capital punishment, so why should female offenders be any different (Stevens, 1992a, 1992b)? A longitudinal study should be conducted examining the relationship between the early prosecution and future criminal activities of females.

REFERENCES

Akers, R.L. (1984). Delinquent behavior, drugs, and alcohol: What is the relationship? *Today's Delinquent, 3*, 19–47.

American Psychiatric Association. (1996). *Diagnostic and statistical manual of mental disorders*. 4th ed. Washington, DC: APA.

Benson, B.L., & Rasmussen, D.W. (1996). Illicit drugs and crime. The Lindersmith Center [online]. Available at //www.soros.org/lindesmith/indep.html.

Boyum, D., & Kleiman, M. (1995). Alcohol and other drugs. In J.Q. Wilson & J. Petersilia (Eds.), *Crime*, pp. 295–327. San Francisco: ICS.

Brown, L.P. (1992). Violent crime and community involvement. *FBI Law Enforcement Bulletin, 61*(5), 2–4.

Bureau of Justice Statistics. (1996). *Sourcebook of criminal justice statistics*. Washington, DC: Department of Justice, U.S. Government Printing Office.

Durkheim, E. (1933, 1984). *The division of labor in society*. New York: The Free Press.

Fletcher, B.R., & Moon, D.G. (1993). Introduction: The population. In B.R. Fletcher, L.D. Shaver, & D.G. Moon (Eds.), *Women prisoners: A forgotten population*, pp. 5–14. Westport, CT: Praeger.

Fletcher, B.R., Rolison, G.L., & Moon, D.G. (1993). The woman prisoner. In B.R. Fletcher, L.D. Shaver, & D.G. Mood (Eds.), *Women prisoners: A forgotten population*, pp. 15–26. Westport, CT: Praeger.

Gibbs, W.W. (1995). Trends in behavioral science: Seeking the criminal element. *Scientific American*, March, 100–107.

Gottfredson, M., & Hirschi, T. (1990). *A general theory of crime*. CA: Stanford.

Green, L. (1995). Cleaning up drug hot spots in Oakland, CA: The displacement and diffusion effects. *Justice Quarterly, 12*(4), 736–754.

Inciardi, J.A. (1996). *A corrections-based continuum of effective drug abuse treatment*. Washington, DC: National Institute of Justice, U.S. Government Printing Office.

Jackson, M.S. (1995). Drug use among black male juvenile delinquents. *Journal of Social Work*, 64–70.

Karmen, A. (1996). What's driving New York's crime rate down? *Law Enforcement News*, November 30. New York: John Jay College of Criminal Justice/CUNY.

Klein, M.W., & Maxson, C.L. (1994). Gangs and crack cocaine trafficking. In D.L. MacKenzie & C.D. Uchida (Eds.), *Drugs and crime*, pp. 42–61. Thousand Oaks, CA: Sage.

Koper, C.S. (1995). Just enough police presence: Reducing crime and disorderly behavior by optimizing patrol time in crime hot spots. *Justice Quarterly, 12*(4), 649–671.

Kristal, A. (1991). You've come a long way, baby: The battered woman's syndrome revisited. *New York Law School Journal of Human Rights, 9*, 111–160.

Liska, K. (1997). *Drugs and the human body*. Upper Saddle River, NJ: Prentice Hall.

Maher, L., & Daly, K. (1996). Women in the street level drug economy: Continuity or change? *Criminology, 34*(4), 465–491.

Miller, D. (1990). Women in pain: Substance abuse/self-medication. In M.P. Mirkin (Ed.), *The social and political contexts of family therapy*, pp. 179–192 . Boston: Allyn and Bacon.

Moon, D.G., Thompson, R.J., & Bennett, R. (1993). Patterns of substance use among women in prison. In B.R. Fletcher, L.D. Shaver, and D.G. Moon (Eds.), *Women prisoners: A forgotten population*, pp. 45–73. Westport, CT: Praeger.

Newton, J. (1996). Number of arrests by LAPD plunges since '91. *Los Angeles Times*, March 13.

Nurco, D.N., Hanlon, T.E., Kinlock, T.W., & Slaght, E. (1996). Variations in criminal patterns among narcotic addicts in Baltimore and New York City, 1983–1984. In *Data Resources of the National Institute of Justice*, 9th ed. NIJ Publication No. 86-IJ-CX-0030 (ICPSR 9586). Washington DC: U.S. Department of Justice.

Sherman, L.W., & Rogan, D.P. (1995). Deterrent effects of police raids on crack houses: A randomized controlled experiment. *Justice Quarterly, 12*(4), 756–781.

Sherman, L.W., & Weisburd, D. (1995) General deterrent effects of police partrol in crime "Hot Spots": A randomized controlled trial. *Justice Quarterly, 12*(4), 625–648.

Stevens, D.J. (1992a). Examining inmate attitudes: Do prisons deter crime? In American Correctional Association (1991), *The State of Corrections*, pp. 272–279.

———. (1992b). The death sentence and inmate attitudes. *Crime and Delinquency, 38*, 272–279.

———. (1994). The depth of imprisonment and prisonisation: Levels of security and prisoners' anticipation of future violence. *The Howard Journal of Criminal Justice, 33*(2), 137–157.

———. (1996). Explanations of homicide: Interviews with female killers. Paper presented at the annual conference of the Academy of Criminal Justice Sciences, Las Vegas, NE.

———. (1997a). Origins and effects of prison gangs in North Carolina. *Journal of Gang Research*, *4*(4), 23–35.

———. (1997b). Influences of early childhood experiences on subsequent criminally violent behavior. *Studies on Crime and Crime Prevention, 6*(1), 14–57.

———. (1997c). Prison regime and drugs. *The Howard Journal of Criminal Justice, 36*(1), 14–27.

———. (1997d). Urban communities and homicide: Why Blacks resort to murder. *Criminologist, 21*(3), 145–157.

———. (1998a). What do law enforcement officers really think about police work? *The Journal: The Voice of Law Enforcement*, *5*(1), 60–62.

———. (1998b). The impact of time-served and regime on prisoners' anticipation of crime: Female prisonisation effects. *The Howard Journal of Criminal Justice, 37*(2), 188–205.

Wright, A. (1994). Black vs. black homicides. *The Charlotte Observer*, January 1.

ENDNOTES

1. For a closer look at how police patrols might reduce social disorder, see Koper (1995). But Koper also argues that the optimal length of time for patrol stops is up to 15 minutes. Continued police presence after 15 minutes brings diminishing returns.
2. Another reason females are involved with drug-related crimes is that society in general is more involved with drugs, especially male criminals who often engage the services of females to help in their criminal activities (BJS, 1996; Moon, Thompson & Bennett, 1993).
3. For other factors that might produce criminal behavior see Gibbs (1995), who presents a host of factors as causal effects with an emphasis on biological contributors.
4. For a more in-depth discussion on career criminals, see Gottfredson and Hirschi (1990, p. 92–93). This study will define criminal lifestyles as those with high degrees of smoking, drinking, sexual relationships, unwanted pregnancies, everyday living expenses from illegal sources, household accidents, and criminal friends.
5. Drug abuse includes, in part, the harmful consequences of repeated use resulting in such experiences as a failure to fulfill major social role obligations and continued drug use despite persistent social problems caused by the effects of the substance.
6. For more detail on prison drug treatment see Inciardi (1996), who suggests that drug-involved offenders who participant in a continuum of prison-based treatment followed by treatment in work release centers have lower rates of drug use and recidivism than drug-involved offenders who participate in a shorter treatment program.
7. The North Carolina Department of Prisons defines violent crime as a category of crime where the victim is a specific person or group of persons, and the crime

results, or could result, in bodily injury. This is considered the most serious category of crime in general. Violent crimes range from misdemeanor assaults that do not result in bodily harm, up to first degree murder. Violent crimes include first and second degree murder, manslaughter, robbery, assault, sexual assault, other sexual offense, abduction, and other offenses against person.

8. Participants could select: always, very often, sometimes, seldom, or never.
9. Yet 4% (3) of the participants were first-time offenders, of which two had been convicted of the crime of murder and one for property crime.
10. The choices of the respondents to the questionnaire were: always, often, sometimes, seldom, never. Although, a control group should have been used as a comparison, further research should be conducted to determine the link between these variables and career criminals. However, the data is consistent with Gottfredson and Hirschi's (1990) notions about career criminals and is, therefore, for the purposes of this limited study, perhaps useful as only an indicator.
11. Of interest here is the data showing that in 74% (50) of the cases, the participants were first given drugs (a trend that continued into their twenties) from males, some of whom were boyfriends, but most were partners of their sisters or intimates, including husbands (and blood fathers of their mothers, too) of their mothers.
12. Chi-Square Tests produce a Pearson value of 520.380 with *df* at 224 and, in a two-sided test, .000 significance level. Also, in paired samples T-Tests, the standard error mean is .50 (addiction) and .43; its paired samples correction is significant at .000, with a mean of 1.37, SD at 1.52, SE at .18, and T at 7.443. These variables are strongly related.

6

Measuring Violent Crime in North Carolina

Laura J. Moriarty and William V. Pelfrey, Virginia Commonwealth University
Michael L. Vasu, North Carolina State University

Methodological Focus. Surveying is a popular way to conduct research, particularly since it can be used in many ways. This article demonstrates how survey research was conducted both by telephone and by mail. Furthermore, **random sampling** was used to determine who should be surveyed. Finally, it offers another look at operationalizing variables.

Abstract

In 1992, a team of researchers was hired to assess violent crime in North Carolina. This paper reports on the process employed to measure such crime, including a detailed explanation of the conceptualization and operationalization of violent crime, the survey methodology, and the results of the research. It concludes with a discussion of the estimates of violent crime in North Carolina. The current research found much higher estimates of violent crime than either the Uniform Crime Reports (UCR) or the National Crime Victimization Survey (NCVS) report.

Violent crime is a public concern. As a result, it has remained one of the most often cited social problems of the twentieth century. It seems every politician running for office, from the smallest local government seat to the President of the United States, has something to say about it.

In 1992, North Carolina was concerned about its rising violent crime rate. Before any crime reduction strategies could be implemented, North Carolina wanted a more accurate assessment of its violent crime problem. To this end, the state assembled eight researchers to develop a research design to study violent crime in North Carolina.

This paper reports the results of that assessment. We begin with an overview of the violent crime problem in North Carolina as determined by the official statistics. Next, the assessment strategy, including the research design, is presented. It is followed by the results of the study, emphasizing the estimates of violent crime in North Carolina.

VIOLENT CRIME IN THE UNITED STATES AND NORTH CAROLINA

Official reports regarding violent crime have shown a steady decrease in the past few years (UCR, 1996; 1995; 1994). However, to understand the concern of the North Carolina citizens, it is necessary to review the statistics available at the time of the study. The available data were from 1990–1992. At that time, the U.S. Department of Justice, Bureau of Justice Statistics released a report indicating there were 6,009,000 victims of violent crime in the United States and twice as many victims of personal property crimes (1992, p. 5).

The violent crime rate had been increasing steadily over the last 30 years, with the only exception being a two-decade decrease in murder following the Second World War (Skogan, 1989). The 1990 violent crime rate of 1,820,127 serious violent crimes was an increase of 22.2% over the 1986 numbers (UCR, 1991).

For many years, North Carolina was considered one of the safest states in the nation. The state's violent crime rate was ranked 20th in the nation, in terms of those states with the lowest violent crime rates. In 1974, the largest amount of violent crime was recorded, and this amount was not exceeded until 1988 (Jones, 1991). However, North Carolina began to experience violent crime more steadily in the latter part of the 1980s and early 1990s. During this time, from 1984 on, the reported North Carolina violent crime rate had increased 52% compared to increases of 45% in the South and 36% in the United States as a whole (Jones, 1991).

The increases in the official statistics of violent crime in North Carolina prompted the Governor to assemble a team of researchers who could better estimate the problem. The Governor funded the project and allowed the researchers to develop the best research design, without being burdened by budget restrictions.

THE ASSESSMENT PROJECT

The process for developing the research design began with several meetings of the research team to discuss possible strategies for capturing a more accurate and complete picture of North Carolina's violent crime problem. It was quickly decided that survey research would be conducted; however, long discussions ensued regarding which type, telephone or mail, would be best. After a thorough review of the advantages and disadvantages of each method, it was agreed that both methods would be used. To our knowledge, no other statewide violent crime assessment has used such an approach. Most states use either the mail survey or the telephone survey, but not both. In addition to using both methods, it was decided to conduct the two modes of research simultaneously.

With the data collection method established, it was now necessary to decide what questions would be used to measure violent crime. Several instruments were collected. They all measured victimization but on various levels; that is, some were state surveys while others were national surveys. The specific questionnaires reviewed included: *The National Crime Study*, *Survey of Crime and Justice in Tennessee*, *Survey of Crime and Justice in Texas*, *The 10th Annual South Carolina Crime Poll*, and *National Opinion Research Corporation (NORC) 1991* national survey.

The researchers voiced a concern after reviewing the surveys. Some of the questions on the surveys specifically stated the crimes under examination without providing a definition of individual crimes, while others never identified the crimes but provided the reader with definitions of such in the questions themselves. Because there is a tendency for the average citizen to misidentify certain crimes (e.g., robbery and burglary), and because in some incidents a more accurate picture is revealed when situations are described and not labeled, the researchers decided to use the format where the definitions are included in the question but the actual crimes are never identified. Since more of the surveys reviewed used this method than did not, the results of the North Carolina research can be compared to other state crime rates.

The mail and telephone surveys were exactly the same for the victimization questions and the demographics. For victimization items, respondents were asked questions that referred to events that happened to them during 1991, that is, between January 1 and December 31, 1991. Because the mail survey could be longer, it included questions concerning fear of crime, perceptions about how well the criminal justice system was working, attitudes toward crime, and implementation of security measures; however, these responses are not discussed here.

The violent crime assessed included robbery, attempted robbery, aggravated assault, simple assault, threats, and rape. Murder was not included for obvious reasons—this is a self-report study, murder victims cannot respond. The legal definitions of the crimes were used to conceptualize the terms. The operational definitions are listed below in Figure 6.1.

The telephone survey was commenced in the spring of 1992. The sampling elements (phone numbers) were computer-generated by Survey Sampling Inc. of Fairview, Connecticut. The sample frame for the study was North Carolina's estimated phone households. The record types were available listed phones. The number of replicates was 350 and the starting replicate was 001. The sampling method was random. The initial sample pool of numbers was 35,000; however, only 16,800 numbers were necessary to generate the required sample size.

The telephone surveys were conducted by the Applied Research Group of the Center for Urban Affairs, North Carolina State University. Here the survey was extensively pretested using a subset of the telephone numbers purchased. The pretesting indicated no problems with the survey.

A decision was made to use the "next birthday" approach to select respondents (Salmon & Nichols, 1983; Lavrakas, 1987). Interviewers asked to speak to the person in the household whose birthday was most recent. This method

Crime	Actual Survey Question
Robbery	Did anyone take something from you by using force, such as by stick up, mugging, or threat?
Attempted Robbery	Did anyone **try** to rob you by using force or by threatening to harm you (other than any incident already mentioned)?
Aggravated Assault	Were you knifed, shot at, or attacked with some other weapon by anyone at all (other than those incidents already mentioned)?
Assault	Did anyone hit, attack you, or beat you up (other than any incidents already mentioned)?
Threats	Did anyone threaten to beat you up or threaten you with a knife, gun, or other weapon, not including telephone threats, other than any incidents already mentioned?
Rape	Did anyone force or attempt to force you to have sexual intercourse with them?

Figure 6.1 Operationalization of the Crime Variables

was selected because it is "nonintrusive, not time consuming and easy for interviews to use" (Lavrakas, 1987, p. 98).

The decision was made to seek a sample of completed interviews of at least 9,604 respondents. The actual number of completed interviews for the telephone survey was 9,774. This allowed for a tolerated error of plus or minus 1% at the 95th confidence level. The response rate was 82% (9774/11873), which is considered extremely high by telephone standards.

The number of completed telephone interviews in terms of contact status frequencies was 58.2% (9774/16800). However, this estimate of response rates does not exclude out-of-service numbers, which were 21.2% (N = 3,572) of the total number of attempts, and business and government numbers, which were 8.1% (N = 1,355) of all attempts. The reported response rate, excluding these two groups of individuals for whom participation in the survey was not possible, is 82%.

The mail survey was entitled "Survey of Crime and Justice in North Carolina, 1992." The respondents were randomly selected from a roster of North Carolina licensed drivers. An initial sample of 2,000 respondents was chosen. The process employed to generate the response rate consisted of five contacts (Dillman, 1978). All 2,000 respondents were mailed a sensitizing postcard alerting the residents that a survey would follow in one week. Seven days later, a full survey packet was mailed, including an introduction letter explaining the purpose of the survey and how the respondents were selected; the survey; a stamped, self-addressed envelope; and a golf pencil. If there was no response within 7 to 10 days, the researchers sent a reminder postcard. If there was no response after 7 additional days, the researchers mailed the full survey packet with a new letter emphasizing the importance of the research and the citizen's participation. Finally, if no response occurred in 7 additional days, a final postcard was sent to the respondents asking that they complete the survey and call a number if they misplaced the survey and needed another one.

This method yielded a response rate of 7%. There were 295 cases of no forwarding addresses and deceased addressees. The adjusted sample size was 1705. The actual number of responses was 1273. This sample size allows for a tolerated error of plus or minus 4% at the 95th confidence level.

The comparison of sample estimates for both the telephone and mail surveys to known state demographics show both surveys to be representative of state demographics. The only demographic variable for which there was variation from known statewide parameters was reflected in the slight overrepresentation of females in both samples. Each sample is described below.

Samples

The mail and telephone surveys are representative of North Carolina. The demographic variables from the telephone survey indicate that 55.9% (5,461) of the sample are female and 44.1% (4,313) are male. The majority of the respondents are White (79.8%), followed by African American (17.6%), Native American (1.2%), Asian (.5%), and Other (.4%). The age range for the respondents is 18 to 92, with the mean age being 47 years.

The mail survey sample is described as follows: there are 691 women (55.1%) and 570 men (44.9%), with 12 cases missing. The race category is broken down into White (82.4%), African American (15.1%), Native American (1.3%), and Other (1.0%), with 11 cases missing. The age range is 16 to 92, with the average age being 45 years.

Estimates of Violent Crime

Table 6.1 shows the breakdown for robbery. Slightly less than 1% of the telephone survey (.8%, $N = 77$) reported that something was taken from them by force in 1991. The mail survey reported a value somewhat higher (1.3%, $N = 16$).

Table 6.2 compares estimates of attempted robbery by mode of interviewing. For the telephone sample, one-half of 1% (.5%, $N = 49$) of the sample reported that someone tried to rob them in 1991 by using force or the threat of force. The mail survey reports a value of 1.2% ($N = 15$).

In Table 6.3, aggravated assault statistics are compared. For the telephone survey, 1.4% ($N = 138$) report that they were attacked. The corresponding percent for the mail survey was 1.2% ($N = 15$).

Table 6.1 Percent of North Carolina Residents Reporting Something Was Taken by Force in 1991

	Telephone		Mail	
	Frequency	Percent	Frequency	Percent
No	9697	99.2%	1251	98.7%
Yes	77	.8%	16	1.3%
Valid Cases	9774	100.0%	1267	100.0%

Table 6.2 Percent of Citizens in North Carolina Reporting That Someone Tried to Rob Them in 1991

	Telephone		Mail	
	Frequency	Percent	Frequency	Percent
No	9725	99.5%	1254	98.8%
Yes	49	.5%	15	1.2%
Valid Cases	9774	100.0%	1269	100.0%

Table 6.3 Percent of Citizens in North Carolina Reporting They Were Knifed, Shot at, or Attacked in 1991

	Telephone		Mail	
	Frequency	Percent	Frequency	Percent
No	9636	98.6%	1252	98.8%
Yes	138	1.4%	15	1.2%
Valid Cases	9774	100.0%	1267	100.0%

Table 6.4 is a comparison of assault victimization estimates for both modes of interviewing. The telephone and mail surveys' estimate were the same, 2.2%.

Table 6.5 presents the breakdown for the sample with respect to threats of violence in 1991. Approximately 3% of the telephone sample (3.1%, $N = 305$) reported that they were threatened with a knife, gun, or some other weapon during 1991. The mail survey reports estimates of 5.1% ($N = 65$).

The next question was designed to measure the incidents of rape. The question was asked of women only in the telephone survey. In the mail survey, it was asked of both genders. Only female responses are reported in the Table. Table 6.6 indicates that approximately 1.0% ($N = 55$) of respondents to the telephone survey answered Yes to the question that someone forced or

Table 6.4 Percent of Citizens in North Carolina Reporting They Were Attacked and Beat Up in 1991

	Telephone		Mail	
	Frequency	Percent	Frequency	Percent
No	9571	97.9%	1240	97.9%
Yes	203	2.1%	26	2.1%
Valid Cases	9774	100.0%	1266	100.0%

Table 6.5 Percent of Citizens in North Carolina Reporting They Were Threatened in 1991

	Telephone		Mail	
	Frequency	Percent	Frequency	Percent
No	9469	96.9%	1202	94.9%
Yes	305	3.1%	65	5.1%
Valid Cases	9774	100.0%	1267	100.0%

Table 6.6 Percent of Females in North Carolina Reporting Someone Forced or Attempted to Force Them to Have Sexual Intercourse with Them in 1991*

	Telephone		Mail	
	Frequency	Percent	Frequency	Percent
No	5406	99.0%	674	97.7%
Yes	55	1.0%	16	2.3%
Valid Cases	5461	100.0%	690	100.0%

*The question was asked of women only in the telephone survey, of whom 5 refused to answer. The mail questionnaire asked both men and women, for whom only female responses are reported above.

attempted to force them to have sexual intercourse. The mail survey reported a rape estimate of 2.2% (N = 16).

DISCUSSION

In order to make sense out of the statistics presented above, it is necessary to compare them to official estimates of violent crime. The Uniform Crime Reports and the National Crime Victimization Survey are the two most often

Table 6.7 Comparison of Crime Rates per 100,000 Population as Reflected by the UCR, NCVS, and the 1991 Telephone Estimates

	1991 UCR North Carolina	1991 NCVS United States	1991 NCVCS (Telephone)
Robbery	178	558	1289
Rape[1]	67[2]	140	1007.1
Aggravated Assault	434	783	1441.9
Assault	N/A[3]	1703	2076.9

1. Rates are shown per 100,000 women.
2. Rate is extrapolated from the rate per 100,000 population and the estimated female population of North Carolina. The assumption is that all the reported rape victims were women.
3. Data on assaults are not available through UCR for any years.

cited official estimates of crime. We use these two estimates to compare and contrast our findings.

Table 6.7 is a comparison of crime rates per 100,000 population by category of violent crime. The telephone survey results are presented because they are slightly more conservative than the mail results. Nevertheless, it is obvious that there is a stair step rise in the magnitude of differences between the various estimates of violent crime in North Carolina for 1991.

The Table graphically displays the underreporting of crime using either UCR statistics or NCVS statistics. The rate at which residents of North Carolina are victims of robbery is approximately seven times that reported by the UCR. The reality of rape is approximately 15 times higher than reported by the UCR, and aggravated assault occurs at a rate approximately 3.2 times that reflected by the UCR. Simple assault cases in North Carolina are approximately 100% higher than those of the United States as reflected by NCVS.

CONCLUSIONS

In the present study, a team of researchers was hired to assess violent crime in North Carolina. The two most often cited statistics, the Uniform Crime Reports and the National Crime Victimization Survey, are estimates of crime with limitations associated with both (for a detailed comparison, see Schmalleger, 1996). For example, the UCR only measures crimes reported to the police. If a crime goes unreported, it cannot be measured. The NCVS was designed to capture that "dark figure" of crime not found in the UCR; however, it has problems as well. For our purposes, the NCVS does not collect state-level data. Obviously, it becomes difficult to estimate a particular state's violent crime level if the data are reported in the aggregate.

In the current study, an assessment of violent crime was undertaken that included using two different modes of interviewing. Additional analysis revealed no statistical difference between the modes of interview (see Vasu, Moriarty & Pelfrey, 1995). The findings indicate that violent crime in North Carolina is underestimated by the official statistics by magnitudes ranging from 7% to 100%.

This more accurate depiction of violent crime in North Carolina underscores the question, What are the correlates or causes of such crime? The variables associated with such high levels of violent crime must be determined before any prevention strategies or policy implications can be employed. The next step in the research process for North Carolina is to identify the causes of its violent crime problem. Some of the information collected on the mail survey can be utilized as a starting point to determine the correlates, but a more in-depth investigation is necessary.

REFERENCES

Dillman, D.A. (1978). *Mail and telephone surveys: The total design method.* New York: John Wiley & Sons.

Jones, D. (1991). Violent crime in North Carolina: An examination of data and trends. Unpublished report presented to the Governor's Crime Commission, May 30, 1991, Raleigh, NC.

Lavrakas, P.J. (1987). *Telephone survey methods: Sampling, selection and supervision.* Newbury Park, CA: Sage.

Salmon, C.T., & Nichols, J.S. (1983). The next birthday method of respondent selection. *Public Opinion Quarterly, 47*, 270–276.

Schmalleger, F. (1996). *Criminal justice today*. Chicago: Prentice-Hall.

Skogan, W.G. (1989). Social change and the future of violent crime. In T.R. Gurr (Ed.), *Violence in America*, pp. 235–250. [Vol. 1, *The History of Crime*]. Beverly Hills, CA: Sage.

Uniform Crime Reports. (1991). Washington, D.C.: Federal Bureau of Investigation.

———. (1993). Washington, D.C.: Federal Bureau of Investigation.

———. (1994). Washington, D.C.: Federal Bureau of Investigation.

———. (1995). Washington, D.C.: Federal Bureau of Investigation.

———. (1996). Washington, D.C.: Federal Bureau of Investigation.

U.S. Department of Justice, Bureau of Justice Statistics. (1992). *Report to the nation on crime and justice: The data.* Washington, D.C.: Government Printing Office.

Vasu, M.L., Moriarty, L.J., & Pelfrey, W.V. (1995). Measuring violent crime in North Carolina utilizing mail and telephone surveys simultaneously: Does method matter? *Criminal Justice Review, 20*(1), 34–43.

7

Correctional Officers' Attitudes toward Delinquents and Delinquency: Does the Type of Institution Make a Difference?

Jill Gordon, Virginia Commonwealth University

Methodological Focus. Regardless of the methodology used, distinguishing between independent and dependent variables, as was done in this article, is always helpful to readers of research. In addition, the research reported here was conducted using a **cross-sectional design** and a **purposive** sample of the complete population of the targets under study. Furthermore, the **hypotheses** are clearly stated. This article also provides a good example of data coding.

Abstract

The institutional experience an inmate undergoes is based on a number of factors. One of the most consistent ingredients that has the ability to influence the inmate's ordeal, either positively or negatively, is the correctional officer. The extent and type of interactions between correctional officers and inmates tend to vary based on the goals and philosophies of the institution. For instance, the level and quality of contact are often regulated by the type of facility an inmate enters (i.e., a custody-oriented institution, where the focus is on security and punishment, versus a treatment-oriented institution, where the emphasis is security with a human service component). It is due to the high level of contact that transpires between inmates and correctional officers that the community should be aware of, and concerned with, the attitudes the correctional officers possess toward inmates and other issues related to criminal justice. This is important, because attitudes often influence one's behaviors toward an issue. This study will examine correctional officers' attitudes toward delinquents and delinquency by considering two differing institutional environments that may shape the inmates stay in the institution.

Institutional detainment can be a vastly different experience for a convicted individual, based on institutional placement, institutional policies, and institutional philosophy. The types of facility an offender is admitted to can produce both positive and negative effects.

Several adverse effects can occur to an individual as a result of the institutionalization experience. In fact, the majority of inmates will encounter some form of psychological and/or physiological stress (Altman, 1975; Bartollas, Miller & Dinitz, 1976; Bonta & Gendreau, 1990; Feld, 1977; Hayduk, 1978; Paulus, McCain & Cox, 1985; Ruback & Innes, 1988; Shopler & Stockdale, 1977; Skovran, 1988). These negative effects have become more pronounced with the onset of prison crowding. Research on the impact of crowding has uncovered (1) a greater inequity in the treatment provided to inmates; (2) further constraints being placed on the inmates ability to access rehabilitative programs; and (3) an increase in violence and victimization among the inmate population (Champion, 1988; Cobb, 1985; Ellis, Grasmick & Gillman, 1974; Frazier, 1989; Gaes & McGuire, 1985; Jacobs, 1980; Lutz, Poole & Regoli, 1985; Skovran, 1988; Singer, 1983). These detrimental institutional events can produce negative outcomes for both the individual and society. These negative outcomes can equate to high recidivism rates, low self-esteem, or negative social adjustment (Frazier & Bishop, 1985; Frazier & Cochran, 1986).

On the other hand, the institutional experience can have a positive impact on a convicted offender. Specifically, studies have revealed favorable outcomes, ranging from increased self-esteem to lower rates of recidivism, for many inmates (Andrews et al., 1990; Garrett, 1985; Gottschalk et al., 1987; Lipsey, 1992). Examinations of the programs which "succeed" at rehabilitating offenders has uncovered facilities with similar treatment and environmental strategies. The treatment strategies tend to emphasize behavioral or social learning techniques (i.e., role-modeling, life-skills development, token economy system), to stress the principle of responsivity, to target high risk offenders, and to focus on relapse prevention (Andrews & Bonta, 1994; Andrews et al., 1990; Garrett, 1985; Gendreau, 1996; Gottschalk et al., 1987; Lipsey, 1992). Additionally, the institutional environment accentuates pro-social activities and interactions at all times, and has a staff that understands and acts according to all facets of the treatment being provided (Gendreau, 1996). Therefore, the correctional officer is a vital component in maintaining the integrity of such an institutional program.

Correctional officers are responsible for the safety and security of the institutional environment along with the custody and care of the detainees. In these roles, correctional officers can have a high level of interaction with the inmates. The type, level, and quality of interaction shown by a correctional officer may be a function of his or her attitudes toward causes and solutions to delinquent behavior (Bazemore, Dicker & Nyhan, 1994). These attitudes may result in the types of behavior a correctional officer expresses toward an inmate.

Correctional officers' attitudes toward inmates, job satisfaction, job stress, punitiveness, and causes of crime have been examined in terms of gender, age, education level, intrinsic and extrinsic rewards, occupational adjustments, and situational factors (Britton, 1997; Crouch & Alpert, 1982; Cullen, Link, et al., 1985; Cullen, Lutze, et al., 1989; Hepburn & Knepper, 1993; Jackson & Ammen, 1996; Jacobs & Kraft, 1978; Johnson & Price, 1981; Jurik & Halemba, 1984; Kasselbaum, Ward & Wilner, 1964; Lindquist & Whitehead, 1986; Poole & Regoli, 1980; Robinson, Porporino & Simourd, 1993, 1997; Toch & Klofas, 1982; Van Voorhis et al., 1991; Whitehead & Lindquist, 1989). The results of these efforts have lead to inconsistencies about correctional officers, especially with regard to the influence of several demographic characteristics (i.e., race, gender, and education). For example, Britton (1997) recognizes that the results of racial or gender differences vary by the method used to examine the issue. More specifically, data that are qualitative in nature consistently reveal gender and racial differences among correctional officers (Jurik, 1985, 1988; Owen, 1988; Zimmer, 1986), whereas quantitative data uncover few outcomes that are related to the race or gender of a correctional officer (Blau, Light, & Chamlin, 1986; Cullen et al., 1985; Jackson & Ammen, 1996; Jurik & Halemba, 1984; Jurik & Winn, 1987; Van Voorhis et al., 1991). This study seeks to add to the correctional officer literature by considering the facility type where a correctional officer is employed.

The purpose of this study is to examine correctional officers' attitudes toward juvenile delinquency at two different types of juvenile detention facilities. The goal is to determine if there is a difference in the correctional officers' attitudes toward the causes and treatment of crime among correctional officers who work in vastly different institutional environments. Prior to discussing the procedures to accomplish this goal, it is important to address the differences among the institutional environments being examined.

ENVIRONMENT OF THE TWO TYPES OF DETENTION FACILITIES

The study centers on the attitudinal differences among correctional officers employed at two types of juvenile detention facilities that differ in appearance and philosophy. However, the institutions house the same type of offender. These offenders are male juveniles who have been convicted of the most serious offense category (Felony 1 or Felony 2), which may consist of crimes such as arson, burglary, robbery, rape, and assault. The institutional environments will be described as an open-security facility and a closed-security facility.

The "open-security" facility has no perimeter fencing, and no perimeter check-in points or structural guarding devices. Security is maintained by offering a highly structured therapeutic environment that focuses on changing the offenders' attitudes from antisocial to prosocial by stressing personal responsibility. The attitudinal and behavioral changes are produced through the implementation of various therapeutic techniques. Some of these techniques are a positive peer culture, role-playing, a token economy system, group therapy, individual counseling, life-skills development, and family counseling. More importantly, the occurrence of prosocial knowledge occurs around the clock at the open security facility. In other words, the strategies learned must be exhibited in the daily behaviors and interactions of the youth. This facility houses approximately 33 juveniles at any given time and has a high staff-to-youth ratio.

The second institutional environment consists of a "closed-security" structure that has perimeter fencing, central check-in points, and electronic monitoring or correctional officer surveillance of the perimeter. The closed-security facility operates more like a traditional training school or traditional juvenile detention facility. The youth are provided education, vocational training, non-theoretically-based programs (i.e., AA [Alcoholics Anonymous], NA [Narcotics Anonymous]), and, for some youth, a limited amount of individual therapy. The facility has a minimal staff-to-youth ratio and houses more than 100 juveniles at any given time.

As demonstrated, these institutions are considerably different. There appears to be three distinguishing differences: (1) the method used to maintain a secure environment; (2) the staff-to-youth ratio; and (3) the overall philosophy of the institutional environment. In short, the open-security facility takes a rather human service approach, where the primary goal is to change the offender's way of thinking about crime in order to reduce or eliminate the youth's cycle of offending. On the other hand, the closed security institution's central emphasis is on the custody and care of the youth.

These theoretical and structural differences have shown to impact the levels of future criminal activity of the youth. Specifically, the youth admitted to the open-security facility have fewer reconvictions upon release than the youth admitted to the closed-security facility (Gordon, 1996; Gordon, Latessa & Wooldredge, 1997). Additionally, youth who successfully complete the entire realm of treatment offered at the open-security facility have a lower probability of being reconvicted of a new offense or recommitted to an institution than a youth who has been admitted to the closed-security facility. This study will add another dimension to the correctional officers' literature by examining and comparing the attitudes of correctional officers employed at varying types of institutions.

METHODOLOGY

Research Design

A cross-sectional design was used. This nonexperimental design was appropriate in order to establish if a relationship exists between the independent variable (facility in which the correctional officer is employed) and the dependent variable (attitudes possessed by the correctional officer), not to explore the cause and effect between the variables. The following lists the three hypotheses that were examined:

1. Correctional officers from the open-security facility are less likely to agree that punishing offenders reduces crime than correctional officers at the closed-security facility.
2. Correctional officers from the open-security facility are less likely to agree that crime is a *result* of environmental/opportunity factors than correctional officers at the closed-security facility.
3. Correctional officers from the open-security facility are more likely to agree that the treatment of offenders can produce change than the correctional officers at the closed-security facility.

The sample consists of all correctional staff members from three juvenile institutions[1] that admit youth who have been convicted of a Felony 1 or Felony 2 level offense.[2] A list of the correctional officer staff was provided by the administrative assistant at each facility. An envelope containing a cover letter, survey, and separate envelope was given to each officer. The correctional officers were to fill out the survey, seal it in the envelope provided, and give it to a designated person at the institution (a clerical staff member who was not being surveyed). Each envelope was marked with an identifying number so the researcher could distinguish who did and did not complete the survey.[3] A reminder letter was sent to all staff members who did not complete the survey approximately two weeks after the original mailing. A final circulation of all original materials (cover letter, survey, and envelope) was provided for all correctional staff who did not respond; this occurred approximately two weeks after the mailing of the reminder letter. The survey process was conducted during the months of June and July 1995.

The various procedures used in the distribution and collection process were conducted due to the reluctance of the institution to provide the researchers with the addresses of all employees. Therefore, the methods utilized to dispense the survey were to certify the confidentiality and anonymity of each correctional officer's response.

The response rates were 86% for the open-security facility ($N = 26$), 31% for one closed-security facility ($N = 86$), and 61% for the other closed-security facility ($N = 41$). For the purposes of the data analysis, the two-closed security facilities were combined, producing a total sample size of 153 correctional officers.

The survey was designed to examine the correctional officers' attitudes toward treatment and punishment. The survey consisted of several attitudinal statements in which the respondents were asked to strongly agree, agree, disagree, or strongly disagree.[4] The survey also examined various demographic and employment characteristic. Table 7.1 describes the pertinent variables and their measurement.

Table 7.1 Variables and Measurement

Variable	Measurement
Attpun	Examines attitudes toward punitiveness.* Higher scores indicate disagreement with punitiveness as a means to reduce crime. Range 3–12, Mean 6.38.
Attdel	Examines attitudes toward delinquency.* Higher scores indicate disagreement that crime is a *result* of environmental or opportunity factors. Range 3–12, Mean 7.49.
Stafphil	Examines attitudes toward treatment of youth.* Higher scores indicate disagreement with the ability of "treatment" programs to change offenders' behaviors. Range 4–16, Mean 10.34
Facility	0 = Open-Security, 1 = Closed-Security
Age	In years
Gender	0 = Female, 1 = Male
Race	0 = White, 1 = Non-White
Education	0 = Less than High School, 1 = High School, 2 = Some College, 3 = Bachelor Degree, 4 = Graduate Degree
Length at current position	In months

* Appendix A demonstrates the statements used to develop the composite attitudinal scales for the variables ATTPUN, ATTDEL, and STAFPHIL.

Table 7.2 reveals the demographic characteristics for the sample. The Table reveals that the majority of staff members are White males in their mid-30s who have completed some college or received a bachelor of arts degree. As expected, the staff members at the closed-security institutions, on average, have been employed with the facility for a longer period of time.[5]

Two analyses were conducted to examine the hypothesis. A test of means for two groups and a logit regression analysis were completed. For the regression model, the ordinal scales were collapsed to nominal scales by using the mean point for each of the dependent variables (ATTPUN, ATTDEL, STAFPHIL).[6]

RESULTS

Table 7.3 examines the percent of agreement on the attitudinal factors for each group. These figures reveal that the majority of staff from the open-security institution disagrees with the attitude toward delinquency and punishment scales (ATTPUN, ATTDEL) and agree with the staff philosophy scale

Table 7.2 Demographic Characteristics

Variable	Open-Security	Closed-Security
Age		
Mean	34.08	37.35
Standard Deviation	12.00	13.06
Gender		
Male	18 (69%)	87 (69%)
Female	8 (31%)	40 (31%)
Race		
White	20 (77%)	68 (53%)
Non-White	6 (23%)	56 (44%)
Education		
Less than High School	0 (0%)	1 (1%)
High School Graduate	6 (23%)	19 (15%)
Some College	8 (31%)	49 (39%)
Bachelor Degree	12 (46%)	42 (33%)
Graduate Degree	0 (0%)	16 (12%)
Length at Current Position (In months)		
Mean	31.23	63.36
Standard Deviation	29.98	80.26

Table 7.3 Percent of Agreement or Disagreement by Facility

	Open-Security		Closed-Security	
Variable	Agree	Disagree	Agree	Disagree
ATTPUN	35%	65%	73%	27%
ATTDEL	16%	84%	48%	52%
STAFPHIL	69%	31%	45%	55%

(STAFPHIL). Each of these outcomes is in the expected direction. For example, the open-security facility places a great deal of emphasis on juveniles accepting personal responsibility and their ability to make right or wrong choices. Therefore, the expectation is that the open-security staff members would disagree with the idea of crime being a result of only environment/opportunity (ATTDEL).

In addition, Table 7.3 shows that 73% of the closed-security staff support the notion that harsh punishment is a way to reduce crime. The closed-security staff members are almost split on their level of agreement with the ability of some facilities to "change" offenders and the likelihood that crime is a result of environment/opportunity.

Although these figures reveal some differences between the two groups, it is important to determine if the differences are statistically significant.

Table 7.4 presents the results of the test of means for two groups. As shown, the facility that an officer is employed at (open-security versus closed-security) is statistically significant, in the expected direction, for all three models. Level of education is also statistically significant in relation to an officer's attitude toward punishment. This positive relationship means that the higher the education level possessed by an officer, the less likely he or she is to agree that punishment will reduce crime.

The statistically significant relationships uncovered in the bivariate models between an officer's attitudes and the facility at which they are employed remain significant in the multivariate models. Specifically, Table 7.5 reveals that the employees at the open-security facility are more likely to disagree (score above the mean) with the notions that environmental factors result in

Table 7.4 T-Test for Attitudes toward Delinquency by Facility

Variable	Attpun	Attdel	Stafphil
Facility	−4.478*	−3.666*	3.433*
Age	1.678	2.637*	−0.247
Gender	−0.780	1.032	0.137
Race	0.071	−1.051	−0.413
Education	2.109*	−0.311	−0.768
Length at current position	−0.249	0.328	−1.030

*Statistically significant at the .05 level.

Table 7.5 Logit Model for Attitudes toward Delinquency by Facility

Variable Pseudo R-squared	Attpun (.35129)	Attdel (.27983)	Stafphil (.24129)
Facility	−1.8870 (.0009)*	−1.5416 (.0055)*	1.2263 (.0239)*
Age	0.0064 (.6856)	0.0242 (.1214)	−0.0189 (.2121)
Gender	−0.2408 (.5722)	0.1106 (.7870)	0.0726 (.8605)
Race	−0.4179 (.3095)	−0.2225 (.5733)	−0.4512 (.2656)
Education	0.4203 (.0587)	−0.1954 (.3494)	−0.1421 (.5058)
Length at current position	−0.0005 (.8562)	−0.0006 (.8075)	−0.0029 (.2889)

*Statistically significant at the .05 level.

criminal activity (ATTDEL) and that the punishment of offenders is a means to reduce crime (ATTPUN). In addition, the officers at the open-security institution are likely to agree that convicted youth can "change" their attitudes and behaviors (STAFPHIL) compared to the closed-security officers.

It is important to note that the facility a correctional officer was employed at is the only significant variable in the logistic regression model predicting attitudes toward delinquency. The results in this model do not support some earlier research indicating that correctional officers' demographic characteristics are related to their attitudes toward causes of crime and/or the treatment of criminals. Moreover, the statistically significant relationship that was present between education level and individual attitudes toward punishment is not significant in the more robust multivariate model.

DISCUSSION AND CONCLUSIONS

Correctional officers are a key component in the institutional experience. The attitudes possessed by a correctional officer can translate into their behaviors toward inmates. Thus, the quality of treatment, if that is a facility's primary goal, may not be fulfilled if the officers do not support the idea that behavioral change can occur among inmates.

This study has uncovered attitudinal differences among correctional officers who are employed at juvenile detention facilities that vary philosophically, structurally, and with regards to the daily regiment of the convicted youth. More specifically, the officers at the open-security facility possess attitudes that do not support punitive ideals. Rather, the open-security staff appears to embrace the belief that the attitudes and behaviors of youth can change from antisocial to prosocial, because the staff understand that engaging in crime is a matter of personal responsibility.

The results uncovered are not surprising, because the open-security facility seeks to change the youth's attitudes (and behaviors) from antisocial to prosocial. These changes are accomplished with a variety of therapeutic techniques that stress the personal responsibility of one's actions, while emphasizing the impact antisocial behaviors have on the victim(s) and the entire community.

The results of this study reveal a lack of influence between the demographic variables and a correctional officer's attitude. Previous research on the influence of demographic characteristics and the impact on correctional officers beliefs have led to inconsistent findings. The current analysis uncovered a significant relationship between an officer's level of education and his or her agreement/disagreement with the ability of punishment to reduce crime. However, the multivariate models did not reveal any significant relationships between the various demographic characteristics and attitudes toward delinquents or delinquency. This inconsistency may be due to the methodology used to collect and analyze the data (see Britton 1997).

This study adds another dimension on the effectiveness of the ability of the open-security facility to change the youth's attitudes and behaviors. As previously discussed, results on the effectiveness of the open-security facility have shown that the youth released from the facility have a lower likelihood of being reconvicted of an offense compared to youth released from the closed-security facility. Thus, the confirmation that the correctional officers are supportive of the goals and philosophy of the program offered at the open-security facility may reflect the institution's actual ability to influence the attitudes of the youth and reduce the youth's future criminal behavior.

In addition, this study has added a rather unexplored dimension into understanding the attitudes of correctional officers by examining the type of facility where the officer is employed. The research revealed that there is a relationship between the type of facility (open-security versus closed-security) and the correctional officer's attitudes toward delinquency and punishment. The primary explanation for this relationship has been based on the fact that the two facility types differ structurally and philosophically. Another possible influence on this relationship is the ability of the open-security officers to exhibit a stronger human service component than the closed-security officers. In this "human service" role, officers have the opportunity to utilize individual skills and aptitude by engaging in a more direct line of communication with the inmates (Lombroso, 1982). This high level of contact allows the officers to serve as advocates for the inmate and enables the officers to truly "assist" the inmates (Lombroso, 1985; Toch, 1978). Thus, it may be the quality and type of interactions that occur that influence the correctional officer's attitudes.

Moreover, the differences in attitudes found between officers may also be a function of the value of intrinsic rewards. The open-security facility provides more opportunities for personal development and better utilizes the correctional officer's strengths and talents. Previous research demonstrates that the intrinsic aspects of the job (i.e., utilization of skills, ability to grow personally) have a stronger influence on job satisfaction than extrinsic factors (i.e., pay, fringe benefits, job security) (Gruenberg, 1980; Hepburn & Knepper, 1993; Mottaz, 1987). It is theoretically plausible that the open-security correctional officers have more opportunities to experience intrinsic rewards that influence their level of job satisfaction, thus, enabling these officers to encompass the goals and philosophies of the institutional environment.

Research needs to continue with regards to correctional officers. It is essential to understand the beliefs possessed by correctional officers because of the direct role they play in shaping the inmate and the institutional environment. Future research needs to consider the possible influence of the type of facility in which an officer is employed when examining attitudes.

APPENDIX A

Components of the Correctional Officers' Attitudes

ATTITUDES TOWARD PUNISHMENT

Most of these kids will return to crime after they leave our program.

Serious juvenile delinquents should be processed as adults.

The only way to reduce crime in our society is to punish offenders.

Codes: 1 = Strongly Agree, 2 = Agree, 3 = Disagree, 4 = Strongly Disagree

ATTITUDES TOWARD DELINQUENCY

Most of our kids are delinquent because they came from bad homes.

Most of our kids are delinquent because they lack the opportunities that other kids have.

Most of our kids are delinquent because their parents neglected or abused them.

Codes: 1 = Strongly Agree, 2 = Agree, 3 = Disagree, 4 = Strongly Disagree

ATTITUDES TOWARD THE TREATMENT OF YOUTH

Our program will help straighten out many of the youths who complete it.

This is a good program.

All of our staff has the same basic treatment philosophy.

All staff members participate in treatment decisions.

Codes: 1 = Strongly Agree, 2 = Agree, 3 = Disagree, 4 = Strongly Disagree

REFERENCES

Altman, I. (1975). *The environment and social behavior: Privacy, personal space, territory, and crowding*. Monterey, CA: Brooks/Cole.

Andrews, D., & Bonta, J. (1994) *The psychology of criminal conduct*. Cincinnati, OH: Anderson.

Andrews, D., Zinger, I., Hoge, R., Bonta, J., Gendreau, P., & Cullen, F. (1990). Does correctional treatment work? A clinically relevant and psychologically informed meta-analysis. *Criminology, 28*(3), 369–404.

Bartollas, C., Miller, S.J., & Dinitz, S. (1976). *Juvenile victimization: The institutional paradox*. New York: Halsted.

Bazemore, G., Dicker, T., & Nyhan, R. (1994). Juvenile justice reform and the difference it makes: An exploratory study of the impact of policy change on detention worker attitudes. *Crime and Delinquency, 40*, 37–53.

Blau, J.R., Light, S.C., & Chamlin, M. (1986). Individual and contextual effects on stress and job satisfaction: A study of prison staff. *Work and Occupations, 13*, 131–156.

Bonta, J., & Gendreau, P. (1990). Reexamining the cruel and unusual punishment of prison life. *Law and Human Behavior, 14*(4), 347–372.

Britton, D.M. (1997). Perceptions of the work environment among correctional officers: Do race and sex matter? *Criminology, 35*(1), 85–105.

Champion, D. (1988). Some recent trends in civil litigation by federal and state prison inmates. *Federal Probation, 51*, 43–47.

Cobb, A., Jr. (1985). Home truths about prison overcrowding. *Annals of the American Academy of Political Science, 478*, 73–85.

Crouch, B., & Alpert, G. (1982). Sex and occupational socialization among prison guards. *Criminal Justice and Behavior, 9*, 159–176.

Cullen, F., Link, B., Wolfe, N.T., & Frank, J. (1985). The social dimensions of correctional officers' stress. *Justice Quarterly, 2*, 505–533.

Cullen, F., Lutze, F., Link, B., & Wolfe, N.T. (1989). The correctional orientation of prison guards: Do officers support rehabilitation? *Federal Probation, 53*, 33–42.

Ellis, D., Grasmick, H., & Gilman. B. (1974). Violence in prisons: A sociological analysis. *American Journal of Sociology, 80*(1), 16–43.

Feld, B.C. (1977). *Neutralizing inmate violence: Juvenile offenders in institutions.* Cambridge, MA: Ballinger.

Frazier, C.E. (1989). Preadjucatory detention. In A.R. Roberts (Ed.), *Juvenile justice policies, programs, and services*, pp. 143–162. Chicago: Dorsey Press.

Frazier, C.E., & Bishop. D. (1985). The pretrial detention of juveniles and its impact on case dispositions. *Journal of Criminal Law and Criminology, 76*(4), 1132–1152.

Frazier, C.E., & Cochran, J.K. (1986). Detention of juveniles: Its effects on subsequent juvenile court processing decisions. *Youth and Society, 17*, 286–305.

Gaes, G., & McGuire, W. (1985). Prison violence: The contribution of crowding versus other determinants of prison assault rates. *Journal of Research in Crime and Delinquency, 22*(1), 41–65.

Garrett, C. (1985). Effects of residential treatment on adjudicated delinquents: A meta-analysis. *Journal of Research in Crime and Delinquency, 22*, 287–308.

Gendreau, P. (1996). The principles of effective intervention with offenders. In A. Harland (Ed.), *Choosing correctional options that work: Defining the demand and evaluating the supply*. Thousand Oaks, CA: Sage.

Gordon, J.A. (1996). *An evaluation of paint creek youth center*. Ph.D. diss., University of Cincinnati.

Gordon, J.A., Latessa, E., & Wooldredge, J. (1997). *Paint Creek youth center: Recidivism study*. Unpublished document for Lighthouse Youth Services: University of Cincinnati.

Gottschalk R., Davidson, W., Gensheimer, L., & Mayer, J. (1987). Community-based interventions. In H. Quay (Ed.), *Handbook of juvenile delinquency*, pp. 266–289. New York: Wiley & Sons.

Gruenberg, B. (1980). The happy worker: An analysis of educational and occupational differences in determinants of job satisfaction. *American Journal of Sociology, 86*, 247–271.

Hayduk, L.A. (1978). Personal space: An evaluative and orienting overview. *Psychological Bulletin, 85*, 117–134.

Hepburn, J., & Knepper, P. (1993). Correctional officers as human services workers: The effects on job satisfaction. *Justice Quarterly, 10*(2), 315–337.

Jackson, J., & Ammen, S. (1996). Race and correctional officers' punitive attitudes toward treatment programs for inmates. *Journal of Criminal Justice, 24*(2), 153–166.

Jacobs, J. (1980). The prisoners' rights movement and its impact, 1960–1980. In N. Morris & M. Tonry (Eds.), *Crime and justice* (vol. 2), pp. 429–470. Chicago: Chicago University Press.

Jacobs, J., & Kraft, L. (1978). Integrating the keepers: A comparison of Black and White prison guards in Illinois. *Social Problems*, *25*, 304–318.

Johnson, R., & Price, S. (1981). The complete correctional officer: Human service and the human environment of prison. *Criminal Justice and Behavior, 8*, 343–373.

Jurik, N.C. (1985). Individual and organizational determinants of correctional officers' attitudes toward inmates. *Criminology, 23*, 523–539.

Jurik, N.C. (1988). Striking a balance: Female correctional officers, gender role stereotypes, and male prisons. *Sociological Inquiry, 58*, 291–305.

Jurik, N.C., & Halemba, G. (1984). Gender, work conditions, and the job satisfactions of women in a non-traditional occupation: Female correctional officers in men's prisons. *Sociological Quarterly*, *25*, 551–566.

Jurik, N.C., & Winn, R. (1987). Describing correctional security dropouts and rejects: An individual or organizational profile? *Criminal Justice and Behavior, 14*, 5–25.

Kasselbaum, G., Ward, D., & Wilner, D. (1964). Some correlates of staff ideology in the prison. *Journal of Research on Crime and Delinquency*, *1*, 96–109.

Lindquist, C.A., & Whitehead, J.T. (1986). Burnout, job stress, and job satisfaction among southern correctional officers: Perceptions and causal factors. *Journal of Offender Counseling, Service and Rehabilitation, 10*, 5–26.

Lipsey, M. (1992. Juvenile delinquency treatment: A meta-analytic inquiry into the variability of effects. In T. Cook, D. Cordray, H. Hartman, L. Hedges, R. Light, T. Louis, & F. Mosteller (Eds.), *Meta-analysis for explanation: A casebook*, pp. 83–127. New York: Russell Sage Foundation.

Lombroso, L. (1985). Mental health work in prisons and jails: Inmate adjustment and indigenous correctional personnel. *Criminal Justice and Behavior*, *12*, 17–28.

Lombroso, L. (1982). Stress, change and collective violence in prisons. In R. Johnson & H. Toch (Eds.), *The pains of imprisonment*, pp. 77–93. Beverly Hills, CA: Sage.

Lutz, R.E., Poole, E., & Regoli, R. (1985). *Juvenile delinquency and juvenile justice.* New York: Random House.

Mottaz, C. (1987). An analysis of the relationship between work satisfaction and organizational commitment. *Sociological Quarterly, 28*, 541–558.

Owen, B.A. (1988). *The reproduction of social control: A study of prison workers at San Quentin*. New York: Praeger Press.

Paulus, P., McCain, G., & Cox, V. (1985). The effects of crowding in prisons and jails. In D. Farrington & J. Gunn (Eds.), *Reactions to crime: The public, police, courts, and prisons*. New York: Wiley.

Poole, E.D., & Regoli, R. (1980). Role stress, custody orientation and disciplinary actions: A study of prison guards. *Criminology, 18*, 215–226.

Robinson, D., Porporino, F., & Simourd, L. (1993). The influence of career orientation on support for rehabilitation among correctional staff. *The Prison Journal, 73*(2), 162–177.

———. (1997). The influence of educational attainment on the attitudes and job performance of correctional officers. *Crime and Delinquency, 43*(1), 60–77.

Ruback, R., & Innes, C. (1988). The relevance and irrelevance of psychological research: The example of prison crowding. *American Psychologist, 43*(9), 6883–69.

Schopler, J., & Stockdale, J. (1977). An interference analysis of crowding. *Environmental Psychology, 1*, 81–88.

Singer, R. (1983). Desert sentencing and prison overcrowding: Some doubts and tentative answers. *Review of Law and Social Change*, I(1), 85–110.

Skovran, S. (1988). Prison crowding: The dimensions of the problem and strategies of population control. In J.E. Scott & T. Hirschi (Eds.), *Controversial issues in crime and justice*. Beverly Hills, CA: Sage.

Toch, H. (1978). Is a "correctional officer" by any other name a "screw"? *Criminal Justice Review, 3*, 19–35.

Toch, H., & Klofas, J. (1982). Alienation and desire for job enrichment among correction officers. *Federal Probation, 46*, 35–44.

Van Voorhis, P., Cullen, F., Link, B., & Wolfe, N.T. (1991). The impact of race and gender on correctional officers orientation to the integrated environment. *Journal of Research in Crime and Delinquency, 28*(4), 472–500.

Whitehead, J.T., & Lindquist, C.A. (1989). Determinants of correctional officers' professional orientation. *Justice Quarterly*, 6, 69–85.

Zimmer, L.E. (1986). *Women guarding men*. Chicago: University of Chicago Press.

ENDNOTES

1. The institutions are located in the same state and in close proximity to each other.
2. Felony 1 and 2 offenses are the most serious offenses and consist of such acts as arson, robbery, rape, and assault.
3. The location and intention of the number was explained to the participants in the cover letter. In addition, the cover letter ensured the confidentiality of the responses and the anonymity of the respondents.
4. Several of the attitudinal statements were combined to develop factors to examine the hypothesis (see Appendix A for the items that make up each factor). Each factor was observed for its independence and significance.
5. This was expected, given the fact that the open-security facility has *not* been in operation as long as the closed-security facilities. The open-security facility opened in mid-1986.
6. A dichotomized variable was created by assigning a score of 0 to the scores that fell below the mean and a 1 to scores that fell above the mean. A score that falls below the mean indicates that the respondents are more likely to agree with the attitudinal statement, and a score that is above the mean indicates the respondents are more likely to disagree with the attitudinal statement.

8

A Survey of Citizen Perceptions of Treatment and Satisfaction with a Telephone Service Option in a Rural Sheriff's Department*

Colleen Fitzpatrick, University of Northern Colorado

Methodological Focus. Research is often conducted in many ways that may allow for the findings to be generalized across a particular population, or that may provide answers to a variety of issues or problems of interest to many. However, sometimes the research is only interested in a particular area, a problem, or in how well something is working for one specific population. This article uses the **case study** method. It also makes use of the **quasi-experimental** approach not often seen in the social sciences. Other highlights include questionnaire construction, research questions, and several aspects of sampling.

Abstract

In mid-1995, a rural sheriff's department in northern Colorado implemented an innovative differential police response protocol that offers citizens the option of problem-solving with an officer over the telephone. Intended to augment the department's community policing model, an evaluation research component was built into this program to assess citizen satisfaction with the service. Using a random sampling technique and a

*Earlier versions of this paper were presented at the 1996 and 1997 Academy of Criminal Justice Sciences annual meetings. Interpretations and analyses are those of the author and do not represent the policies or points-of-view of the Larimer County Sheriff's Department nor of the University of Northern Colorado. Thanks are offered to Drew Davis, Nancy Brex, Laurie Reichert, and Michael Maestas for their valuable assistance.

> standardized telephone questionnaire, data on perceived deputy demeanor, departmental problem-solving skills, and overall citizen satisfaction were collected. Analyses of the data reveal that most sociodemographic factors make no significant difference in the degree to which citizens are satisfied with problem-solving services offered by the department. The exception is found in age and education. Age makes a difference in the degree to which citizens are satisfied with the overall service received, and overall satisfaction from beginning to end of the problem-solving process is dependent on education, but only for those receiving "telepolicing" service.

PROBLEM-ORIENTED COMMUNITY POLICING

Law enforcement agencies across the nation are discussing the need to provide citizens with alternate forms of policing. Much of this need has arisen in response to actual or perceived increases in crime and violence over the past couple of decades (Maguire & Pastore, 1995; Warr, 1995), as well as a recognized need to improve relationships between police and community (Bobinsky, 1994). Concomitantly, citizens have grown to expect policing agencies to provide more and more services, such as tending to noise disturbances, neighbor problems, family problems, suspicious vehicles, phone harassment, and so on. However, law enforcement organizations may be faced with considerable difficulty in responding to increased demands for service that are often the result of changes in responsibilities once assumed by other social institutions (Brown, 1990; Monk, 1996).

> Under a variety of names—strategic policing, problem-solving policing, neighborhood-oriented policing, community policing, and others—police agencies are developing new concepts to betterh satisfy the demands and needs of the citizens they serve. In the course of the self-examination and creative thinking that are taking place, fundamental questions have been raised about the basic purpose and responsibilities of the police, the capabilities they possess, the types of contributions they can make to society, the optimum methods of their organization and deployment, and the relationship that they have with the communities that employ them. In contrast to a philosophy of "business as usual," police executives sense the need to "redeploy the money and authority entrusted to them in hopes that their organizations will produce greater value for society" (Meese, 1993, p. 1).

In a broad sense, community policing

> refers to a philosophical position which holds that the goals of policing, the conditions which it addresses, the services it delivers, the means used to deliver them and the *assessment of its adequacy* [emphasis added] should be formulated and developed in recognition of the distinctive experiences, mores, and special structures of local communities. (Weisburd, McElroy & Hardymann, 1988, p. 30)

Furthermore,

> Although the concept is defined in varying ways and its ability to meet its goals remains largely untested, community policing has gained widespread acceptance. According to one source, about 40% of the Nation's larger police departments have adopted it. (Sadd & Grinc, 1996, p. 1)

A somewhat innovative aspect of problem-oriented community policing is found in differential police response.

DIFFERENTIAL POLICE RESPONSE

Clearly, policing departments across the nation are facing a growing number of calls for service and shrinking budgets. Many fear that community policing may produce more frustration for police and community members alike (Worsnop, 1993). The overriding concern, however, has to do with fiscal constraints. To help combat the additional costs of community policing, Differential Police Response (DPR) programs have been developed in some departments.

Differential Police Response (DPR) is used as a way to address public demands for more service without necessarily increasing patrol strength and the number of field operations personnel. The principle objective of DPR is to efficiently provide increased police service with proportionately fewer resources. DPR enables a police department to restructure its response protocol by differentiating calls for service from other types of needs; it essentially involves a delayed response when a nonemergency response is called for. In the event that health and safety are at issue, or the apprehension of offenders is a direct possibility, DPR alternatives would not be initiated.

DPR consists of a variety of programs such as substations, using nonsworn personnel for services like traffic control, walk-in/mail-in reporting options, call stacking, and telephone response. Perhaps the one DPR strategy with the greatest cost effectiveness, but also the greatest potential for problems with citizen satisfaction, is found in the telephone response strategy, or telepolicing.

Telepolicing

Telepolicing involves using trained personnel to handle requests for help with noncriminally related problems over the phone. The need for such programs stems largely from an inability of staffing levels to efficiently respond to additional community needs as the result of population increases and shrinking per capita budgets. The idea is that many calls for service can be handled entirely over the telephone, the result of which would be an increased availability of patrol officers to engage in self-initiated policing. However, much of the effectiveness of this alternate form of policing may be dependent on the sociodemographic characteristics of the community being served. But to conclude confidently that any DPR option is citizen effective is not appropriate without implementation of research methods designed to aid in drawing such conclusions.

EVALUATION OF PILOT PROGRAMS

The National Institute of Justice (NIJ) has sponsored perhaps the most comprehensive research on DPR strategies to date. NIJ funded three studies in Greensboro, North Carolina, Toledo, Ohio, and Garden Grove, California. Evaluations of these three cities have been generally favorable. All three sites experienced considerable reduction in the amount of direct response to nonemergency calls and a concomitant increase in the time available for self-initiated patrolling. Preproject and postproject reviews found that more than 90% of the citizens served by the agencies were satisfied with the convenience found in DPR alternatives (MacEwen, Connors & Cohen, 1986).

The reviews also found that citizens accepted the program more when they were notified in the beginning that delays may occur when calling the departments. It was also found that the demeanor of personnel in the communications centers greatly reflected the acceptance rate of the program. Citizens who reported experiencing courteous, friendly, and attentive operators tended to show higher levels of respect for the program than those citizens who had less understanding of the goals of the program. These programs were refined and now serve as models for departments wishing to carry out similar policing programs (MacEwen, Connors & Cohen, 1986).

One potential area of concern, not well-addressed by current research, relates to issues of equality. No matter what DPR procedures are used, it is likely that some individuals will receive police services disproportionately. For example, race or ethnicity, sex/gender, age, and education may provide a subtle basis for creating an unequal response effect. Thus, while DPR appears to be inherently nondiscriminatory, there is a possibility that procedures used to differentiate calls will represent a higher quality of service to one person or group over another (Flanagan, 1985).

Though research regarding DPR is limited, some generalizations are offered. It can be assumed that DPR does save departments money and resources as related to patrol costs. Firm calculations regarding how much time and money saved varies, but obviously the savings do exist. Quick responses are not always the most effective responses, and it is not necessarily an important factor in citizen satisfaction. What may be the most important factor is how the police respond to citizens once in contact with them, which provides a base upon which citizens form perceptions of treatment and ultimately are or are not satisfied with the service provided.

Perceptions of Treatment and Satisfaction with Service

There are many variables that can affect the formation of perceptions and satisfaction with the services citizens have received. For example, preexisting sociodemographic factors (i.e., ethnicity, gender, age, education, and primary life residency) can influence how citizens perceive themselves as being treated by officers assisting them in the problem-solving process. Perception formation operationally amounts to the degree to which citizens think an officer was courteous, provided useful solutions, understood their problem, and took their problem seriously. Furthermore, citizens' sense of satisfaction with the department (i.e., satisfaction with how the problem was resolved, the services received, the options for handling the problem, whether they would feel comfortable calling upon the department in the future, and their overall degree of satisfaction) is similarly influenced by sociodemographic characteristics.

The development of perceptions and satisfaction is, therefore, the result of a complex process involving the influence of sociodemographic factors. Sociodemographic factors thus directly influence the formation of perceptions derived from interacting with departmental personnel, as well as citizens' degree of satisfaction with the service(s) received and their overall assessment of the department. For example, could gender play a role in determining one's sense of being treated courteously and being taken seriously during the problem-solving interaction with the officer? Could age also be an influential factor in the outcome of the process? Or could ethnicity make a difference in how citizens view themselves as being treated and in their degree of satisfaction with the services received?

In addition, the type of service received (i.e., telepolicing vs. in-person) may influence citizens' sense of treatment and level of overall satisfaction with the department. For example, whether citizens receive in-person or telephone policing may make a difference in their satisfaction with the department's ability, as a whole, to help them resolve the problem.

Thus, the principle research questions at hand are twofold: (1) Does age, gender, ethnicity, education, or primary life residency (i.e., having mostly resided in an urban or rural area) make a significant difference in perceptions of treatment and/or satisfaction with services received? and (2) Does the primary type of service received (telepolicing vs. in-person) make a significant difference in perceptions of treatment and/or satisfaction with services received?

A Rural Example

A case example of the dilemma of stagnating budgets and population growth is found in the sheriff's department of Larimer County, Colorado. Located in northeastern Colorado, ranging across plains and mountains, Larimer County encompasses 2,640 square miles with 1,090 miles of county maintained roads. Geographically, it is the second largest county in the state of Colorado (Larimer County Planning Division, 1991). In addition to law enforcement responsibilities for all unincorporated areas of the county, the sheriff's department is responsible for civil defense, civil process serving, court security, jail operations, search and rescue, and traffic direction and control. Fulfillment of these responsibilities is accomplished with approximately 145 sworn full-time employees, of which 45% work in field operations, 5% work in administration, 2% provide technical support, 46% are in jail operations, and 2% are in court operations, all together at a cost of approximately $50.00 per citizen per annum (Reaves & Smith, 1995).

Larimer County is in the midst of steady growth. Its 1990 population was 186,136 (49.5% female, 50.5% male) with a median age of 31.1 years, where 25.3% were under the age of 18 and 9.6% were 65 or older. A large majority of county residents are White (90.9%), 6.5% are classified as Hispanic, followed by 4.5% Native American, Eskimo or Aleut, 1.43% Asian or Pacific Islander, .56% African American, and .06% other (U.S. Department of Commerce, 1993). As a whole, the county has experienced more than a 14% population increase since 1990 (Coloradoan, 1995).

Unincorporated Larimer County represents 28.8% (53,557) of the total county population (U.S. Department of Commerce, 1992). Rural growth is on the rise, increasing at a conservative estimate of an average 3% annually (Larimer County Planning Division, 1993). All of which amounts to the sheriff's department being faced with a considerable surge in demands for service, and thus a need to increase its response capabilities.

Approximately 85% of calls the department receives from citizens typically involve minor traffic offenses, misdemeanors, civil matters, equipment repair, noise disturbances, missing persons, family problems, and other such service requests. This leaves about 15% of the calls directly related to criminal offenses. From 1988 to 1994, the number of calls for service had increased 97%, while the patrol staff had only increased by 26% (Larimer County Sheriff's Department, 1993). With such an increase in demand for services and a staff growth rate not commensurate with the demand, the department's ability to respond to calls in a timely manner became problematic. The availability of deputies to patrol and respond quickly to criminally related matters could be compromised when officers are increasingly required to respond to noncriminal concerns. The department thus chose the telephone reporting option within the DPR strategy as a way to reduce the workload of the patrol deputy.

EVALUATING THE DPR PROGRAM

"How are we doing?" How the public answers this question can determine police strategies and, ultimately, their success or failure. Research teaches that many popular yardsticks of police performance—speedy response to calls for service, for example—tell little about law enforcement's true effectiveness in reducing crime and the fear of crime. Some evidence suggests that door-to-door surveys by police officers are enough by themselves to reduce crime and fear and enhance citizen attitudes toward police, independent of any information they gain or what police do with it. Surveys can also help measure the characteristics of neighborhood residents, the background of crime victims, or the background of offenders. They can supplement and help interpret other, more readily obtainable information, such as census data, arrest reports, or complaints of crime (Bureau of Justice Assistance, 1993, p. ix).

Virtually all public service organizations are being confronted with the need to demonstrate the effective use of taxpayer dollars. Such demands for accountability serve to accentuate the need for law enforcement agencies to incorporate research protocols into their operations management strategies. A considerable amount of literature on the basic concepts and strategies of community oriented policing and on police attitudes exists (Bayley, 1994; Fielding, 1995; Goldstein, 1987; McElroy, Cosgrove & Sadd, 1993; Meese, 1993; Rosenbaum & Lurigio, 1994; Sadd & Grinc, 1996; Skolnick & Bayley, 1988; Travis, 1995; Trojanowicz, 1985). But a relatively scant amount of research on citizen experiences and perceptions of policing has been accomplished (Correia & Lovrich, 1997; Flanagan, 1985; Fluellen, Renauer & Duffee, 1997; Flynn, 1993; Fox & McDonough, 1993; Percy, 1980; Reisig & Giacomazzi, 1997). As a result, it is difficult to determine what to expect in terms of public acceptance of innovative programs such as telepolicing.

It is important that policing programs be subjected to scrutiny to learn the degree to which the goals of the department coincide with the needs of the community it serves. By necessity, the problems of the community and the department must be monitored and analyzed if effectiveness of community oriented policing strategies are to be determined (Fielding, 1995; Furstenburg & Wellford, 1973; Johnson, Misner & Brown, 1981; Rosenbaum & Lurigio, 1994). Furthermore, citizen experiences with the service must be specifically studied to identify problem areas and to fine-tune the program to provide optimal service (Flynn, 1993). Thus, in recognition of the need to understand the public's point of view, the sheriff's department developed a research partnership with a sociologist from a local university and strategies for monitoring the new DPR program were designed.

METHODOLOGY

Research Design

The department introduced its telepolicing program to the citizens of unincorporated Larimer County in June 1995. A research protocol was designed to provide randomly selected citizens, who had phoned the department for assistance, an opportunity to express feedback on their experiences with the department. The goal was to evaluate citizens' perceptions of how they were treated by departmental personnel with whom they had contact, and to measure their satisfaction with the services provided. It was determined that the most prudent way to systematically research citizen satisfaction with the newly introduced telepolicing program was to telephone survey those citizens who had requested services, then to compare citizens subjected to telepolicing with those who received in-person response.

Data was in no way meant to offer a basis for evaluating individual departmental personnel performance. Instead, it was meant to provide an overall view of citizen perceptions of the department derived from their recent contact with on-duty personnel. However, an inherent tendency to use the data to scrutinize individual officer performance may exist. To guard against this inclination, information that could identify individual officers was not recorded in the data-set.

Measuring the Concepts

A telephone questionnaire was designed to collect data on the major concepts of interest in assessing citizen satisfaction, particularly in reference to perceptions of treatment.

Sociodemographics and Type of Service Received. Measuring sociodemographics was straightforward and was accomplished by simply asking respondents their year of birth, ethnicity, education, gender, and so forth, then coding the responses into a numeric scheme for classification and analysis. Type of service was measured similarly, by recording whether the citizen had predominantly received telepolicing or in-person service.

Perceptions of Treatment and Satisfaction with Service. Citizen satisfaction with the department is thought to be formed out of perceptions of how they were treated by the person with whom they had primary contact, either in-person or over the telephone. The measurement of perception of treatment included asking several questions related to such things as officer courteousness, understanding, providing useful solutions, if they thought their problem was taken seriously, and if the citizen felt as if the department could help. Satisfaction was measured by soliciting responses to questions related to being satisfied with how the problem was resolved, satisfaction with service options (i.e., telepolicing or in-person), willingness to call upon the department in the future, and degree of overall satisfaction.

The actual measuring of the concepts of perceived treatment and satisfaction required a bit of complexity. It was necessary to break each primary concept into subconcepts that cumulatively would represent the major construct of focus. The subconcepts were measured by asking respondents the extent to which they agreed or disagreed with a series of statements constructed to measure each of the subconcepts. Responses were coded in such a way that the lower the number, the less a respondent agreed with the statement. Each statement could be scored across a range of 1 to 5. When summed, the variables form a scale designed to measure total perceived treatment and total amount of satisfaction with the overall service(s) received. Table 8.1 depicts the six interview items used to create a score representing perceived treatment for each type of service experienced.

Two distinct variables were devised, one representing total perceived treatment in reference to telepolicing service, and the other in reference to in-person service. Each composite score could range from a minimum of 6 (very strong disagreement with the statements) to a maximum of 30 (very strong agreement). Overall satisfaction with the services received from beginning to end of the problem-solving process was measured in a fashion similar to those measuring satisfaction with telepolicing and in-person services. The score

Table 8.1 Interview Items Measuring Perceived Treatment

Do you:	Strongly Disagree	Disagree	No Opinion	Agree	Strongly Agree
That the officer assisting you (on the phone/in-person) was polite and courteous.	1	2	3	4	5
That the officer understood your problem.	1	2	3	4	5
That the officer (on the phone/in-person) provided useful solutions to your problem.	1	2	3	4	5
That the Department could help you with your problem.	1	2	3	4	5
That the officer (on the phone/in-person) recorded your problem accurately.	1	2	3	4	5
That your problem was taken seriously by the officer (over the phone/in person).	1	2	3	4	5
Total					30

Table 8.2 Interview Items Measuring Overall Satisfaction with Service Received from Beginning to End of the Problem-Solving Process

Question	1	2	3	4	5
Overall, do you consider the service you received to have been:	Poor	Below Average	Average	Above Average	Excellent
In terms of calling upon the Sheriff's Department in the future, would you be .... asking the Department for service again?	Very Reluctant	Reluctant	No Opinion	Comfortable	Very Comfortable
All in all, what degree of satisfaction do you feel with the way your problem was handled from beginning to end? Were you	Very Dissatisfied	Dissatisfied	Somewhat Dissatisfied	Satisfied	Very Satisfied
Total	3				15

resulting from summing three interview items designed to measure the concept of overall satisfaction with the department as a whole could range from a minimum of 3 to a maximum of 15 (see Table 8.2).

Training and Pretesting

During a six-month period prior to implementation of the telepolicing service, the instrument was pretested on citizens calling the department for assistance of some sort. Interviewers were also trained during this time, and the questionnaire was assessed for face validity in terms of determining if citizens' definitions of concepts coincided with the research team's definitions. The wording of questions were fine-tuned until we thought we had an acceptable data collection instrument. Prior to pretesting, the instrument was distributed to all department heads who provided input on question wording as well as use of vocabulary. The telephone questionnaire was approved for use on human subjects by the University's internal review board.

The instrument became fully operationalized with respondents sampled from the July 1995 pool of callers. All citizens agreeing to participate were queried in a standardized manner. Previous to asking any substantive questions, participants were requested to voluntarily participate and were given an opportunity to decline.

Populations and Samples

The unit of analysis was citizens of Larimer County who had telephoned the sheriff's department for assistance in solving a problem of some sort. A comprehensive listing of the population of citizens who called the department for help was generated at the beginning of every month following the preceding month. This listing served as a sampling frame from which to choose respondents. Callers were randomly selected by going through the sampling frame systematically. Such a sampling method was accomplished by developing a sampling interval according to a predetermined percentage of the population needed for inclusion in the study and the total size of the monthly population. Resources in both time and money led us to decide that it was feasible to collect data from approximately 10% of the population calling the department for assistance.

If the population for a given month was 200 callers and the sample size needed was 10% of the population, then the sampling interval became the proportionate sample size multiplied by the monthly population total (i.e., [.10][200] = 20, which is the minimum sample size needed; the sampling interval became 200/20 = 10, therefore every 10th element was selected until the sample size of 20 had been achieved). For this procedure to be random, the beginning element must be selected in a truly random manner. To meet this requirement when developing the sampling frame every month, the population was numerically identified and a random number was generated by a hand held calculator, the resulting number thus decided the beginning point of the list from which to proceed.

This systematic random selection strategy produced a proportionate monthly representation of citizen callers across time. In other words, the sample size for the busiest months of the year would be larger than the size for the less busy months. This provided adequate representation across the population of citizens from month to month throughout the course of a year and potentially from year to year. This sampling technique was also designed to ensure that citizens differing on various characteristics would be adequately represented. Such a procedure also could allow for generalizing the sample findings to the larger population of callers from which the sample was drawn.

RESULTS

The focus of this analysis was to determine the variables important to satisfaction with services received and those affecting development of perceptions. The major independent variables under consideration were broadly categorized as sociodemographics and service type. The principal research questions will be addressed in the following ways: (1) the sample characteristics of the citizens interviewed and the types of service received are presented; (2) the analyses to determine the major sociodemographic variables influencing citizen perceptions of treatment are presented in reference to telepolicing and in-person service; and (3) an analysis of satisfaction with the entire process from beginning to end in reference to services provided by the department as a whole is offered.

A variety of analytic techniques are used, depending on the level of data a particular variable possesses. Since the sample has little variance in race, for the purposes of analysis, race was dichotomized as either White or non-White.

The sample was divided into a telepoliced group and an in-person policed group. This analytic approach could also lend itself well to making comparisons between telepoliced and in-person respondents. Such a quasi-experimental design created an experimental group (i.e., telepoliced) and a control group (i.e., in-person). Therefore, three samples are amenable to being analyzed separately: (1) a group representing those who primarily received in-person service—such participants may have also received telepolicing, but for one reason or another they were eventually serviced in-person; (2) a group representing those who had only received telepolicing; and (3) the entire sample, composed of both in-person and telepoliced respondents. For the most part, only analyses resulting in a 95% or better level of confidence ($a \leq .05$) are presented in table form.

Sample Characteristics

The entire sample for the period of July 1, 1995 through January 31, 1996 consists of 164 cases, or 12.6% of the 1,305 citizens who called the department during this period requesting service. Basic sociodemographic characteristics for both the in-person and the telepoliced samples are found in Table 8.3. Also included are *Chi*-square statistics to aid in determining if having been serviced in-person or over the phone was dependent on any such factors.

More than half of the sample (51.2%) had initially received telepolicing, but some were eventually serviced in-person. For analytic purposes, a respondent was classified as a citizen receiving in-person service if at any time during the problem-solving process he or she met with an officer face-to-face. Thus, 62.2% of the sample was serviced in-person and 37.8% were serviced strictly over the telephone.

The sample, as a whole, is composed of 46.3% males and 53.7% females. The mean year in which respondents were born is 1955, with a median age of 38 years. The average number of years of education is 13.7, with 36.6% possessing a high school education and 57.3% a college degree or graduate school training. A large majority of respondents identified themselves as being White (85.7%). More than half of the respondents (56.3%) indicated that they had spent most of their adult lives living in urban areas and 43.7% were predominantly rural dwellers.

Sociodemographic Differences in Type of Service Received

It is instructive to know if a caller's sociodemographic characteristics might somehow make a difference in the type of service he or she ultimately received. For example, could it be that a significantly larger number of females received telepolicing than males? A crosstabulation of the basic sociodemographics and the type of service received was accomplished to examine this curiosity.

When comparing respondents in light of race, gender, primary life residency (i.e., urban vs. rural), and level of education, no significant tendency for one type of characteristic seemed to be operating to determine whether a caller chose to be serviced in-person or over the telephone. Thus, the type of service received was independent of a respondent's basic sociodemographic profile (see Table 8.3).

Both White and non-White respondents were equally likely to receive in-person or telepolicing service as were males and females. While a simple majority of respondents had lived most of their lives in urban areas (56.3%), there was no significant relationship between the type of service received and whether a respondent had lived most of her or his life in an urban or rural area. Furthermore, the type of service received was independent of the level of education a respondent possessed. All-in-all, it appears as if little or no bias, in terms of the basic sociodemographics measured, was operating to influence whether a caller received in-person or telepolicing service. While many other unmeasured factors may have been operating to influence such a bias, it is safe to assume that the determination of whether to send an officer in-person was based on the type of problem presented as well as the expressed wishes of the caller.

Perhaps, whether a caller receives telepolicing or in-person service makes a difference in satisfaction ratings. The following examines the degree to which satisfaction with services, or perceptions of treatment, might be influenced by sociodemographic factors. Each type of service offered (i.e., telepolicing or in-person) is analyzed separately.

Table 8.3 Crosstabulations of Sociodemographics with Type of Service Received

Sociodemographic	In-Person	Telepoliced Only	Total
Race/ethnicity	% (*n*)	% (*n*)	% (*n*)
White	51.6 (83)	34.2 (55)	85.7 (138)
Non-White	10.6 (17)	3.7 (6)	14.3 (23)
Pearson $c^2 = 1.588$; $df = 1$; $p = .208$			
Gender	% (*n*)	% (*n*)	% (*n*)
Female	31.1 (51)	22.6 (37)	53.7 (88)
Male	31.1 (51)	15.2 (25)	46.3 (76)
Pearson $c^2 = 1.452$; $df = 1$; $p = .228$			
Primary Residency	% (*n*)	% (*n*)	% (*n*)
Urban	33.8 (54)	22.5 (36)	56.3 (90)
Rural	27.5 (44)	16.3 (26)	43.8 (70)
Pearson $c^2 = .135$; $df = 1$; $p = .713$			
Education	% (*n*)	% (*n*)	% (*n*)
Less than High School	1.9 (3)	0.0 (0)	1.9 (3)
High school	25.5 (40)	12.7 (20)	38.2 (60)
College	27.4 (43)	17.8 (28)	45.2 (71)
Grad School	6.4 (10)	8.3 (13)	14.6 (23)
Pearson $c^2 = 5.708$; $df = 3$; $p = .127$			

Telepolicing Service

During the period sampled, 62 respondents received only telepolicing and experienced no face-to-face interaction with an officer. A very large majority (94.1%) indicated that the phone-officer was courteous and polite, and when asked if they felt the phone-officer understood their problem, 90.5% agreed at some level. However, respondents did not necessarily assess the phone-officer as being able to provide useful solutions to their problems; 47.5% disagreed, strongly disagreed, or had no opinion that the officer could provide useful solutions over the phone. Perhaps this is reflective of no solution being possible. For example, a respondent may have called to report mailbox vandalization where no direct solution is available for such a problem.

When asked if the phone-officer took their problem seriously, 82.2% agreed. Almost everyone (91.5%) indicated that the phone-officer adequately explained the procedures for dealing with their problem. And when asked if they felt the department, as a whole, could help them with their problems, 61.9% agreed. As a whole, telepoliced respondents rated the phone-officer as being courteous and polite as well as understanding of their problem.

Nevertheless, factors such as race, residency, gender, age, and years of education may significantly impact citizens' perceptions of how well they were treated and their satisfaction with services received during the course of problem resolution with an officer over the telephone.

Influence of Race on Telepolicing Satisfaction. A two-tailed *t*-test for equality of means revealed no difference between White and non-White telepoliced citizens in how they rated their level of satisfaction with telepolicing service ($t = -0.143$; $df = 6.096$; $a = 0.891$), in particular, and, in general, with overall services received from beginning to end of the problem-solving process ($t = -0.345$; $df = .806$; $a = 0.774$). While White respondents rated satisfaction on both service indicators slightly higher than non-Whites, the difference was negligible and most likely due to chance alone.

Influence of Primary Life Residency on Telepolicing Satisfaction. The idea behind primary life residency is that people who have spent most of their lives residing in an urban area will have different expectations of policing services than those who have lived mostly in rural areas. This is particularly germane to differential police response strategies in that the ability of rural sheriffs' departments to be able to provide full response capabilities to all residents, even those living in outlying areas, may be quite different from the response capabilities of urban police agencies.

The majority (56.3%) of respondents indicated that they had spent most of their lives living in urban settings but had recently moved to a rural area. However, no significant difference between urban and rural dwellers in satisfaction with services received was revealed in the data. It appears as if having lived primarily in urban or rural areas has no meaningful influence on the degree to which citizens are satisfied with either the telepolicing service ($t = -0.788$; $df = 57.748$; $a = 0.434$) or with the overall services they received from beginning to end of the process ($t = -0.668$; $df = 56.004$; $a = 0.434$).

Influence of Gender on Telepolicing Satisfaction. It was also thought that gender might somehow influence the degree to which citizens were satisfied with the services received from the department. For example, males and females might differ in their expectations of what the department could provide in their problem-solving situation. However, no significant difference between males and females on expressed satisfaction with either telepolicing services ($t = -0.148$; $df = 56.933$; $a = 0.883$) or the overall services ($t = -0.602$; $df = 59.464$; $a = 0.549$) received from the department was revealed. While males scored slightly lower on both satisfaction scales, the difference is negligible and is likely due to measurement error or simply chance alone.

Influence of Age and Education on Telepolicing Satisfaction. A person's age and years of education might also influence the degree to which they were satisfied with services received. Table 8.4, presenting Pearson correlations, reveals that neither age nor years of education had any significant effect on satisfaction with telepolicing services specifically.

Table 8.4 Influence of Age and Years of Education on Perceptions of Treatment/ Satisfaction with Services for the Telepoliced Sample Pearson Correlation

	Satisfaction with Telepoliciing		Satisfaction with Overall Service from Beginning to End	
Sociodemographic	r	*p*	r	*p*
Age	0.221	0.090	0.362	0.004
Years of Education	0.081	0.536	0.292	0.022

	n	Mean	Standard Dev	Var	Min	Max
Age	61	44.02	12.91	166.62	18	84
Years of Education	61	14.25	2.71	7.36	10	22
Sat/w Telepol	61	23.72	3.77	14.2	10	30
Sat/w Overall Service	62	11.95	2.81	7.92	3	15

Interestingly, both age and years of education did provide a direct and positive influence on satisfaction with overall services received from beginning to end of the problem-solving process for the telepoliced sample. The age variable had the strongest influence, indicating that older citizens were more likely to express greater satisfaction with the department as a whole than were younger respondents.

Education influenced the process in a fashion similar to age. As education increased, overall satisfaction increased. Which is to say that the lower the level of education, the less satisfied a respondent was with the overall services offered by the department.

Clearly, age and years of education are the best predictors for determining the degree to which a telepoliced citizen will be satisfied with services offered by the sheriff's department from beginning to end of thc problem-solving process. It could be that as citizens grow and mature, they become more realistic in their expectations of what policing can do for them and are thus less critical of the type of services offered and the manner in which they are offered. It could also be that older citizens are more inclined than younger citizens to take personal responsibility for problem-solving and are therefore less likely to rely on the problem-solving skills of public servants such as police officers.

In-Person Officer Service

The analytic criteria for inclusion in this sample was having met with an officer in-person at some point in the problem-solving process. Nearly two-thirds

(62.2%) of the total sample, or 102 respondents, experienced face-to-face interaction with an officer. The vast majority (93.9%) of participants indicated that the in-person officer was polite and courteous, and that he or she understood their problem (96.1%). Slightly more than two-thirds (68.6%) felt as if the in-person officer gave useful solutions to their problems, however 9.8% disagreed and 22.0% had no opinion. Respondents also largely agreed (90.2%) that the in-person officer took their problem seriously, and 87.7% indicated that the in-person officer adequately explained procedures.

As with the telepoliced sample, it could be that factors such as race, primary life residency, gender, age, and years of education might significantly influence citizens' perceptions of how well they were treated during the course of problem resolution with an in-person officer.

Influence of Race on Satisfaction with In-Person Services. A difference of means test between White and non-White respondents for the in-person sample revealed that race made no significant difference in the degree to which a citizen was satisfied with the in-person service received (t = 0.65; df = 23.14; a = 0.52) as well as with the overall services received from the department as a whole (t = 0.11; df = 20.91; a = 0.92). Any differences between White and non-White respondents were virtually nonexistent and therefore had no apparent bearing on a citizen's satisfaction with services received.

Influence of Primary Life Residency on Satisfaction with In-Person Service. Whether respondents had primarily spent their lives living in an urban versus a rural area made no significant difference in the degree to which they expressed satisfaction with the services received (t = 0.735; df = 77.117; a = 0.465). Primary life residency also made no significant difference on satisfaction with overall services received from beginning to end of the process (t = 0.569; df = 89.821; a = 0.571). Thus, any observed variance in satisfaction cannot be attributed to primary life residency for the in-person sample.

Influence of Gender on Satisfaction with In-Person Services. As with race and primary life residency, gender made no difference in whether or not respondents receiving in-person service were satisfied with their experiences with the department. Females were negligibly less satisfied ($\bar{x}$ = 24.08) with services provided by in-person officers than were male respondents ($\bar{x}$ = 24.50), but any observed difference was not significant (t = 0.590; df = 97.744; a = 0.557). While females expressed a slightly greater level of satisfaction ($\bar{x}$ = 12.27) with the services received from beginning to end of the process than did males ($\bar{x}$ = 12.06) in the survey, any noted difference was not significant (t = 0.384; df = 99.999; a = 0.702) and must be attributed to chance alone.

Influence of Age and Years of Education on In-Person Satisfaction. Unlike the telepoliced sample, those respondents receiving in-person services revealed no significant influence from age and years of education on either the degree to which they were satisfied with the services offered or with the overall services

Table 8.5 Influence of Age and Years of Education on Perceptions of Treatment/ Satisfaction with Services for the In-Person Sample Pearson Correlation

	Satisfaction with In-Person Service		Satisfaction with Overall Service from Beginning to End	
Sociodemographic	*r*	*p*	*r*	*p*
Age	0.029	0.774	0.029	0.791
Years of Education	0.113	0.264	−0.037	0.714

	n	Mean	Standard Dev	Var	Min	Max
Age	99	37.68	10.66	113.69	16	73
Years of Education	100	13.41	2.95	8.73	2	22
Satisfaction with In-Person Service	101	24.28	3.58	12.85	12	30
Satisfaction with Overall Service	102	12.17	2.82	7.96	3	15

received from beginning to end of the process. Table 8.5 reveals that while both age and years of education were very slightly and positively correlated with satisfaction, the influence of either factor was not statistically significant.

Influence of Race, Primary Life Residency and Gender on Overall Satisfaction. The basic sociodemographic factors of race, having primarily lived in an urban versus a rural area, and gender made no measurable difference in whether or not a citizen was satisfied with the overall services received from beginning to end of the problem-solving process. Table 8.6 reveals that none of the sociodemographics measured provided a basis for understanding any differences people might possess in being satisfied with the services received. While non-Whites were slightly more satisfied, urban dwellers and rural dwellers were equally satisfied, and males were slightly more satisfied than females, none of these factors made any significant difference in ratings of satisfaction.

Influence of Age and Years of Education on Overall Satisfaction. When analyzing the entire sample, age had a direct, positive, and significant influence on the degree to which respondents were satisfied with the overall services received from beginning to end. But years of education had no significant influence on satisfaction when analyzed for the entire sample. However, when viewing Table 8.7 it is important to keep in mind that the lack of influence from age and education for the in-person sample likely deflated the influence noted for the telepoliced sample. Nevertheless, it is instructive to note that age is a surviving influence on the entire sample's degree of satisfaction with overall services received.

Table 8.6 Difference of Means Test between Race, Primary Life Residency, and Gender of Respondents on Perceptions of Treatment/Satisfaction with Services for the Entire Sample

Satisfaction with Overall Services Received from Beginning to End (minimum = 3; maximum = 15)

Race	***n***	**Mean**	**Standard Dev.**	**Standard Error**
White	138	12.05	2.78	0.24
Non-White	23	12.26	3.22	0.67

t-test for Equality of Means

t	*df*	2-Tail Significance	Mean Difference
0.30	27.53	0.77	0.21

Residency	***n***	**Mean**	**Standard Dev.**	**Standard Error**
Urban	92	12.04	2.82	0.30
Rural	70	12.03	2.84	0.34

t-test for Equality of Means

t	*df*	2-Tail Significance	Mean Difference
0.04	147.96	0.97	0.02

Gender	**n**	**Mean**	**Standard Dev.**	**Standard Error**
Female	88	12.07	2.95	0.32
Male	76	12.11	2.66	0.31

t-test for Equality of Means

t	*df*	2-Tail Significance	Mean Difference
−0.09	161.68	0.93	−0.04

If nothing else can be said, when rating the level of overall satisfaction with services received from beginning to end of the problem-solving process, age provides a positive, significant, and surviving influence. Older respondents were consistently more likely to rate their overall experiences with the department slightly higher than younger respondents. And while education appears to lose its influence in the entire sample as a result of taking into account the in-person sample, it, too, must be considered an influential variable.

Clearly, age is a very important factor influencing satisfaction, followed closely by the influence of education. It can be safely said that older county residents who call upon the sheriff's department for service are more likely to be satisfied with services received than younger residents. It can be tentatively

Table 8.7 Influence of Age and Years of Education on Perceptions of Treatment/ Satisfaction with Services for the Entire Sample Pearson Correlation

Satisfaction with Overall Services Received from Beginning to End		
Sociodemographic	*r*	*p*
Age	0.152	0.027
Years of Education	0.075	0.172

	n	Mean	Standard Dev	Var	Min	Max
Age	160	40.09	11.94	142.49	16	84
Years of Education	151	13.73	2.89	8.32	2	22
Satisfaction with Overall Services	164	12.09	2.81	7.91	3	15

said that the higher the educational level of the citizen calling upon the department for service, the more likely the department will receive high satisfaction ratings.

CONCLUSION

The basic intent of this paper has been to present a contemporary rural example of a law enforcement agency's need to initiate a DPR strategy with telepolicing at its core, and its efforts at simultaneously evaluating citizen satisfaction with this innovative community-oriented policing initiative. I have sought to demonstrate the usefulness of developing a research protocol for providing objective data on citizen perceptions and satisfaction with services. Such research can simultaneously be used by the agency to fine-tune its community policing program as well as to be responsive to the changing needs of the community it serves.

In general, the major findings coincide somewhat well with the findings of Worden (1993) and of MacEwen, Connors, and Cohen (1986), thus serving to confirm the anticipated usefulness of DPR initiatives. These findings also correspond well to the findings of recent research by Reisig and Giacomazzi (1997), who found that "the level and quality of participation [in community policing programs] is likely to be greater in those neighborhoods characterized by older, longer term, and better educated residents" (p. 22).

The research presented herein extends the base of community policing research by focusing on a specific DPR strategy, namely telepolicing, and by pointing to specific sociodemographic characteristics likely to influence public receipt of problem-oriented community policing initiatives. From an overall citizen perspective, the DPR strategy of telepolicing is useful and was well-received by the citizens of the unincorporated rural county studied. And when comparing in-person service to phone service, there was little difference in terms of satisfaction with services and perceptions of treatment.

While the factors of gender, primary life residency, and race provided no basis for explaining any significant differences in satisfaction with services received from the sheriff's department, the influences of age and education are undeniable, particularly in the context of telepolicing. Both factors had a direct and positive influence on levels of satisfaction with services offered, especially for those respondents experiencing only telephone contact, absent of any in-person influences. For the telepoliced sample, as both age and education increased, the level of satisfaction simultaneously increased. But for the in-person sample, these two factors had no significant influence on levels of satisfaction.

Age and education may provide for a more articulate person who is able to effectively and satisfactorily deal with problem-resolution without personal contact. Or it could be that once a citizen comes into personal contact with an officer, the importance of age and education tends to diminish during the problem-solving process and other factors that the measuring instrument failed to detect become important in determining levels of satisfaction with offered services.

It is apparent that the two basic sociodemographic factors of age and education are influential in determining a public's receipt of newly introduced telepolicing services. These two factors may provide an ongoing effect as well, but this study was not designed to allow such an inference to be drawn. However, these findings might be brought to bear on decision-making about appropriate service strategies to develop in various communities. In extending these findings to other areas and service strategies, the importance of specifically taking into consideration the characteristics of age and education in a community when making decisions about what type of DPR strategy to introduce is apparent. For example, environments predominantly occupied by a younger, less educated citizenry might best be served by locating substations in the area that would facilitate in-person service. On the other hand, areas characterized by middle-aged to older citizens who are relatively well-educated might best be served with the telepolicing option in a department's array of community policing services. It would, therefore, behoove law enforcement managers and planners to take into consideration the sociodemographic profile of the target community when making decisions on what community-oriented policing strategies to initiate.

REFERENCES

Bayley, D.H. (1994). *Police for the future.* New York: Oxford University Press.

Bobinsky, R. (1994). Reflections on community-police oriented policing. *FBI Law Enforcement Bulletin, 63*(3), 15–19.

Brown, L.P. (1990). The police-community relationship. *The Police Chief, 58*(12), 8.

Bureau of Justice Assistance. (1993). *A police guide to surveying citizens and their environment.* Washington, DC: U.S. Department of Justice, Office of Justice Programs.

Coloradoan. (1995). State population up 11%, Larimer grows 14%. 27 May.

Correia, M.E., & Lovrich, N.P. (1997). Building a sense of community: Assessing the strength of social capital and sense of community on community policing programs. Paper presented at the 34th Annual Meeting of the Academy of Criminal Justice Sciences, Louisville, KY.

Federal Bureau of Investigation. 1994. Who is the customer. *FBI Law Bulletin, 64*(3), 24–26.

Fielding, N. (1995). *Community policing.* Oxford, England: Clarendon Press.

Flanagan, T. (1985). Consumer perspectives on police operational strategy. *Journal of Police Science and Administration, 13*, 10–21.

Fluellen, R., Renauer, B., & Duffee, D. (1997). Community variables in community policing. Paper presented at the 34th Annual Meeting of the Academy of Criminal Justice Sciences, Louisville, KY.

Flynn, J.F. (1993). *Community policing: The use of questionnaire results in program evaluation.* Master's thesis, Department of Sociology, University of Northern Colorado.

Fox, D.M., & McDonough, K. (1993). Evaluation of annual citizen survey: 1993 Greeley Police Department. Paper presented at the annual meeting of the Academy of Criminal Justice Sciences, Chicago, IL.

Furstenburg, F., & Wellford, C. (1973). Calling the police: The evaluation of police service. *Law and Society Review, 7*(3), 393.

Goldstein, H. (1987). Toward community-oriented policing: Potential, basic requirements, and threshold questions. *Crime and Delinquency, 33*, 60–80.

Johnson, T.A., Misner, G.E., & Brown, L.P. (1981). *The police and society.* Engelwood Cliffs, NJ: Prentice-Hall.

Larimer County Sheriff's Department. (1993). *Analysis of 1988–1993 call statistics for the Larimer County Sheriff's Department.* Fort Collins, CO: Research and Development Section.

Larimer County Planning Division. (1991). *Larimer County demographics: A summary of population and economic information.* Fort Collins, CO: Larimer County Commissioners Office.

MacEwen, J.T., Connors, E.F., & Cohen, M.F. (1986). *Evaluation of DPR field fest.* Washington, DC: National Institute of Justice.

Maguire, K., & Pastore, A.L., eds. (1995). *Sourcebook of criminal justice statistics, 1994.* U.S. Department of Justice, Bureau of Justice Statistics. Washington, DC: U.S. Government Printing Office.

McElroy, J.E., Cosgrove, C., & Sadd, S. (1993). *Community policing: The CPOP in New York.* Thousand Oaks, CA: Sage.

Meese, E., III. (1993). Community policing and the police officer. *Perspectives on policing*, No. 15. A publication of the National Institute of Justice, U.S. Department of Justice, and the Program in Criminal Justice Police and Management, John F. Kennedy School of Government, Harvard University.

Monk, R.C. (1996). *Taking sides: Clashing views on controversial issues in crime and criminology.* 4th ed. Guilford, CN: Dushkin Publishing Group.

Percy, S. (1980). Response time and citizen evaluation of police. *Journal of Police Science and Administration, 8*, 75–86.

Reaves, B.A., & Smith, P.Z. (1995). *Law enforcement management and administrative statistics, 1993: Data for individual state and local agencies with 100 or more officers*. U.S. Department of Justice, Office of Justice Programs, Bureau of Justice Statistics. Washington, DC: U.S. Government Printing Office.

Reisig, M.D., & Giacomazzi, A.L. (1997). Neighborhood attitudes and community policing. Paper presented at the 34th Annual Meeting of the Academy of Criminal Justice Sciences, Louisville, KY.

Rosenbaum, D.P., & Lurigio, A.J. (1994). An inside look at community policing reform: Definitions, organizational changes, and evaluation findings. *Crime and Delinquency, 40*(3), 299–314.

Sadd, S. & Grinc, R.M. (1996). *Implementation challenges in community policing*. Washington, DC: National Institute of Justice.

Skolnick, J.H., & Bayley, D.H. (1988). *Community policing: Issues and practices around the world*. Washington, DC: National Institute of Justice.

Travis, J. (1995). Community policing: A focal point of innovation. *Searching for answers: Criminal justice research, development and evaluation, 1995 annual report to Congress*. Washington, DC: National Institute of Justice.

Trojanowicz, R. (1985). *Job satisfaction: A comparison of four patrol versus motor patrol officers*. Flint, MI: Michigan State University, National Neighborhood Foot Patrol Center.

U.S. Department of Commerce. (1991). *Social and economic characteristics of Colorado*. Washington, DC: Bureau of the Census, Economic and Statistics Administration.

U.S. Department of Commerce. (1992). *U.S. census 1992 update*. Washington, DC: Bureau of the Census, Economic and Statistics Administration.

U.S. Department of Commerce. (1993). *1990 census of population and housing characteristics*. Washington, DC: Bureau of the Census, Economic and Statistics Administration.

Warr, M. 1995. Poll trends: Public opinion on crime and punishment. *Public Opinion Quarterly, 59*, 296–310.

Weisburd, D., McElroy, J., & Hardymann, P. (1988). Challenges to Supervision in Community Policing: Observations on a Pilot Project. *American Journal of Police, VII*(2), 29–50.

Worden, R.E. (1993). Toward equality and efficiency in law enforcement. *American Journal of Sociology, 12*, 1–32.

Worsnop, R.L. (1993). Community policing: Is it the best answer to the nation's crime problem? *CQ Researcher, 3*(5), 99–119.

9

Women as Organized Criminals: An Examination of the Numbers Gambling Industry in New York City

Donald R. Liddick, Jr., University of Pittsburgh—Greensburg

Methodological Focus. Although surveying is a popular research methodology, there are times when it is not necessary because the data is already available. This article demonstrates the use of **secondary data** (Records research) as a means of researching an area of interest.

Abstract

The part played by women in organized crime is a largely unexplored issue and is, therefore, a topic worthy of study. Using official reports derived from police investigations in the 1960s in New York City, a database of 1666 numbers gamblers was compiled. An analysis of the data revealed that 13.3% of the gamblers identified by police were women, many of whom filled management-type positions in the gambling operations. However, men were proportionately far more likely to hold management positions. Women who did perform management functions were almost exclusively African American and Hispanic.

While there are well-known examples of females in organized crime like Harlem's "Madam Queen of Policy" Stephanie St. Clair, or, more recently, escort service entrepreneur Heidi Fleiss, conventional wisdom suggests that organized crime is dominated by males, with the participation of females a rare exception. Countless prosecutions of male organized crime figures and some other limited data do suggest that the participation of women in organized crime is very rare. For example, a survey of the 1980 report of the Pennsylvania Crime Commission revealed that only two of the 357 persons (0.56%) identified as organized criminals were women (Lyman & Potter, 1997). Historically, Progressive Era reformers envisioned the participation of females in criminality as confined to prostitution, their role one of subservience to men involved in the White slave trade (Block, 1980). Nevertheless, there is enough evidence to indicate that the traditional and Progressive Era assumptions about female participation are inaccurate. Asbury's *The Barbary Coast* (1933), Turkus and Feder's *Murder Inc.* (1951), and Teresa and Renner's *My Life in the Mafia* (1973) all provide anecdotal glimpses of women who were not only involved in a wide range of criminal activities in addition to prostitution, but who also actively managed certain enterprises and were at times more hard-nosed than their male contemporaries (Block, 1980).

Although research in this area is slim, we fortunately do not have to rely entirely on mere anecdotes. Two successive articles by Alan Block (1980) review historical documents that cast some doubt upon the conventional view of female organized criminality as a rare occurrence typified by low-level servitude. Rather, Block suggests that female involvement in organized crime is explained best as "a rational method of adaptation to urban opportunities and institutions" (Block, 1980, p. 202). In this context, Block observed that female providers of gambling and prostitution services in 1930s New York City played a major role in resisting takeover attempts by infamous and ultrapowerful gangsters like "Lucky" Luciano (who tried to centralize prostitution) and Dutch Schultz (who for a short time successfully centralized a portion of Harlem's numbers trade). In addition to occupying key roles in prostitution and gambling enterprises, women were also quite important in the writing of bail bonds, an industry intimately linked to organized crime and official corruption. A list of bail bond racketeers derived from an investigation by New York City's special prosecutor Samuel Seabury revealed that nearly 44% of the named criminals were women (Block, 1980).

Another good scholarly source examining the nature of female organized criminality is Potter and Gaines' (1992) study of rural organized crime in eastern Kentucky. They found that 82.14% of the rural crime networks examined had women who filled management or coordination roles. Put another way, 19 of 97 (19.6%) criminals examined were female, a significant percentage given that the researchers included in their analysis only upper-level or management-type personnel. The researchers concluded that "female leadership roles in organized crime are a peculiarly rural phenomenon," shaped by rural society generally and, in their study, by "the cultural norms in eastern Kentucky" (Potter & Gaines, 1992).

THE PRESENT STUDY: GOAL, DATA, AND METHOD

The few scholarly studies available suggest that conventional wisdom concerning female participation in organized crime may be inaccurate. The participation of women in criminal enterprises is fairly common, and sometimes they even assume management roles. The goal of this project is to assess the degree to which women participated in New York City's numbers gambling industry.

Of particular interest is the degree to which females filled management positions in numbers firms. The study will also try to determine if there is a relationship between the gender of numbers workers and the roles they occupied. First, however, it is necessary to briefly examine the structure of numbers enterprises.

THE STRUCTURE OF NUMBERS FIRMS

Numbers gambling is a simple form of an illegal lottery where bettors usually wager a small amount of money on a three-digit number. Numbers firms are headed by a "banker," the person behind the enterprise who provides the necessary capital reserve to ensure continued solvency. In the authority structure, the next level down comprises "middle-managers" called controllers (Reuter, 1983). Controllers are appointed by the banker and are responsible for the timely movement of betting information between the accounting center and the collectors of bets on the street. Numbers collectors or runners are the street-level retailers of the operation and report directly to their designated controller. Other low-level salaried employees are bank workers or clerks, who tabulate the daily winnings, and pick-up persons, who move money and betting information between various parties. The structure of numbers firms and the tasks assigned to the different personnel indicate that bankers and controllers should be considered management positions. In fact, economist Peter Reuter has arrived at this conclusion and sees controllers as something like mid-level managers below bankers in the authority structure (Reuter, 1983).

THE DATA

The data on female numbers gamblers used in this study were derived from New York City Police Department reports. Police reports are not readily accessible to the public and are often confidential, so the acquisition of the files used in the present research was fortunate. The reports were obtained through an academic liaison, who requested them from a former assistant district attorney in Manhattan. Success in accessing the data can be attributed to a well cultivated relationship with Manhattan's municipal authorities, and the fact that the data in the reports contained no information concerning an active or ongoing investigation.

In all, 51 police reports were used in the present study. After a thorough reading of the reports, it became evident that they contained a gold mine of potentially useful information. Most of the reports were authored by the commanders of special plainclothes units called "bank teams." These police squads were created and grafted onto each borough command in 1963 as a response to heightened awareness of the problem of illegal gambling in New

York City. Each bank team consisted of about six to twelve plainclothes officers led by a lieutenant. The mission of the teams was not only to arrest and deter numbers gambling activity, but also to gather information about the numbers enterprises—the individuals involved, their places of operation, the extent of the enterprises, and so forth. Additional reports were also provided by the Police Commissioner's Confidential Investigating Unit (PCCIU), the Chief Inspector's Investigating Unit (CIIU), and the Internal Revenue Service.

The police reports provided detailed information about the personnel involved in the delivery of numbers gambling services. Their residences, areas of illegal operation, ethnic identity, gender, organizational affiliation, roles within the given numbers enterprise, age, and classification numbers assigned by the police were provided for many of the subjects. In some cases, relatives, legal employment or businesses, automobiles used, dates and places of birth, places frequented, criminal and noncriminal associates, aliases, and physical descriptions were also provided. The arrests made by the investigative teams were also recorded. The arrest data included the dates of the arrests, the names of the arrested individuals, the locations of the arrests, the arresting officers, and the number of slips, ribbons, plays, envelopes, cash, and personal property seized in each arrest. Unfortunately, the disposition of arrests and the sentences given to those convicted were rarely included in the reports.

The structural characteristics of each targeted numbers enterprise was outlined, and in some cases a schematic was included with the police report. Many of the reports contained the identity and number of collectors, controllers, pick-up men, bank clerks, bankers, and other personnel associated with each numbers firm. The area of operation for each enterprise was described in great detail, including the exact street addresses of drop spots, pick-up spots, collection sites, and accounting centers. The methods employed by the organizations in the actual delivery of their gambling services to the public were also described, including how the numbers wagers were collected, transferred, and processed by the numbers personnel, and the various and often creative adaptive measures employed by the numbers personnel as a result of police pressure. Information concerning the pay-out rates established by the numbers entrepreneurs, organizational policies concerning "cut numbers," the acceptance of other types of numbers wagers (such as single action), and the use of layoff services was mentioned less frequently.

In addition to describing in detail the structure and functioning of the numbers enterprises, the police reports also contained information explaining and describing the nature of the relationships that existed within and between the various numbers firms. Some of the data described territorial disputes, factional conflicts within organizations, internal problems between management and lower level personnel, the withdrawal of certain individuals from the illegal numbers market, the emergence of independent numbers operators, the absorption of numbers operations by other entities in the market, and incidences where lower-level personnel switched allegiances. Separate investigations and the methods employed by the investigators were also recorded in great detail in the PCCIU and policy bank team reports.

Typically, police investigations were initiated by gathering all available information concerning numbers gamblers from numerous sources, including FBI files, CIB (Criminal Identification Bureau) files, "U.F. 44 cards," departmental files, telephone listings, and the personal knowledge of officers. Analysis of known data was then utilized to target certain areas and persons deemed to be significant.

Plainclothes officers employed various investigative techniques, primarily the constant surveillance of numbers personnel and the notation of their activities. Officers tailed suspects on foot and in private cars, public buses, and taxicabs. Departmental trucks and some private trucks were also used for tailing and standing observations. Departmental walkie-talkies were used for car-to-car communications while tailing suspects, and for communications from rooftops or indoor observation sites. As cover, police would distribute pamphlets, advertisements, and various other forms of literature inside suspected buildings; they would also solicit tenants to contribute clothing for the needy or safeguard discarded refrigerators. Investigators often resorted to the utilization of disguises, including mail man, auto mechanic, delivery man, butcher's apron, firemen, porters, customers, handball players, and in several notable instances, a baby carriage on the sidewalk and the use of a "Trojan-horse-like" box in which police hid. Policewomen were used in many situations, and often disguised themselves as maids, housewives, and charity workers. Many observations were made from rooftops through binoculars. The police also had the backing of the local judiciary, and were granted numerous ex parte orders allowing for the interception of telephone communications between numbers operators. In addition, the police made widespread use of confidential informants.

Most of the police reports used in this study are dated from 1962 to 1966. They are essentially the product of round-the-clock surveillance of numbers operators for a period of several years. In addition to the thousands of events observed and recorded, the police seized millions of numbers plays, adding machine ribbons, and other "policy work." These gambling records were analyzed by police gambling specialists and the Department's own handwriting expert, Max Renner. Renner could look at the seized records and determine who accepted the wagers, who tabulated the daily play, and what organization was handling the play. This invaluable tool allowed the police to ascertain the extent of many numbers operations, and to make inferences about the organization of the gambling market.

While all of this information could be used to address numerous research questions, the present study is limited to the gender distribution of numbers gamblers (with special attention paid to female criminals), their ethnicity, and the roles they filled within gambling enterprises. Before describing the method of the study, however, it is first necessary to answer a very important question: can the data be trusted? The use of police reports raises serious questions of validity. Most of the concerns revolve around the issue of the integrity of the police who authored the reports. Independent sources such as The Knapp Commission Report and articles in *The New York Times* indicate that the NYPD officers often made phony arrests while protecting actual gamblers. The possibility that these activities contaminated the data is a reason for concern. Fortunately, a thorough assessment of the reports indicates that the data used in this study accurately reflect the nature of numbers gambling and the gender distribution of numbers gamblers.

First, the bank teams were new units attached to the borough commands, but which operated independently. These special squads would not have been immediately compromised. Also, the Police Commissioner's Confidential Investigating Unit, from which many of the reports were derived, was well-known to be one of the few police commands that was not easily corrupted. Many of these arrests must have been the real thing. Another important point is that much of the data used in this study would not have been compromised even if the police were corrupt. For example, the gender, ethnicity, and organizational role of numbers gamblers are pieces of information not likely to be falsified by police because it would have served no logical purpose. Also, much of the data is based on hundreds of hours of street-level observations corroborated by other police units, wiretap information, confidential informants, and the analysis of betting documents. Police might lie about areas of operation to protect gamblers; however, the extent and precise nature of the observations—corroborated by other police commands and independent sources including the newspapers—suggest that the data used in the present study is sound.

Concerns about the validity of the police reports were alleviated further by an interview with Jeremiah McKenna, a former assistant DA in south Manhattan who oversaw some of the same investigations reflected in the police reports. Mr. McKenna seemed confident that the data are reliable, and that the police who observed events on the street were the same ones who provided the information contained in the reports.

All that aside, a crucial element of the present study was one of verification. In a secondary analysis of existing data, certain questions should be asked of the source:

What is the source?

What does it state?

Who is the author?

What do we know about the author?

Is the author a credible source?

How do the author's assertions compare with others on the same point?

Are the author's statements logical and possible?

What is the relationship in time and space between the author and his observations? (Block, Hallowell & Inciardi, 1977)

The data were consistently viewed with these questions in mind, with favorable results. Not only are the authors credible, but their observations and conclusions make sense and are corroborated by independent sources. Of course, the issue of time and space between observer and author could not be more favorable. The police were right there on the street making real-life observations. Many of the reports contained lengthy and detailed narratives that were so precise in their observations (exact street addresses, time of day, etc.) that the possibility that the information was fabricated is practically nil. Consider the following narrative quoted directly from a police report on the Mazzarati-Somma numbers operation:

> On August 11, 1966, an ex-parte order was applied for and granted by Judge Robert Dempsey, Westchester County Court, to intercept and record all telephone messages over instruments 655-9378 and 655-9992 listed to Burke's stationery store, 655 Burke Avenue and in addition, instruments 547-5983, 547-7799 and 547-7913, listed to the Romano Funeral Home, 3254 White Plains Road, Bronx, New York. Telephone instrument 655-9992 was used exclusively as a policy "trouble phone" receiving only incoming calls. From these interceptions and the resulting surveillance, it was determined that this operation extends across a large and widely scattered area, including parts of Westchester, north Bronx, and sections of Harlem, midtown Manhattan, also the lower west side of Manhattan along Little West 12th Street. During the initial stage of the investigation, Frank Justo (B#564132) was placed under surveillance and was observed leaving his residence, 3617 Willet Avenue, Bronx, daily approximately 11:00 a.m. and proceeding directly to Caruso's stationery store where he would meet with Caruso and receive his daily instructions. At about 1:00 p.m. Justo would leave the store in his auto, a 1962 blue Oldsmobile convertible, license #4221BC, and utilizing various deceptive routes would proceed to pick up the daily policy play from intermediate pick-up personnel such as Nicholas Cioli, a.k.a. "Chippy" B#130408, and a female negress identified only as "Thelma." Various locations and methods were used to effect this pick-up including floating meets and often the use of a "stash" vehicle. An abandoned vehicle a 1955 blue and white chevrolet, license #BX9582, registered to Alice Mazza, 3232 Barker Avenue, Bronx, N.Y., would be parked at various locations in the east Bronx, predominantly along Waring Avenue or near St. Raymond's Cemetery on East 177th Street. Cioli and Thelma would stash the policy inside the abandoned vehicle and Justo would reclaim it and proceed directly to Caruso's stationery store. Nicholas Cioli would receive the policy in the first instance from one Eugene Esposito B#432705, a pick-up man for the area of the Little West 12th Street market. Esposito would transfer the daily play to Cioli at various locations in the Bronx including but not limited to the following locations: Howard Johnsons, Bruckner Boulevard and East 177th Street, various gas stations along the route of the Bronx River Parkway, and a Carvel, located at the end of Gunhill Road. Thelma would receive her policy from one Constance Mitchell B#316318, a policy controller in the area of 133rd Street and 7th Avenue, including 149th Street and 8th Avenue and would

> also deposit the policy play in the aforementioned vehicle. Justo after returning to the stationery store would remain thereat until approximately 5:30 p.m. at which time Caruso would telephone his number services to obtain the winning number for the day over telephone instruments 583–1442 listed to John Cassamassine, 2015 Southern Boulevard, Bronx, and 862–8200 listed to Mitchell's Laundry, 2258 7th Avenue, Manhattan. Immediately after the number was obtained, Justo would assist Gina Somma, an employee of the store and also a co-conspirator in the policy operation, to close the store and then he would proceed directly to his residence. At approximately 6:30 p.m. Justo would leave his residence and go straight to 3215 Olinville Avenue, Bronx and enter apartment #3E where he would remain until approximately 9:15 p.m.. After leaving this apartment he would go to Burke's Restaurant, 3204 White Plains Road where he would meet and converse with Caruso, Annatone, and either Somma or Mazzarati or both. When this meeting was concluded both Justo and Annatone would depart presumably to deliver the policy ribbons to the controllers.
>
> Surveillance of Frank Caruso revealed the following pattern. Caruso would arrive at 665 Burke Avenue at approximately 11:00 a.m. daily and remain thereat for the entire day with the exception of short trips to expedite the policy operation. A number of calls would be received for Caruso at this location but he would very seldom speak on the phone preferring instead to have the aforementioned Gina Somma accept all calls and relay messages to the various policy personnel. On October 13, the day after the arrest of Annatone, Caruso, through Gina Somma, directed the various persons calling to deliver their policy play directly to 665 Burke Avenue. It was subsequently learned that whenever Caruso desired to return a call he would use a telephone booth located in the street at Burke Avenue and Whiteplains Road. On October 14th, an ex-parte order was requested and granted by Judge Dempsey to receive and record all messages over telephone instrument 655–9666. The resulting interceptions revealed that Caruso was also accepting wagers on race horses and sports. During the World Series, Caruso contacted a "Mr. White" in Westchester to obtain the line, Caruso was referred to as "Mr. Blue."

The purpose of this somewhat tedious excerpt is to demonstrate the obvious veracity of the information contained in the police reports. The police obviously did not just make up these events. Further, this kind of detailed narrative was typical of the reports. The detail of the information strongly suggests that the cops who authored the reports used here were not on the take, but were doing their job as assigned. In many cases, they were not immediately concerned with making arrests, but were more interested in gathering information.

Police reports have also been questioned as to their utility because of the law enforcement goals of the data collectors. Police normally gather information merely for the purpose of presenting a case in court. However, as evidenced by the above excerpt, the plain clothes investigators who authored the reports were oriented toward gathering all kinds of descriptive information about gambling enterprises, not just the suppression of those activities. As a final note in defense of police reports, one historian noted that police reports are built up over time, "layer upon layer," and are far more accurate than the corporate annual reports commonly used in the sociological study of complex organizations (Block, 1991).

In addition to satisfactory answers related to the important issue of verification, the probity of the present research is further bolstered by innate advantages that the secondary analysis of existing data manifests for any researcher. For example, while the present study does not conform to any conventional social scientific sampling techniques, the data collection method that was employed negated the possibility of a selection bias on the part of the researcher. The veracity of findings is enhanced further by the fact that the analysis of existing data is an unobtrusive and nonreactive method for gathering and interpreting data.

While the police reports used were a tremendous source of valid information, it must be noted that the data do present difficulties. For example, some of the files collected for this project were merely undated biographical sketches of various organized crime figures active in the New York metropolitan area. A major difficulty of the police reports was the uneven nature of the data. While one report might contain detailed information on all aspects of a given numbers enterprise, others were quite sketchy and disjointed. For example, information pertaining to one Sebastian Aloi might include his weight, age, place of residence, frequented locations, relatives, associates, and other data of a highly personal nature, in addition to more relevant data (from the police investigator's viewpoint) such as prior arrests, areas of illegal gambling operations, and trusted personnel. On the other hand, a separate report from an entirely different police command and on a different target might include only the barest of information. Also, because the actual documents in question were copies of the actual police reports, the quality and legibility of some of the files was problematic. In addition to those files with scanty data to begin with, the result was that for certain organizations and subjects, there were missing values. The ethnicity, position within the given organization, and especially the ages of the numbers personnel mentioned in the police reports were often nonexistent.

Another problem with the data was that in addition to those items that were directly observed, much of the information was based on the conjecture of police gambling specialists. Also, some of the intelligence concerned subjects and events beyond the scope of this inquiry, such as the bookmaking and narcotics activities of some of the numbers entrepreneurs. Therefore, information in the police files had to be carefully scrutinized for data relevant to the object of interest. In all cases, concrete observations and the suppositions of police personnel were carefully delineated. Those items based on theory were recorded as such.

Although the police squads who were responsible for the data may not always have been corrupted, as human beings capable of making errors, some of their observations and recordings were probably faulty. At times, the police investigations were apparently hampered by a lack of coordination. In fact, several different investigating units may have been pursuing the same target simultaneously. Aside from the Policy Bank Teams created in the early 1960s, the Police Commissioner's Confidential Investigating Unit (PCCIU), the Chief Inspector's Investigating Unit (CIIU), and, at the federal level, the Internal Revenue Service (in search of violators of the Federal Wagering Tax law) were all investigating known gamblers in the New York City region listed in the files of the CIB and the FBI. For example, in a report dated July 13, 1966, the Assistant Chief Inspector of the Policy Bank Team #2 (assigned to the Avitabile target) noted that additional quality arrests might have been made had it not been for other divisions (PCCIU and CIIU) initiating arrests in areas under observation by the bank team. These arrests caused pick-up and personnel changes that apparently cost the bank team weeks of wasted surveillance.

Finally, another point that must be made is that the observations made by the police and compiled in the reports used in this project were undoubtedly a fraction of all numbers activity in New York City during the 1960s. Nevertheless, the volume and specificity of the data do make it possible to draw reliable conclusions about the totality of the numbers industry and the role of females.

After reading through the police reports several times, a large database was compiled of 1666 numbers workers. This table contained fields for the name of the individual, place of residence, place of illicit work activity, organizational affiliation, gender, race, alias, and organizational role. Using a database management tool, queries were made of the data and frequency distributions were tabulated for the items of interest, including the gender distribution, the distribution of roles occupied by males and females in numbers firms, and the ethnic distribution of female numbers workers.

The principal goal of this study was to see if the gender (independent variable) of numbers workers was related to the position they occupied (dependent variable) within the enterprise. Since the variables used were nominal, contingency table construction and analysis were appropriate. For the sake of clarity, the exact methods used will be discussed in the next section.

RESULTS

Of the 1666 numbers workers identified, 222 (13.3%) were females. The organizational roles of many of these women could not be ascertained from the police reports. However, the police did identify 83 collectors, 59 pick-up persons, 12 bankers, 26 controllers, and 19 bank clerks who were female. This looks like a typical distribution of roles within numbers firms, with low-level collectors and pick-up persons comprising the majority of personnel. (See Figure 9.1.)

The ethnicity of the females involved in numbers gambling was also an item of interest. Unfortunately, the police did not record the ethnicity for

31.1% of the females workers observed. For those subjects whose ethnicity was determined, the largest percentage were African American (31.1%), followed by Hispanic (18.9%), Italian-American (14.9%), and Jewish (4.1%). (See Figure 9.2.) This is somewhat surprising, because the ethnic distribution of the entire sample, male and female, reveals that the most prevalent group overall was Italian-American (36.6%), followed by African American (22.9%), Hispanic (15.2%), and Jewish (5.2%).

Having established the above frequency distributions, the construction of contingency tables was undertaken. While there is some limited research that suggests that women play a more prominent role in organized crime than traditional wisdom suggests, the present hypothesis will be that women are proportionately less likely than men to fill management positions in numbers firms. To test this notion, a contingency table was constructed, with sex as the independent variable and role as the dependent variable.

Row percentages would not be very useful here, because it is already known that most of the numbers workers in this time and place were male. The percentages reflected in Table 9.1 are column percentages, which clearly demonstrate that women were proportionately less likely to fill both banker and controller (management) positions: males identified by the police were classified as bankers 11.4% of the time, females only 6% of the time; 19.8% of men were controllers, while for women the figure is 13%. Also notice that women were proportionately more likely than men to fill low-level positions like collector, pick-up person, and bank clerk.

It is useful to know whether the relationship observed in the contingency table can also be found in the population. Therefore, a chi-square analysis was conducted. The null hypothesis states that there is no relationship between sex and role, and the research hypothesis says that there is a relationship. With the level of error set at .01 and the degrees of freedom equaling

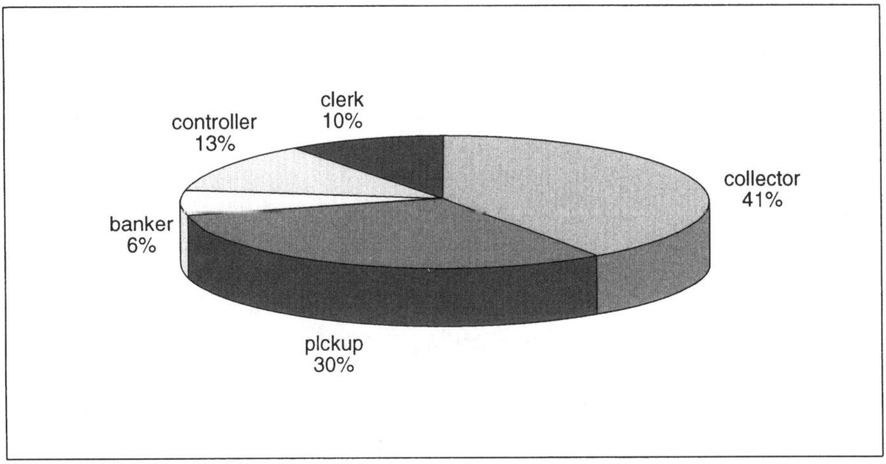

Figure 9.1 Roles of Female Numbers Workers

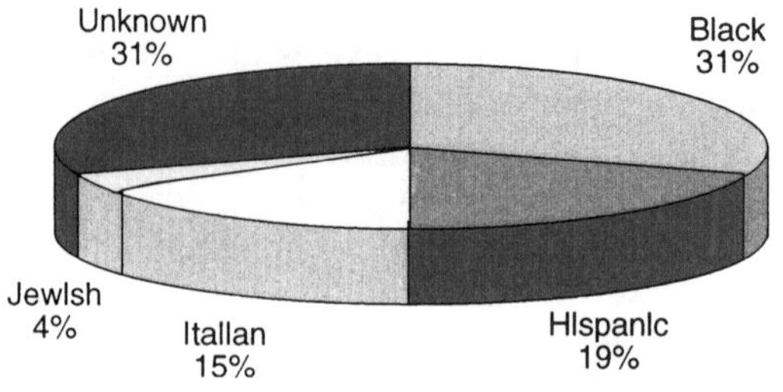

Figure 9.2 Ethnicity of Female Numbers Workers

Table 9.1 Male and Female Roles in Numbers Firms

Role	Male	Female	Total
Banker	138 (11.4%)	12 (6%)	150
Controller	239 (19.8%)	26 (13%)	265
Collector	398 (33%)	83 (41.7%)	481
Pick-up	330 (27.4%)	59 (29.6%)	389
Clerk	100 (8.3%)	19 (9.5%)	119
Totals	1205	199	1404

four, the computed chi-square statistic was 13.748. This exceeded the chi-square sampling distribution parameter of 13.277. Therefore, the null hypothesis was rejected.

After completing the above computation, a new contingency table was constructed with roles coded as either management or non-management. (See Table 9.2.)

Once again the column percentages reveal that men were proportionately more likely to hold a management position in the numbers firms examined. A new chi square statistic was computed at 12.18, with degrees of freedom equal to one and the level of error set at .001. The computed statistic exceeded the figure of 10.827 found in the chi square distribution table. Once again, the null hypothesis was rejected. At this point in the investigation it was tempting to conclude that there was indeed a relationship between the sex of numbers workers and the roles they filled. Still, other variables must be considered before one's hypothesis is accepted as true.

Before considering other variables, the strength of the observed relationship was measured. Because the chi square test is not a good way to measure the strength of a relationship, Cramer's V was computed for the second contingency table. The results were V = .0931, which indicates that the relationship between the gender of numbers workers and the roles they filled was very weak. Cramer's V was only slightly better for the original contingency table (.09895).

Since the relationship between gender and role was so weak, it seemed obvious that the relationship between the two was dependent on some third variable. Therefore, yet another contingency table was constructed, this time controlling for ethnicity. (See Table 9.3.)

Now it can be seen that women are indeed unlikely to be numbers managers, not just because of their sex, but because of their sex and their membership in certain ethnic groups. The police identified no cases where either Italian-American females or Jewish females filled management roles in numbers firms. African American and Hispanic women contributed all cases where females filled management roles. In fact, 56.8% of all African American females identified filled management positions, compared to only 45.8% for African American males; 44.8% of Hispanic females filled management roles, compared to only 26.8% for Hispanic males. One might conclude that the overall finding that women are proportionately less likely than males to fill management positions in numbers firms is because of ethnic or cultural norms or biases between Italian-American and Jewish gamblers.

DISCUSSION

Before interpreting the results, several points need to be made. The first and most obvious problem is that there are many missing values. Of the 1666 men and women identified as numbers workers, the police reports assigned roles to only 1404 of them. The ethnic identity of 20.1% of the entire sample is unknown, while for women the figure is even higher—31.1%. It is also curious that only four ethnic types were identified by the police. Certainly other ethnic groups must have been represented in the ranks of numbers workers, but probably in fewer numbers than the four groups prominently observed.

Obviously, the police could not observe all numbers activity occurring in New York City at this time. It seems likely that they concentrated their efforts on the more active or prominent operations and personnel. For this reason, the frequency distribution of roles comes out top heavy. Nearly one out of every three males and one out of every five females filled a management position based on the observations in the police reports. This is clearly not plausible. Numbers operations are high-volume enterprises dependent on many low-level collectors and runners who service customers at the street level. Some of the larger collectors must have had several runners working for them who were never identified by the police. The proportion of collectors within numbers organizations must have been well over half of all employees. This means that the true number of collectors and pick-up persons employed in the numbers industry must have comprised a greater proportion of all

Table 9.2 Males and Females in Numbers Firms: Management and Nonmanagement Frequencies

Role	Male	Female	Total
Management	377 (31.2%)	38 (19.1%)	415
Nonmanagement	828 (68.7%)	161 (80.9%)	989
Totals	1205	199	1404

Table 9.3 Ethnicity, Gender, and Role

	Italian		Black		Hispanic		Jewish	
Role	M	F	M	F	M	F	M	F
Management	150	0	88	25	45	13	13	0
Nonmanagement	304	33	192	44	168	29	45	9
Totals	454	33	280	69	213	42	58	9

numbers workers than represented in the data used here. The police also observed more bankers than bank workers. This is also implausible. Perhaps the problem lies in how the police assigned certain roles to arrested numbers workers—that is, mistakenly. Many bank clerks were arrested as bankers probably because that is the only charge New York penal law provided for persons arrested in accounting rooms of numbers enterprises. Many individuals charged with operating a numbers bank were probably clerks who tabulated daily wagers. The banker of an operation would rarely appear in the accounting center. However, because the clerks had to be arrested for something, they were charged with the only crime in the New York Crimes Code that came close to describing their role. The true number of bankers must have been far less than the number (150) identified by the police, while the number of bank clerks (119) must have been substantially greater.

Limitations in the observations of police officers gives reason for pause. Nevertheless, it is still possible to draw some broad conclusions with security. The data clearly indicate that the industry was dominated by males. Nevertheless, women did comprise a considerable minority of all numbers personnel observed. Due to frequent arrests, male functionaries were replaced by lesser-known females in some organizations. These women often resorted to the use of disguises or moved numbers play in the company of other women or children. On occasion, pregnant women were used to pick up and deliver wagering information. However, women were not employed merely as low-level workers and replacements. The police identified 12 females as bankers (again, however, it is quite possible that some if not most of these were merely clerks) and 26 as controllers. Nevertheless, women were proportionately less likely to fill management positions than were men. The data suggest that the difference is due to preferences among Italian-American and Jewish gamblers, who did not allow females to assume management roles. The other two major ethnic groups identified, Hispanic and African American, contributed all of the female numbers managers.

Given the nature of these findings, the present research does not agree with Potter and Gaines' assertion that "the appearance of females in leadership roles in organized crime is a peculiarly rural phenomenon" (1992, p. 46). Police observed females in leadership roles in the highly urban environment of New York City. It does seem as if cultural norms deriving from geographic regions generally (urban vs. rural) and specifically (eastern Kentucky vs. New York City) must play a part in determining the frequency and position of females in criminal enterprises. However, the findings here suggest that cultural norms based on ethnic background may also be a good predictor of whether females will assume management roles in criminal enterprises. Based on what has been observed here and what is known about African American culture in general, it is no great leap to conclude that the absent-father/strong-mother pattern so common to the African American community is partly responsible for the relatively strong showing of African American females in management positions in numbers enterprises. Likewise, the patriarchal tradition of the Italian (especially the southern Italian) culture taken to extreme in the "mafia" mind-set would explain why no Italian-American females were employed as numbers managers. Ethnicity aside, the present study does indicate that it is no longer realistic to view the participation of women in criminal enterprises as rare. Depending on cultural, economic, and geographical factors, it may even be presumptuous to characterize their participation as subservient. Of course, the lack of an EEOC presence in illegal market sectors and the penchant for the use of physical force by organized criminals may mean that organized crime's "glass ceiling" could be even more difficult to crack.

REFERENCES

Asbury, H. (1933). *The Barbary Coast: an informal history*. New York: Capricorn Books.

Block, A.A. (1980). Searching for women in organized crime. In S.K. Datesman (Ed.), *Women, crime and justice*, pp. 192–213. New York: Oxford University Press.

———. (1991). *The business of crime*. Boulder, CO: Westview Press.

Block, A.A., Hallowell, L.A., & Inciardi, J.A. (1977). *Historical approaches to crime: Research strategies and issues*. Beverly Hills, CA: Sage.

The Knapp Commission report on police corruption. (1972). New York: George Braziller.

Liddick, D. (1995). Telephone interview with Jeremiah McKenna, May 5.

Lyman, M., & Potter, G.W. (1997). *Organized crime*. Upper Saddle River, N.J.: Prentice Hall.

Potter, G.W., & Gaines, L.K. (1992). Country comfort: Vice and corruption in rural settings. *Journal of Contemporary Criminal Justice*, *8*(1), 36–61.
Reuter, P. (1983). *Disorganized crime: The economics of the visible hand*. Cambridge, MA: MIT Press.
Teresa, V., & Renner, T.C. (1973). *My life in the mafia*. Garden City, NY: Doubleday.
Turkus, B.B., & Feder, S. (1952). *Murder Inc.: The story of "the syndicate."* London: Gollancz.

10

A Cross-Sectional Quantitative Analysis of Federal Asset Forfeiture

Greg L. Warchol, Bureau of Justice Studies
Brian R. Johnson, Grand Valley University

Methodological Focus. The previous article was one example of research using secondary data. Another example of using **secondary data** is demonstrated in this article. However, a major difference between the two is that this article's research uses a **cross-sectional** sample design and a large *N*. It also helps reinforce the identification of variables.

Abstract

The objective of this study is first to describe the different types of federal asset forfeiture law, then explore the practice of how property seized under the forfeiture laws for drug law violations is proceeded against by the federal government. The methodology, which is primarily exploratory, utilizes quantitative data. More than 6,000 federal administrative and judicial drug forfeiture cases are described and then analyzed to construct a profile of the federal government's use of this policy. Findings raise questions about the use of forfeiture and the government's intent.

One of the most unique of the different narcotics controls policies employed by federal law enforcement in the War on Drugs is asset forfeiture. The forfeiture laws provide the federal government with the authority to seize property used to facilitate drug trafficking or that representing the proceeds of drug trafficking. The Department of Justice (DOJ) favors this economic approach to drug enforcement because money drives the narcotics business. By depriving traffickers of profits and the instrumentalities of crime, it is believed their criminal organizations will be immobilized (Executive Office for Asset Forfeiture [EOAF], 1993). Accordingly, the U.S. Attorney General's primary goal for the program is "to punish and deter criminal activity by depriving criminals of property used or acquired through illegal activities" (DOJ, 1990, p. 2).

Aside from its ability to deprive drug traffickers of their illegally obtained assets, the other significant benefit of forfeiture is the large amount of revenue it generates for the government. Following the 1984 legislation designed to strengthen forfeiture laws, the cumulative net value of property forfeitures in the United States increased from $27,196,168 in Fiscal Year 1985 to $3,768,040,757 as of Fiscal Year 1994, eventually providing the government with approximately $500,000,000 annually (DOJ, 1990, 1995). Property and cash transfers to state and local law enforcement agencies (through the Equitable Sharing Program) also increased from $22.5 million to $195 million during this same time period (DOJ, 1990, 1994).

As the use of asset forfeiture increased it attracted much attention and criticism. Critics from academia, the defense bar, the media, and Congress have expressed reservations about the utility and fairness of this policy (Bauman, 1995; Burnham, 1996; Hyde, 1995; Miller & Selva, 1994; Warchol & Johnson, 1996a, 1996b; Warchol, Payne & Johnson, 1996). However, rather than quantitative empirical analyses, the majority of this literature questioning asset forfeiture is in the law journals. This research questions the constitutionality of asset forfeiture and examines its potential for infringement on civil liberties (Durkin, 1990; Goldsmith & Linderman, 1989; Kasten, 1991; Wilson, 1991–1992; Yoskowitz, 1992). Another common source is stories in the print media that highlight select forfeiture cases to illustrate problems with this policy (Bauman, 1995; Burnham, 1996; Chapman, 1993; Enders, 1993; Greenburg, 1995). Empirical analysis of the use of forfeiture is a very limited subject in current drug and police literature (Miller & Selva, 1994; Warchol & Johnson, 1996a, 1996b; Warchol, Payne & Johnson, 1996; Zalman, 1996).

Even given the attention this policy has generated, there are still many issues yet to be addressed. This is especially obvious in light of the complexity of the federal and state forfeiture statutes and the diverse nature of the complaints about these laws. As a result, an apparent need exists to conduct further research on this topic. This study contributes to the current literature by examining the different types of federal asset forfeiture and their application crossnationally. The interest is in the types of seized assets, their economic values, the manner in which they are proceeded against, and the disposition of the proceeding.

CURRENT LITERATURE ON ASSET FORFEITURE

Law-related articles comprise the majority of the literature on asset forfeiture. Durkin (1990) examined the impact of the shifting burden of proof requirement with civil actions. Once an asset is seized based only on probable cause, the burden in a civil action shifts to the party asserting a claim of ownership on the property. Thus, the claimant must prove the "innocence" of the asset with a preponderance of the evidence in civil court. This requirement can place a severe financial burden on claimants attempting to recover seized property from the government. The cost of the litigation may exceed the value of the asset. Yoskowitz (1992) addressed the impact of the civil forfeiture of federally-assisted housing on the poor. He contends that this practice may actually violate the Eighth Amendment's prohibition of excessive punishment. The issue of the forfeitability of attorneys' fees has also been questioned (Mass, 1987). Mass argues that a defendant's right to counsel is the right to an effective counsel (p. 676). The forfeiture of attorneys' fees may result in a loss of this right given the burdens on public defenders.

Similarly, other law-related analyses have addressed the issue of the rights of third-party owners following an asset seizure (Enders, 1993; Goldsmith & Linderman, 1989; Stahl, 1992). The difficulties encountered by third-party claimants trying to recover seized property can be substantial given the nature of civil forfeiture proceedings. In calling for reform, Goldsmith and Linderman (1989) advocated changes in the burden of proof allocations and the pretrial restraint of assets by the government. Kasten (1991) called for increasing constitutional safeguards to be applied to civil proceedings.

A highly controversial aspect of the forfeiture statutes is the seizure of property under the facilitation theory. Since 1984, federal agencies could seize property that facilitated the violation of the drug laws (CCCA, Title 21, U.S.C. Sect.881 (a)(7)). Burnham (1996) notes that Congressional action extending this provision to real property seizures has become highly problematic. Law enforcement can now readily justify the seizure of high value assets without having to establish that they represent the proceeds of illegality.

There are some empirical studies examining how the use of forfeiture alters the roles and strategies of drug enforcement agents (Dombrink, 1988; Hyde, 1995; Miller & Selva, 1994; Zalman, 1996). Hyde concluded that provisions allowing police agencies to keep confiscated monies and properties, combined with the lack of legislative oversight as to how they are to be used, creates a conflict of interest "of the first magnitude" (Hyde, 1995, p. 30). Police agencies now have an incentive to "push for more and more valuable forfeitures" (Hyde, 1995, p. 30). Hyde also uncovered evidence of police preplanning seizures based partly on the value of the asset (1995, p. 31).

Miller and Selva's (1994) qualitative study found evidence that forfeiture has resulted in local law enforcement agents assuming the role of revenue collection officers selecting targets based on the value of their property rather than the seriousness of their offenses, if any. The authors argue that forfeiture gives "drug enforcers a powerful incentive to maintain and manage economic institutions that allow the illegal drug market to continue" (p. 333).

Dombrink (1991) contended that the equitable sharing of assets gives police an incentive to be more proactive in narcotics enforcement, seeking out offenders based more on the value of their assets than the seriousness of their offense. Similarly, Zalman (1996), in his critique of asset sharing, notes that this practice can influence the role of police in drug enforcement. He states:

"Asset sharing also has a way of helping to institutionalize this never ending war, as it promotes institutional self-aggrandizement that turns police into a special interest. The 'profits' they make become so alluring that they lose judgment and perspective about any weakness in the laws they are sworn to uphold" (p. 37).

The literature examining the merits of the different types of forfeiture shows there are significant advantages for law enforcement and disadvantages for the property owner with administrative and civil-judicial proceedings (Massey, 1993; Warchol & Johnson, 1996a, 1996b; Warchol, Payne & Johnson, 1996). Though criminal proceedings are better suited to meet the law enforcement objectives of the federal forfeiture program, administrative and civil-judicial forfeiture were by far the most frequently used types (Warchol, Payne & Johnson, 1996).

METHODS OF ASSET SEIZURE AND FORFEITURE

Property can be forfeited through either a civil or criminal proceeding. Prior to 1970 the only forfeiture statutes in the U.S. legal code were civil. Civil forfeitures are in-rem (against a thing) proceedings brought against the subject property in question (Loui, 1988). This concept is based on the legal fiction that the property itself is guilty, that is, the asset involved in the illegality is tainted by guilt (*The Palmyra,* 1827). There are currently three types of civil forfeiture proceedings: summary, administrative, and civil-judicial, and one type of criminal forfeiture. Summary and administrative proceedings do not involve the district court. Rather, they are conducted by the federal law enforcement agency that seized the asset (Asset Forfeiture Office [AFO], 1994). Civil proceedings also include a judicial procedure filed by the U.S. Attorney's Office against the property and adjudicated in federal district court—civil-judicial forfeiture. The final type is criminal forfeiture. Criminal forfeiture was included with the Racketeer and Influence Corrupt Organizations (RICO) Act in 1970. These proceedings are implemented in conjunction with the criminal prosecution of the defendant. The proceedings require that the property used or derived from the crime be indicted with the defendant (DOJ, 1990).

Nonjudicial Civil Proceedings

Nonjudicial civil proceedings include summary and administrative forfeitures (AFO, 1994). A summary forfeiture is only applied to contraband and is defined as "property the possession or production of which is illegal in all circumstances" (19C.F.R. Sect. 162.45(a)). Since no person may assert a legal ownership in contraband, its forfeiture can be effected without the need for formal process (19 U.S.C. Sect.1607). Administrative proceedings are conducted by a federal law enforcement agency (EOAF, 1993). These forfeitures do not involve the federal district court unless the seizure is contested, at which point it may be filed as a civil-judicial action. Administratively forfeitable property includes: (1) merchandise prohibited from importation; (2) conveyances used for the transport, import, or storage of controlled substances; (3) monetary instruments; or (4) other property that does not exceed $500,000 in value (DOJ, 1994). Such administrative proceedings are a fast, efficient, and a cost-effective manner to forfeit property.

JUDICIAL CIVIL PROCEEDINGS

When a claim is filed following an administrative seizure, or the property is real estate or otherwise falls outside of the statutory requirements, the asset must generally be forfeited through the civil court proceeding (DOJ, 1990). A criminal charge against the owner is not necessary. A civil forfeiture has the significant advantage of a shifting burden of proof. The government needs only to show probable cause that the asset in question was used to violate federal law (*U.S. v. $250,000 USC*, 1987). Following seizure, the burden of proof shifts to the person claiming an interest in the property to prove its "innocence" by a preponderance of the evidence (*U.S. v. A Single Family Residence,* 1986).

The justification for this proceeding is premised on the theory that many owners of forfeitable property are narcotics traffickers residing outside the United States, thus making civil forfeiture a highly valued strategy. If the criminal forfeiture proceeding was the only strategic option available, considering its requirement of conviction as a prerequisite to a forfeiture, international criminals could conduct their business with impunity by staying outside of U.S. borders and employing intermediaries in this country (DOJ, 1990). Civil proceedings effectively remove this option from the high-level narcotics' trafficker (Valukas & Walsh, 1988).

Judicial Criminal Proceedings

Criminal forfeiture was included with the RICO Act in 1970 and subsequently strengthened with the passage of the Comprehensive Forfeiture Act (CFA) as part of the Comprehensive Crime Control Act of 1984 (CCCA). Criminal forfeitures authorize an *in personam* liability against the criminal defendant and are conducted in conjunction with the criminal prosecution of the defendant (Loui, 1988). The success of a criminal forfeiture depends on the conviction of the defendant (*Calero-Toledo v. Pearson Yacht Leasing Co.,* 1974). If a jury finds the property forfeitable, the court issues an order of forfeiture (DOJ, 1994).

Criminal forfeitures also offer more protection to the defendants and innocent third-party owners. The burden of proof in these matters is beyond a reasonable doubt, and the full range of legal protections is provided to the defendant. Furthermore, a criminal conviction is a threshold requirement in a criminal forfeiture, and unless the government obtains a seizure warrant for the asset, it cannot take possession until there is a conviction (DOJ, 1994). In accordance with the Speedy Trial Act, criminal cases tend to be resolved faster than civil actions (AFO, 1991). This provides for faster resolution of third-party interests. Because punishment is the core of the criminal forfeiture, only property in which the defendant has a bona fide interest is forfeitable (DOJ, 1994). This requirement helps reduce the number of innocent owners caught up in this prosecution. As a result of these characteristics, criminal forfeiture is a complete sanction with its ability to incapacitate both the defendant and the asset, while offering a full range of constitutional protections.

METHODOLOGY

Population and Sample

The limited number of quantitative analyses of asset forfeiture may be due, in part, to difficulties in obtaining valid and reliable data from law enforcement agencies. Fortunately, the problem was overcome in this study as the authors received permission to obtain federal forfeiture data from the United States Marshal's Service (USMS). The USMS role in the federal forfeiture program is that of a property custodian. With this responsibility, it is required to maintain detailed data on each seized asset, the date of seizure, the seizing agency, the asset's owner(s), the economic value, the legal proceeding used to forfeit the asset, and the asset's final disposition. USMS data also contained detailed records of the population of individual properties seized and disposed of in the United States by fiscal year for all of the federal judicial districts.

Four federal judicial districts were selected for this analysis. They were the Southern Districts of California and Florida, the Northern District of Illinois, and the Eastern District of Michigan. These districts were distinct from one another in terms of their geographic location and level of drug trafficking. The Southern District of Florida and the Southern District of California have been identified as "high-intensity drug trafficking areas" and serve as ports of entry, being border districts on different coasts (Bureau of Justice Statistics [BJS], 1992). The centrally located districts of Northern Illinois and Eastern Michigan were not identified as ports-of-entry or major drug distribution centers and were selected because they may exhibit different characteristics than the border districts. This cross-section of districts was included in the analysis to develop an initial profile of how the use of forfeiture varies across districts rather than to draw specific conclusions about forfeiture activities by district. Data from FY 1991 and FY 1992 were used in this study. These years were selected since they marked the financial high-water point for the federal forfeiture program (EOAF, 1993).

The data source has several advantages. The population of cases was selected for each of the four districts to provide a large sample (n = 6,000) to generalize to other districts. Within the data, definitions of property type, dollar value, time, and disposition are specific and unambiguous. Terms are clear and accurate, and such definitions provide a level of scientific virtue that was considered a strength for comparing activities across the four districts.

Variables

To address the research question, eight variables were created. They included:

District: The four federal judicial districts (Southern District of Florida, Southern District of California, Eastern District of Michigan, and the Northern District of Illinois).

Asset: The type of seized asset (conveyances, real property, monetary instruments, lab equipment, and other).

EstValue: The initial estimated dollar value of the seized asset as determined by the USMS.

Appvalue: The formal, precise appraisal of the seized asset's dollar value as determined by the USMS.

Amtdep: The final dollar amount deposited by the USMS into the Assets Forfeiture Fund as a result of the forfeiture case.

Prosecution Time: The amount of elapsed time (in days) from date of asset seizure to date of final disposition of the forfeiture case.

Legal Proceeding: The type of forfeiture proceeding used against the asset (administrative, civil-judicial, and criminal forfeiture).

Disposition: The final outcome of the asset forfeiture case (not forfeited, forfeited/sold, forfeited/retained, and forfeited/substitute asset).

Procedures

The specific methodological approach employed in this research is exploratory in nature. Nonparametric statistical tests were selected for the analysis since the data were not normally distributed. The first phase of this analysis includes an examination of the nature of the property seizure, including type of asset, its economic values, and the type of police investigation leading to the seizure. Chi-square and Kruskal-Wallis Anova tests are used to determine whether there are significant differences in the seizure cases relative to these characteristics.

The second phase of the analysis focuses on the manner in which the case was prosecuted. Included in this phase of the analysis is the legal theory supporting the property seizure and the amount of time required to reach a disposition. Chi-Square and K-W Anova tests are again conducted on whether there are any significant differences as to how different types of seizures are processed by federal authorities. Differences over time for each variable are also included in the analysis.

The final phase of the analysis examines asset forfeiture case dispositions in relation to the type of asset, the police investigation leading to its seizure, and the legal theory used to support the seizure and forfeiture action. Non-parametric tests are also used to determine whether there are any significant differences within and between variables.

ANALYSIS AND FINDINGS

Identifying Asset Types by District

The data in Table 10.1 illustrate the relationship between district and asset for 1991 and 1992. The most striking finding (in Table 10.1) is the overall relative

Table 10.1 Asset Type by Federal Judicial District (*1991*/1992)

	Florida		Illinois		Michigan		California	
Asset Type	%	*N*	%	*N*	%	*N*	%	*N*
Monetary	*47.4*	*391*	*35.4*	*169*	*48.9*	*224*	*58.8*	*979*
	40.0	335	34.5	186	42.8	148	52.0	592
Real Prop.	*15.0*	*124*	*11.3*	*54*	*16.4*	*75*	*01.6*	*26*
	16.2	136	15.4	83	16.5	57	03.3	38
Conveyance	*30.2*	*249*	*48.1*	*230*	*24.5*	*112*	*26.8*	*447*
	36.4	305	42.9	231	24.6	85	32.2	366
Lab Equip.	*0.0*	*0*	*0.2*	*1*	*0.0*	*0*	*0.3*	*5*
	0.0	0	0.2	1	0.6	2	0.1	1
Other	*7.4*	*61*	*5.0*	*24*	*10.3*	*47*	*12.5*	*209*
	7.3	61	7.1	38	15.6	54	12.4	141
Totals	*100*	*825*	*100*	*478*	*100*	*458*	*100*	*1666*
	100	837	100	529	100	346	100	1138
Cramer's V = *.176*			Chi-square = *319.368*			*df* = *12 p* < *.001*		
.148			188.483			12 p < .000		

similarity of the four districts, with monetary instruments and conveyances comprising the highest percentage of seized assets. The variation between districts is in terms of these specific asset types, with Northern Illinois having the highest percentage of conveyance seizures (48.1%) in 1991 and (42.9%) in 1992. Additional variation is found in Southern California. This border district stands out, with the highest percentage of monetary asset seizures and the lowest percentage of real property seizures. The 1991 results are confirmed by their resemblance to the 1992 data. Real property, a critical asset, never exceeds more than 16.5% in any of the districts. Of note, Southern California, with only 1.6% in 1991 and 3.3% in 1992 in real property and monetary assets comprised more than 50% of its seizures for both years.

Lab equipment seizures never exceed .6% of all asset types for either year. Conveyances constitute a frequently targeted type of asset, comprising no less than 24.5% of seizures to a maximum of 48.1% in Northern Illinois for 1991. Interesting is the high percentage of seizures of "other" types of assets (electronics, jewelry, clothing, art, etc.) in Southern California and Eastern Michigan. Though these districts are distinct from each other geographically and in terms of the extent of narcotics trafficking, these data suggest that there is an overall similarity in terms of the most common asset types they are targeting.

Value of Seized Assets

Three dollar values were identified and used in this analysis. These consist of the initial appraisal or estimated value of an asset (estvalue), the more precise appraised value (appvalue) made by the USMS after custody, and the dollar amount deposited to the Assets Forfeiture Fund (amtdep). The data (see Table 10.2) indicate the disparity of property values between two border districts considered to be high drug trafficking areas.

One finds a high mean value of seized property in Southern Florida and a surprisingly low value in Southern California. There is an $8,000 and $10,000 dollar difference between the two central districts of Illinois and Michigan for 1991 and 1992. While the data in the previous section revealed the types of assets in each district are relatively similar, their values differ considerably.

A more precise comparison of the four districts is accomplished by the Kruskal-Wallis onc-way analysis of variance. The results of the test (see Table 10.2) confirm the earlier observation that the four districts are different from one another on all three asset values.

The analysis of the value of forfeited and nonforfeited assets and the difference between the estimated and appraised values of an asset could be viewed as a measure of efficiency of the government in judging the value of property. Of note is the minimal disparity between the estimated and appraised value of the assets, showing the accuracy of these early estimates of the value of an asset. There is little variation among the four districts in this respect. While these approximated values are considerable, the mean amount

Table 10.2 Estimated, Appraised, and AFF Deposits, Mean Dollar Values by Asset (1991–1992)

District	Est. Value	App.* Value	Amt. Dep.
1991			
FL	76,963	73,977	43,015
IL	27,656	26,332	14,222
MI	35,767	34,518	12,156
SC	18,136	18,396	2,781
1992			
FL	79,597	76,269	44,305
IL	42,033	42,239	24,383
MI	31,848	31,082	13,212
SC	16,742	15,676	7,762

	F-Ratio	$p <$	F-Ratio	$p <$
Est. value	252.706	.0000	278.134	.0000
App. value	226.197	.0000	260.272	.0000
Amt. dep.	968.566	.0000	70.228	.0000

*6 missing cases for 1991.

deposited to the AFF is substantially lower. However, when comparing the two years, the mean amount deposited to the AFF increased for every district.

Another approach shown (see Table 10.3) is to compare the values of assets that are forfeited to those that are returned to the owners. These data suggest that for currency seizures in all the districts, the estimated value appears related to disposition with the higher value monetary assets being forfeited. However, this pattern changes as one examines the four other types of assets. In 1991, Southern Florida and Northern Illinois are more successful with higher value real property. However, by 1992, all districts have forfeited the lower value real property. Even more surprising, for both years, only Illinois in 1991 has forfeited the more valuable vehicles. The pattern is less distinct with the low numbers of lab equipment seizures and other types of property fluctuating from 1991 to 1992.

Time Requirements for Processing Forfeiture Cases

The data (see Table 10.4) reveal that, with the exception of Southern Florida, it takes approximately one year to process a forfeiture case. An interesting finding is that the mean amount of time increased for every district except Southern California. Time requirements in Southern Florida showed the greatest increase, to more than 100 days from 1991 to 1992. Included with

Table 10.3 Mean Estimated Dollar Values Comparisons: Forfeited (F) and Not Forfeited (NF) Assets by District (1991–1992)

Asset Type	Florida	Illinois	Michigan	California
Monetary				
1991F	77,757	34,720	30,355	18,349
NF	60,892	13,219	26,951	16,597
1992F	99,089	55,413	29,180	12,399
NF	82,607	15,745	48,323	9,210
Real Property				
1991F	230,097	122,466	92,907	198,900
NF	175,055	72,500	109,085	269,281
1992F	168,923	120,294	83,973	159,700
NF	170,770	134,934	104,362	222,566
Conveyances				
1991F	22,966	10,319	14,617	8,724
NF	38,015	9,196	16,355	11,794
1992F	33,623	8,103	12,004	8,550
NF	35,836	12,319	14,016	15,629
Lab Equipment				
1991F	N/A	N/A	N/A	14,686
NF	N/A	N/A	N/A	8,000
1992F	N/A	15,000	36,675	1,000
NF	N/A	15,000	N/A	N/A
Other				
1991F	8,031	3,048	20,200	5,338
NF	21,553	13,117	6,446	13,122
1992F	33,623	7,823	7,988	3,065
NF	14,810	5,525	12,812	5,626

Table 10.4 Mean Processing Time by District (1991–1992) ANOVA Test

Year	District	Mean Days	S.D.	N
1991	Florida	427.66	392.89	825
	Illinois	332.02	328.43	478
	Michigan	318.67	265.50	456
	California	383.72	348.45	1666
1992	Florida	528.55	438.16	837
	Illinois	356.15	391.06	539
	Michigan	397.66	388.75	346
	California	328.62	363.70	1138
1991	F-Ratio = 12.994	$p < .0000$	Levene Stat = 23.013	$p < .00$
1992	F-Ratio = 44.180	$p < .0000$	Levene Stat = 16.487	$p < .000$

Table 10.5 Legal Proceeding by Judicial District (1991 and 1992)

	Florida		Illinois		Michigan		California	
Type	%	*N*	%	*N*	%	*N*	%	*N*
1991								
Admin.	56.2	463	50.6	242	56.8	260	82.9	1381
Civil/JD	43.2	357	46.2	221	40.8	187	17.1	285
Criminal	0.5	5	3.1	15	2.4	11	0.0	
1992								
Admin.	55.2	461	53.8	290	51.4	177	74.9	852
Civil/JD	44.0	369	44.5	240	47.4	165	25.1	286
Criminal	00.8	7	01.7	9	01.2	4	00.0	

1991	Cramer's V = .219	Chi-square = 137.569	$df = 6$	$p < .0000$
1992	Cramer's V = .225	Chi-square = 350.000	$df = 6$	$p < .0000$

these findings is an analysis of variance results and the Levene Test. This post-hoc procedure tests the hypothesis that the groups come from populations with the same variances in the one-way ANOVA. The observed significance levels are small for both years, thus allowing for a rejection of the null hypothesis that all variances are equal.

Examining Forfeiture Case Characteristics in the Districts

A more in-depth look at two important characteristics of individual cases provides additional insight into the operation of this program. These characteristics are the type of legal proceeding—administrative, civil-judicial, or criminal—and the case disposition. To provide the greatest detail in this analysis, disposition values include not forfeited, forfeited with the asset sold, forfeited with the asset retained by the government for its own use, and forfeited with the owner forfeiting substitute assets for the original seized property.

The data (see Table 10.5) indicate that criminal forfeiture is seldom used by any of the four districts. The emphasis is on the faster administrative and civil-judicial proceedings. Southern Florida, Northern Illinois, and Eastern Michigan are quite similar, however Southern California again is very distinct with its high percentage (82 .9% in 1991 and 74.9% in 1992) of administrative forfeitures. It also shows minimal use of civil-judicial proceedings. Overall, the four districts are very similar to one another, and these results are statistically significant.

Based on the data (see Table 10.6) the four districts are similar in that they all have more forfeitures than nonforfeitures. They also all have low percentages of retained assets and the forfeiture of substitute assets. Retained assets accounted for less than 8% for both years in all districts. However, Southern

Table 10.6 Disposition Types by Judicial District (1991 and 1992)

	Florida		Illinois		Michigan		California	
Disposition	%	*N*	%	*N*	%	*N*	%	*N*
1991								
Not Forfeited	29.2	241	34.3	164	21.4	98	17.0	283
Forfeited Sold	69.8	576	59.4	284	65.3	299	71.4	1189
Forfeited Retained	00.8	7	03.8	18	07.4	34	11.6	194
Forfeited Substitute	00.1	1	02.5	12	05.9	27	00.0	
1992								
Not Forfeited	263	220	28.6	154	29.5	102	23.9	272
Forfeited Sold	71.1	595	61.0	329	57.5	199	69.4	790
Forfeited Retained	02.4	20	07.6	41	07.8	27	06.7	76
Forfeited Substitute	00.2	2	02.8	15	05.2	18	00.0	
1991	Cramer's V = .169		Chi-square = 295.429		*df* = 9		$p < .001$	
1992	Cramer's V = .116		Chi-square = 115.47		*df* = 9		$p < .000$	

California is again distinct, forfeiting at least 75% of all seized assets for both years. This district also has the lowest percentage of nonforfeitures for each year.

DISCUSSION AND CONCLUSION

The objective of this study was to present a cross-national quantitative analysis of a frequently questioned federal government drug enforcement policy—asset seizure and forfeiture. The findings of this study need to be considered in context, as the forfeiture activities of four federal judicial districts for two years were analyzed. This research, however, addressed a policy that has attracted considerable attention and criticism, yet has been subject to few empirical studies. Furthermore, this study is unique in that it examines all three types of federal forfeiture in a cross-section of judicial districts. Finally, unlike law reviews and much of the current empirical research, this study uses quantitative data to build upon and complement existing research in this area.

The findings allow for a profile to be constructed of how federal authorities in these four major judicial districts used asset forfeiture during this time period. The results indicate that with the exception of Southern California, there was little variation in terms of the percentages of the types of seized assets, even given the districts' distinctly different locations and level of drug activity. The concentration across districts was on monetary instruments and conveyances, with real property seizures accounting for a very low number of seizures for all districts. During this time period, the program did not appear to be tailored to address the unique nature of each region. However, the high frequency of monetary instrument seizures, the second most valuable of all five types, is in accordance with the program's objectives.

The emphasis on conveyances may be indicative of a law enforcement concentration on the transportation end of the drug-trafficking business. Conveyance seizures may disrupt the operations of traffickers. A concentrated emphasis on depriving traffickers of the means to move their illegal goods may have long-term benefits not yet apparent in the data on drug control efforts. However, such seizures also have a lower rate of forfeiture compared to monetary assets. The higher number of such seizures may offset the value of the monetary asset seizures.

The rather low frequency of real property seizures is an interesting finding. This could be attributed to the high cost of seizing real property and the requirement for a judicial proceeding. Alternatively, it could be a function of the nature of the drug trade in these districts, or a reluctance by federal prosecutors to seize property that frequently involves innocent owners (Valukas & Walsh, 1988).

Data also reveal that while there was a decline in the number of seizures from 1991 to 1992, there was an increase in the amount deposited to the Federal Assets Forfeiture Fund. This may suggest more careful case selection and prosecution. Furthermore, the results of the analysis showed considerable variation on asset dollar values between districts. While Southern California had the highest frequency of monetary seizures, they were of the lowest value of the four districts.

Several questions relating to the use of forfeiture in this unique district should be examined: (1) Is this district seizing more assets than the other three to keep pace in terms of revenue? (2) Are they intentionally targeting lower-level dealers, which could account for the lower value of the monetary assets? (3) Is there an overrepresentation of lower-level traffickers in this district? and (4) Are these values a function of this region bordering Mexico? Southern California had a high mean value of real property, but experiences few seizures of this type. Southern Florida has the most valuable monetary and real property assets.

One important finding was the difference between appraised value and the final amount deposited to the Assets Forfeiture Fund. This represented approximately one-half of the appraised values. The difference between values is due in part to the need to pay the claims of innocent lien holders. Overall, the four districts did manage to deposit to the Assets Forfeiture Fund $15,316 in 1991 and $22,248 in 1992 per asset seizure.

Dollar results also provide a measure of program profitability. The mean value of seized assets increased from 1991 to 1992, as did Assets Forfeiture Fund deposits in light of a decrease in overall seizures. This could indicate that the government became more selective and precise in targeting higher value assets in order to have a greater impact on the drug trafficker. Alternatively, it also raises the question of whether the government was shopping for the most valuable property.

Similar to the property values, the processing times also varied between the districts from 1991 to 1992. A striking feature with these findings is the exception of Northern Illinois. The districts required more time for nonforfeitures than forfeitures. Northern Illinois disposed of nonforfeitures in about one-third of the time required for forfeitures. Under these conditions, districts are holding and maintaining assets for extended periods of time that will eventually be returned to their owners. Such a situation supports current criticism of the program.

The analysis of the legal proceedings and dispositions reveal additional implications relevant to the use of this program. Perhaps most striking was that more than 70% of all asset seizures resulted in a forfeited disposition. The results also reveal an emphasis on the more economically efficient, but heavily criticized, administrative seizures, which account for over one-half of all types of proceedings. The extensive use of administrative forfeiture indicates that a large percentage of asset seizures are not contested. This could be a function of the drug trade in these areas, with traffickers writing off the loss of select assets as a cost of doing business. However, another explanation suggests that a significant number of owners of seized property may choose not to contest the seizure to avoid costly and lengthy litigation.

The almost negligible use of criminal forfeiture across the four districts is a cause for concern. Of the three types of proceedings, only criminal forfeiture can effectively incapacitate both the asset and the offender. Given the full range of constitutional protections afforded the defendant inherent in a criminal trial, critics are less likely to question a forfeiture when it follows the conviction of a defendant. An increased use of this proceeding may allow the Department of Justice to attain the primary goal it established for the asset forfciturc program.

With many unanswered questions, the opportunities for future research are extensive. To date, there are no studies specifically examining the impact of federal forfeiture on the illegal drug trade. Additionally, research needs to be done on both police and prosecutor decision-making in selecting assets for seizure. Finally, more research should focus on the influence of asset sharing on state and local police departments cooperating with federal authorities in property seizures.

REFERENCES

Asset Forfeiture Office. (1991). *Asset forfeiture news.* Washington, DC: United States Department of Justice. July-August.

——. (1994). *Asset forfeiture manual: Law and practice.* Washington, DC: U.S. Department of Justice.

Bauman, R. (1995). Take it away. *National Review*, 20 February, 34–38.

Bureau of Justice Statistics. (1992). *Drugs, crime, and the justice system* (NCJ-133652). Washington, DC: U.S. Government Printing Office.

Burnham, D. (1996). *Above the law.* New York: Scribner.

Chapman, S. (1993). Seizing property: Law enforcement's dangerous weapon. *Chicago Tribune*, 7 March, 3.

Comprehensive Crime Control Act of 1984, Title 21, U.S.C. Sect. 881(a)(6)(7) (1988).

Department of Justice. (1990). *Annual report of the department of justice asset forfeiture program.* Washington, DC: Office of the Attorney General.

——. (1994). *A guide to the equitable sharing of federally forfeited property for state and local law enforcement agencies.* Washington, DC: Office of the Deputy Attorney General.

——. (1995). *Audit report: Asset forfeiture program.* Washington, DC: Office of the Inspector General.

Dombrink, J. (1988). The touchables: Vice and police corruption in the 1980s. In D. Carter and T. Barker (Eds.), *Police deviance*, pp. 61–99. Cincinnati, OH: Anderson.

Durkin, C. (1990). Civil forfeitures under federal narcotics law: The impact of the shifting burden of proof upon fifth amendment privilege against self-incrimination. *Suffolk University Law Review, XXIV*, 678–709.

Enders, J. (1993). Opposition growing to nation's drug forfeiture laws. *Chicago Daily Law Bulletin*, 11 February, 2.

Executive Office for Asset Forfeiture. (1993). *Annual report of the department of justice asset forfeiture program.* Washington, DC: U.S. Department of Justice.

Executive Office for Asset Forfeiture. (1992). *Criminal vs. civil forfeiture: Evaluating the options.* Report of the Assistant Director, September. Washington, DC: U.S. Department of Justice.

Goldsmith, M., & Linderman, M.J. (1989). Asset forfeiture and third party rights: The need for further law reform. *Duke Law Journal,* 1253–1301.

Greenburg, J.C. (1995). Hyde: Ease recovery of seized property. *Chicago Tribune*, 22 June, 14.

Hyde, H. (1995). *Forfeiting our property rights.* Washington, DC: The Cato Institute.

Johnston, D. (1991). Illegal drug sales in the U.S. put at over $40 billion in '90. *New York Times*, 20 June.

Kasten, L. (1991). Extending constitutional protection to civil forfeiture that exceeds rough remedial compensation. *The George Washington Law Review*, *60*(1), 194–244.

Loui, M.P. (1988). *Glossary of forfeiture terms.* Washington, DC: Criminal Division, Asset Forfeiture Office, U.S. Department of Justice.

Mass, R. (1987). Forfeiture of attorneys' fees: Should defendants be allowed to retain the "Rolls Royce of attorneys" with the "fruits of the crime"? *Stanford Law Review, 39*, 662–687.

Massey, J. (1993, November). *Justifying Civil Forfeiture*. Paper presented at the Annual Meeting of the American Society of Criminologists, Phoenix, AZ.

Meyer, C. (1991). Zero tolerance for forfeiture: A call for reform of civil forfeiture law. *Notre Dame Journal of Law, Ethics and Public Policy*, *5*, 853–887.

Miller, J.M., & Selva, L.H. (1994). Drug enforcement's double-edged sword: An assessment of asset forfeiture programs. *Justice Ouarterly, 11*(2), 313–335.

Racketeer and Influenced Corrupt Organizations Act of 1970, 18 U.S.C. Sect. 1963.

Stahl, M. (1992). Asset forfeiture, burdens of proof and the war on drugs. *The Journal of Criminal Law and Criminology, 83*(2), 274–337.

Valukas, A.R., & Walsh, T.P. (1988). Forfeitures: When Uncle Sam says you can't take it with you. *Litigation, 14*, 31–37.

Warchol, G.L., & Johnson, B.R. (1996a). Ensuring the future of asset forfeiture programs. *The Police Chief, XIII* (3), 49–53.

——. (1996b). Guilty property: A quantitative analysis of civil asset forfeiture. *American Journal of Criminal Justice, 21*(1), 61–81.

Warchol, G.L., Payne, D.M., & Johnson, B.R. (1996). Criminal forfeiture: An effective alternative to civil and administrative proceedings. *Police Studies*, *19*(3), 51–66.

Wilson, D. (1991–1992). Drug asset forfeiture: In the war on drugs, is the innocent spouse the loser? *Journal of Family Law, 30*, 135–153.

Yoskowitz, J. (1992). The war on the poor: Civil forfeiture of public housing. *Columbia Journal of Law and Social Problems, 25*, 567–600.

Zalman, M. (1996). Judges in their own cases: A Lockean critique of law enforcement asset sharing in drug forfeiture law and practice. *Criminal Justice Review, 21*, 2.

List of Cited Cases

Calero-Toledo v. Pearson Yacht Leasing Company, 94 S. Ct. 2080 (1974).

The Palmyra, 25 U.S. (12 Wheat) 1 (1827).

U.S. v. One 1941 Pontiac Sedan, 83 F. Supp. 999 (SD NY, 1948).

U.S. v. Sandini, 816 F.2d 869 (3rd Cir. 1987).

U.S. v. A Single Family Residence, 803 F.2d 625 (llth Circuit, 1986).

U.S. v. $250,000 USC, 808 F.2d.895 (1987).

11

Accessing Data: Procedures, Practices, and Problems of Academic Researchers*

Chrisann M. Flanyak, University of Illinois Chicago

Methodological Focus. This last article is somewhat special, because it is an excellent example of **qualitative** research using **in-depth interviewing** as well as a **snowball and convenience sample**. Furthermore, it offers readers insight into conducting research that is rarely found in the literature.

Abstract

A study of how academic researchers in criminal justice, and related fields, gain access to data and data sites for research was completed using a qualitative methodology of in-depth interviewing. Interviews were conducted with 19 academic researchers from four Illinois universities. Information on the practices they utilize to facilitate their access to data and data sites were obtained. Descriptions of the barriers and procedures researchers used to overcome them were collected.

General accessing issues were presented first. Academic researchers revealed several techniques they utilized in order to facilitate their access, including the use of their personal networking skills and role negotiation to gain permission from agency gatekeepers. Researchers discussed hurdles that may delay their access to data, including gatekeepers, and various organizational, institutional, and personal barriers. Procedures involved in accessing the data for this study were included. Many similarities in techniques, practices, and problems were found among the academic researchers interviewed in regards to issues of gaining access to data.

---

*The author would like to give special thanks to Michael Maltz, Joseph Peterson, and Mindie Lazarus-Black for their guidance and support with this project.

The following study is predicated on several observations. In order to do academic research, data must be collected for analysis. All researchers have to gain access to sources (i.e., settings, data banks, individuals) to obtain their data, and this may be done by various methods. For example, to receive permission to enter an institution for data collection, researchers may correspond with the appropriate gatekeepers of that institution by mail, phone, or on-site meetings (Patton, 1990; Punch, 1986). A researcher who wishes to gain access to police records may call or write the appropriate superintendent of police. A researcher who intends to gain access to social work data may go to the local branch of the Department of Children and Family Services and speak to an official.

Researchers may also use personal networking as a tool to gain access to their data source (Department of Communications [DOC], 1972; Gordon & Heinz, 1979; Weiss, 1994; Westin & Baker, 1972). For example, in order to receive permission to participate in police ride-alongs, a researcher may contact a former student who is currently employed by a police department and who can arrange an introduction to a superior. In order to gain access to school records, a researcher may contact a colleague in his or her university's College of Education who has had experience in dealing with the district's Board of Education.

As they endeavor to collect data, researchers may encounter bureaucratic obstacles that may delay or impede their access. These barriers may include destroyed or damaged records, unwilling gatekeepers, and restrictive guidelines and statutes (Duncan, Jabine & de Wolf, 1993; Gordon & Heinz, 1979; Hagan, 1993; Maltz, 1976; Wilson & Smith, 1983). Further, once these initial barriers are overcome, agencies and institutional review boards may still prevent or delay data collection by imposing restrictions concerning the confidentiality and privacy of the subjects involved. Requirements may include obtaining the informed consent of the subjects, using coded identifiers, and utilizing anonymous data collection procedures (Babbie, 1992; Boruch & Cecil, 1979; Duncan, Jabine & de Wolf, 1993; Hagan, 1993; Maltz, 1976).

Hurdles, such as these discussed, are virtually always present, and often complicate the conduct of the research. Yet, in the final reports of their findings, very few academic researchers present details of the procedures they used to gain access to the data for their studies. Their presentations of methodology and data collection are usually limited to description of the types of data they collected, the research methods they utilized, and the subjects or records studied. Generally, academic researchers acknowledge and thank the appropriate gatekeepers, funders, and respondents for their participation in their study, but do not describe the procedures taken to gain their confidence, cooperation, and support. The purpose of this study is to provide an increased understanding of how academic researchers in criminal justice and related fields gain access to the data for their studies.

PRIOR RESEARCH

Research on the question of how academic researchers gain access to data is limited. Most studies have dealt with the ethical issues surrounding the use of different types of data (e.g., records, human subjects, computerized data banks) for social science research. Such studies have provided discussions about the privacy and confidentiality of data kept by various agencies and the steps involved in maintaining this privacy without limiting access to information.

Few studies or publications have specifically dealt with the methodology researchers use to gain access to the data they collect and analyze for their research. Patton (1990) described the process of "entry into the field" as the first and most uncomfortable stage of fieldwork for evaluation research (pp. 250, 252). He presented issues regarding the need for role manipulation of researchers to overcome barriers to gain access to settings; however, his discussion is limited to that practice and its place in evaluation research (Patton, 1990, pp. 252–54).

Further, Punch (1986) presented several factors that may influence fieldwork and successful access to data and data sites, including the personalities and personal characteristics of researchers, the makeup of the research site, and the expectations of team research (pp. 22–23). The author's analysis raised many issues regarding the need for trust between the researchers and their subjects. However, his discussion is limited to that of the political influences, moral obligations, and ethical considerations of the researchers in the field (Punch, 1986, p. 29) This study will primarily investigate the procedures academic researchers utilize to facilitate access, such as role negotiation or manipulation, and the techniques they use to overcome barriers encountered.

ETHICAL ISSUES SURROUNDING DATA

Many studies have reviewed the ethical issues involved in the use and access of data for social science research. Through results obtained by on-site visits to organizations and analyses of procedural techniques for anonymity and confidentiality, researchers have stressed the importance of maintaining confidentiality when studying human subjects, and have often implied that the informed consent of any human subjects is desirable (Babbie, 1992; Hagan, 1993; Westin & Baker, 1972). These studies emphasized the need for a balance between individuals' privacy and society's benefits from research, and discussed techniques for maintaining that balance (Bower & de Gasparis, 1978; Duncan, Jabine & de Wolf, 1993; O'Brien, 1981). These authors principally address the high demand for access to information and the availability of reliable data for research purposes (Boruch & Cecil, 1979).

Several studies have discussed the ethical issues involved in what has been described as an individual's or organization's right to public information, specifically that which is kept on record and in data banks by criminal justice and other governmental agencies. Researchers have struggled to interpret how the various freedom or privacy acts and the different codes, guidelines, and restrictions imposed by agencies and institutional review boards have defined private, sensitive, or public information and regulated researchers' access to it (Babbie, 1992; Duncan, Jabine & de Wolf, 1993; Hagan, 1993; Maltz, 1976; Westin & Baker, 1972). Other researchers have strived to analyze the argument of whether the First and Fourth Constitutional Amendments may or may not guarantee the public's right to access information controlled or generated by the government (Bower & de Gasparis, 1978; O'Brien, 1981, p. 132). This study will provide techniques utilized by academic researchers to overcome barriers and address ethical concerns, such as these, to gain access to data successfully.

THE COMPUTERIZATION OF DATA

The effects of the increased computerization of data on the privacy, security, and accessibility of such data have been discussed by researchers. Computerized data banks used for record-keeping purposes by various agencies and institutions present questions concerning the positive and negative aspects of data-sharing between agencies and researchers, and among the researchers themselves. Studies have generally concluded that when proper measures are taken to assure confidentiality, and justifiable reasons for accessing the data exist, data sharing can be very beneficial to society, as well as to agencies and institutions (David, 1980; Maltz, 1976; DOC, 1972; Westin & Baker, 1972).

ACCESS TO DATA

As stated previously, few studies or publications have specifically dealt with how researchers in the area of criminal justice and social science gain access to data for their research. Gordon and Heinz (1979) conducted experiments in order to analyze which methods are most effective in gaining assess to general information from twenty-six bureaucracies in Illinois. The researchers created fictitious, and mostly politically neutral organizations, on whose behalf the information was requested (Gordon & Heinz, 1979). Through results obtained from letter writing and on-site visits, the authors made general conclusions regarding the successes and failures of their accessibility to data. They focused particular attention on the explanations given by agencies for denial or refusal of access to the data requested and other reasons why data was not obtained in some situations. Gordon and Heinz (1979) found many agencies claimed they felt threatened politically at the time of request and often quoted access laws, acts, and statutes to deny access (pp. 200–207, 223–227, 378).

More recently, Wilson and Smith (1983) investigated the accessibility of income tax returns and other tax data by the public and various federal statistical agencies (p. 595). The authors discussed how the history of congressional restrictions, federal acts, and constitutional amendments have affected access to tax data (Wilson & Smith, 1983, p. 595). The researchers concluded by stressing the importance of increased access to tax returns for statistical purposes and interagency data sharing, while maintaining the confidentiality and security of information through guidelines, restrictions, and sanctions (Wilson & Smith, 1983, pp. 598, 600). This paper will discuss procedures used by researchers to ensure the confidentiality of their subjects and, more importantly, how they assure gatekeepers of this in order to facilitate access to data. In contrast to previous research, this research utilized the method of interviewing to obtain access information from 19 academic researchers.

METHODOLOGY

In order to study how academic researchers gain access to data, I employed the qualitative research method of in-depth interviewing (Briggs, 1986; Hagan, 1993; Patton 1990). This method provided a high response rate and allowed me to have personal contact with and observation of my subjects (Hagan, 1993). The use of an interview guide instrument permitted me to maintain a general outline and framework of questions to ensure that specific topics were investigated (Patton, 1990, p. 284). The guide also provided me with the opportunity and discretion to explore or probe respondents for detail in specific areas (Babbie, 1992; Briggs, 1986; Hagan, 1993; Weiss, 1994).

A pilot study of 4 of the respondents was conducted in order to test the interview guide and develop the third and final revision of the instrument used for data collection (Weiss, 1994). I then conducted my interviews with each subject, which generally lasted from 45 minutes to 75 minutes, the longest being two hours in length. Follow-up interviews were completed as needed and lasted approximately 15 minutes.

Each interview was tape recorded and transcribed by me in order to provide accuracy in data collection (Briggs, 1986; Patton, 1990; Weiss, 1994). Sanjek (1990) related the importance of these practices in that they allow researchers to check for errors in their interpretations of data and to use extensive quotations in their texts (p. 115). Field notes (scratch or jotted notes) were taken during the interviews to record meaningful interaction between subjects and the interviewer (Sanjek, 1990, p. 93). Transcriptions were coded and categorized inductively using content analysis to organize data (Babbie, 1992; Charmaz, 1983; Emerson, 1983; Patton, 1990; Weiss, 1994). An analyses of the interview and observational data, in concurrence with the literature reviewed, are presented herein.

Fieldwork was conducted between the months of October of 1994 and April of 1995. Most interviews for the initial pilot study were conducted with subjects from a major public research institution in Illinois. Other interviews were completed with respondents from the Criminal Justice and Sociology departments of four other major universities in the state. Subjects were interviewed at their own academic institutions and usually in the privacy of their offices.

In total, 19 respondents were interviewed for the research. Respondents consisted of those sampled from a study population of academic researchers in the fields of criminal justice, sociology, and criminology who, at the time of the study, were teaching and conducting research at an Illinois institution of higher education. All subjects expressed prior to the interview that they experienced the need to access data and data sites for their research.

Snowball (chain) sampling and convenience sampling methods were utilized to obtain 22 subjects from the study population (Babbie, 1992; Hagan, 1993; Patton, 1990). The sampling frame consisted of lists of Sociology and Criminal Justice department faculty members in several universities in Illinois. Initial interviews for the pilot study were conducted with respondents at my academic institution. These respondents advised me of other potential subjects. Additional subjects were chosen from the faculty of my undergraduate institution to ensure a high response rate.

Those interviewed for the study consisted of a panel of 14 male and 5 female academic researchers. These respondents, with the exception of one, possessed doctoral (Ph.D.) or law (J.D.) degrees, and their areas of expertise in research and teaching covered a number of disciplines, including criminology, sociology, law, criminal justice, psychology, political science, social work, criminalistics, and law and society research. To maintain the anonymity of my subjects, I will refer to them as sociologists, criminologists, and social scientists when quoted verbatim. Subjects will also be identified by gender, as this issue will be discussed further as a possible factor that may influence successful access to data.

Seventeen of the academic researchers interviewed were Caucasian, (13 male and 4 female) and two subjects (1 male and 1 female) were African American. Fourteen of the respondents (12 Caucasian males, 1 African American male, and 1 Caucasian female) were tenured at their educational institutions, while 5 respondents (3 Caucasian females, 1 Caucasian male, and 1 African American female) were not. Approximately half of the sample (10 of 19 respondents) reported having been previously employed in some form of "practical" experience (e.g., lawyer, engineering consultant, youth prison guard, police officer) before teaching and researching in the university setting. Fifteen of the 19 interviewees had 10 or more years of research (field) experience, and 13 respondents reported they had been teaching for 10 or more years prior to being interviewed for this study.

Access

While gaining access to data for this study, many of the same procedures were utilized, and many of the same barriers were encountered, as those described by the researchers interviewed. For example, when calling university offices, I negotiated my role as a student researcher and used networking techniques to facilitate access to department faculty lists. Further, assurances of confidentiality and anonymity were purposely and specifically stated in the introduction letters sent to researchers, as well as the forms sent to the Institutional Review Board (IRB) for approval.

The academic researcher refusing to be interviewed for this study displayed a common barrier reported by many of the subjects. She stated she was "uncomfortable and unwilling to discuss [the topic]" with me because she felt it would be "inappropriate" to speak to a *graduate student* about the issue. Here, this gatekeeper did not believe that I was legitimate or credible enough as a researcher to allow access to her information.

Time constraints imposed on this study proved to be a major concern in this research. IRB approval required approximately two months time and was necessary before data collection could begin. Interviews with the subjects were often postponed or rescheduled due to their "grant work," "busy weeks," vacations, unexpected trips, and deaths in their families, among other personal issues. Interviews were also commonly interrupted or ended abruptly due to long distance calls, meetings, and busy schedules. Respecting and understanding these time constraints were crucial to the successful access of data for this study. Such procedures and barriers as experienced by academic researchers are discussed at length in this study.

FINDINGS AND ANALYSIS

Research Backgrounds

The 19 respondents interviewed were initially asked questions about their personal research backgrounds and current research endeavors. Subjects' descriptions of their areas of specialty in research varied greatly, with 11 respondents each citing at least four areas of specialty. Specialty areas included: rape and the psychological effects of crime; minorities' theories of adolescent delinquent behavior; qualitative social control; legal anthropology; comparative criminology; linguistics and social interaction in the courtroom; policing agencies; corrections and punishment; and crime-mapping.

Three of 19 interviewees strictly reported they specialized in quantitative research methods, while 5 stated that they specialized solely in qualitative research. Ten subjects responded that they engaged in both quantitative and qualitative research, and 4 stated they had only specifically analyzed archival data. Approximately half of the researchers (9 of 19) related that their research methods of specialty had changed over the years; several stated that they felt this was due to a turn in academic research toward qualitative data collection and analysis and away from quantitative research.

At the time of the interviews, 12 of 19 respondents expressed that they were currently engaged in qualitative research or "the original collection of data," as described by one male sociologist. Their research included fieldwork in foreign courts; interviews of battered women, police officers, and street gang members; and observations of middle-school students. Five researchers described their current studies as quantitative, including surveys of minority police officers and adolescent students, and data from school, police, and court records. Six interviewees described their current research as "archival" or "historical," such as that involving the secondary analysis of "banked" and "canned" crime statistics (existing data sets) from state or federal agencies and analysis of nineteenth-century newspaper articles. Eleven respondents reported they were currently involved in multiple studies, and 2 stated they had put their current research on hold due to administrative duties or personal reasons.

GENERAL ACCESSING ISSUES

Regardless of their research specialties or preferred research methods, all of the subjects interviewed reported they had been required to secure permission from a person or persons in order to access data for their current or previous studies. These gatekeepers have control over information or entry into the field and protect the data (Patton, 1990). Gatekeepers must first be identified and then contacted before data collection can begin. Interviewees also reported having to acquire approval or exemption from their universities' Institutional Review Board (IRB) before beginning research with human subjects. Academic researchers find it necessary to facilitate this process, and to overcome any barriers that might hinder their access to data.

IDENTIFICATION OF THE GATEKEEPERS

According to several interviewees, identifying the gatekeepers is a complicated process that requires them to learn from their prior research experiences. One female sociologist recalled that after she had successfully gained access to observe courtrooms in one city's jurisdiction, she attempted to utilize the same procedures to gain access to courts in another district. She related:

> In [the first jurisdiction], the head deputies had the power. I wanted to do the same thing in Chicago, and I found the head deputy and he seemed

> reluctant. Well, I finally realized I had originally gone to the wrong person . . . In Chicago, it's a fishing expedition to find the right person.

Other academic researchers reported they utilized their networking skills and personal acquaintances in order to identify gatekeepers. The interviewees described the efforts they made to contact former students, employers, relatives, mentors, and co-workers who might have knowledge of, or were personally known to, those in control of the data desired. A male sociologist recalled how he identified and then utilized his personal relationship with his uncle, a judge, in order to gain simple access to court transcripts. Another male criminologist discussed the complications involved in identifying the gatekeeper of local school records he wished to access. He explained:

> [The access] really took a long time, and it had to do with the changing of the guard of the school board, until I met a friend of mine at a Christmas party. She worked for the school board. She gave me the name of acting director of research and evaluation and I gave her my [business] card. The next day, he gave me a call and said come on in . . .

Many academic researchers offered diverse views of how gatekeepers should be identified and contacted. One male criminologist offered this advice:

> Go to the top [of the organization] first to get approval, and go through the proper channels. To interview correctional officers, I went through their union representatives.

Still, another male criminologist suggested:

> Meet a number of the individuals in the field to gain their confidence so the agency heads see a need [for the research]. Talk to the attorneys and police officers first, and later go to the judge so as to not cause complaints from the bottom [of the organization].

FACILITATING ACCESS TO DATA AND DATA SITES

After the identification of the official guardians of the data, academic researchers must next acquire their permission, as well as that of informants and the institutions' internal review boards to access data and data sites. Interviewees described several methods they have utilized to facilitate this process and related that the permission was secured through various procedures, including letter writing and obtaining active or passive (negative) consent of subjects. These practices required the researchers to have extensive knowledge of the data site and to present their studies to watchdogs and informants in a convincing and credible manner. Researchers also had to provide them with assurances of confidentiality or anonymity and the importance of the experts' work and the respondents' participation. One male criminologist described this process as the "staging or selling" of his research and explained:

> You really have to know the organization you research in. All the things happen around this knowledge. You have to know the ecology of the environment and stage your research around that. Integrate your research with the environment.

Several academic researchers similarly emphasized the importance of the investigators' understanding of the language and culture of the gatekeepers and informants at the data sites. A male anthropologist related:

> I always suggest you do a pilot project for ethnographic longitudinal research. You need to go to the [research site] and look around, read a lot about it and have a feeling of what life is like there. The more prepared, the better off you are.

Further, the same researcher recalled this about her field research in a foreign community:

> It's a country that very much takes pride in its Christian morality. I'm Jewish and people would ask me a lot of questions about it, but I didn't have to go to church on Sunday. I could use Sunday to transcribe tapes, while everyone else dutifully went to church.

Many interviewees stated they often hired students and assistants of different races and who possessed bilingual skills in order to facilitate access to informants and diverse gatekeepers. Researchers believed these practices permitted easier entries into the settings, provided them with the opportunity to show respect and legitimacy to the different cultures and environments, and allowed for more accurate data collection. A Caucasian, female criminologist reported she had hired an African American woman, an advanced undergraduate student, to conduct the interviews of minority respondents for one of her studies, and a bilingual Latino student to collect data in a Latino shelter. She explained:

> When you are looking at a more diverse population, I would really want to have some legitimate interviewers in the minds of the respondents. Otherwise, it just looks like "these white professors ripping us off."

A male sociologist similarly stated:

> Generally, it's good to have people of similar race or ethnicity collect data because they can relate better to the subjects if they speak the language and have the right style, but if you have people of a similar race or

> ethnicity that don't know how to handle themselves, that's not going to help you.

While recalling survey research he conducted of local high school students, another male sociologist concurred:

> I sent a White female undergraduate student to an all-Black high school and they expected a Black person. The teacher refused data collection at first, and I almost quit the research, but later got her permission. She was the last gatekeeper.

Several of the academic researchers also reported that their own gender or race, and the presentations of themselves to gatekeepers and informants, facilitated their ability to obtain permission to gain access to subjects. Interviewees explained that when they were of similar race or gender as the gatekeepers or the subjects in a specific setting, this added greater legitimacy and credibility to their research. According to Punch (1986), the researchers' sentiments are accurate in that successful access to data sites can be affected by many factors, including age, sex, status, and ethnic background (p. 23).

For example, a Caucasian, male sociologist stated that he felt both his race and gender facilitated his access to police department records because the department administration was predominantly made up of Caucasian males. An African American, female criminologist described her similar situation when gaining access to school records:

> The woman at the administrative position was an African American female who had just finished her dissertation herself. She understood the process of research and collecting data. I don't think I would have had as much support if it was someone else.

Furthermore, one Caucasian, female sociologist stated that her race influenced her access to court records and recalled: "By virtue of being white, I was considered part of the power structure. I could just go in and ask for any file I want and get it."

Regarding gender, a female anthropologist involved in research in a small, foreign community reflected: "Gender is an issue. In that society, it was very legitimate for a woman to be a student or teacher, and I was that." A male criminologist expressed similar feelings regarding his gender and access when he discussed his computer-related research: "I couldn't do it if I were a woman. Being a male in the computer stuff helps. It's a male world. We have things in common and [a] culture I could share with them."

Each academic researcher interviewed explained the importance of their utilization of networking skills and personal contacts in order to gain permission or approval from gatekeepers to access data. This use of personal networking has been discussed in previous literature (Gordon & Heinz, 1979;

DOC, 1972; Weiss, 1994; Westin & Baker, 1972) Several interviewees referred to the importance of "keeping in touch" with significant, employed student and agency contacts in such ways as sending Christmas cards, exchanging publications, and writing thank-you notes. Other researchers stressed the significance of "not burning any bridges" behind them after successfully gaining access to data sites as they might wish to access the same data sites for future research. Interviewees explained that networking allowed them to verify their identity and establish their credibility and legitimacy to the various guardians of the data. They described this practice as "having someone to vouch for you," "having someone to play the politics," and "using connections." As one male sociologist who gained access to records from a city's police headquarters suggested: "Have connections with the key people in law enforcement agencies. In Chicago, it's who you know that counts."

Academic researchers expressed that they related their connections to significant acquaintances to gatekeepers through the use of letters of approval or support of the research, "meeting people who seem to know people," and "throwing out names" of those already established or known in the setting. One female sociologist described how she felt networking allowed her access to the data site:

> I was in the master calendar court . . . I would just go in there and sit down and orient myself. I identified who the main players were and I introduced myself to [the prosecuting attorney] and asked if I could sit with him. He took me under his wing and I got to meet the judge. I also met three female attorneys . . . I wanted to do [research] on rape and one of the women came in to speak to my students, so I had a little connection. I called her and used her name later to get court transcripts.

A male social scientist seemed to agree:

> In order to get permission to look at [city] Police Department data, I needed permission from the Chief Judge. My access was contingent on getting a letter signed by the Chief Judge. I met with his administrator and brought my graduate student who already knew him and got permission. Connections really helped.

Each of the interviewees expressed that they felt their perceived levels of prestige, their reputations and "track records" as competent researchers, influenced their data access and often revolved around the assurances of confidentiality, protection, and anonymity given to watchdogs and subjects during previous studies. Many researchers related that they hoped and expected they had been perceived in the eyes of gatekeepers as "established and experienced," "a known quantity," "someone with clout," "a professional," "honest," and "nonthreatening." One female sociologist explained that since she had been in a setting before to collect data, and had not "run to the media" with any negative findings, she would most likely be given permission to access the environment again. A male criminologist further explained:

> I try to incorporate [the agency's] intentions and their questions into my research . . . and share draft and preliminary findings with [gatekeepers] and ask them, "what does this mean to you?" and then present the results fairly and evenly, and hopefully the results will have positive results . . . [so] as to not burn or blast the agencies.

Another criminal justice researcher expressed a similar view:

> So much of it [access] has to do with reputation. Critics would say I probably bend over backwards to protect the organization. I have been able to be critical and yet not blow the organization, the individuals, out of the water. A lot of it had to do with the presentations of the findings, where I explain why something didn't come out the way it was supposed to. I provide an "out" for the administration . . .

Additionally, many academic researchers reported how negotiating their roles as researchers, and the ways they presented themselves to informants and guardians of the data, influenced their ability to access information, as discussed in previous literature (David, 1980; Hagan, 1993; Patton, 1990; Punch, 1985). Some interviewees discussed how they often had to present themselves to gatekeepers as nonthreatening, agreeable, and accommodating. Furthermore, many researchers stated that they felt it was not of importance to reflect their own personal views and opinions of the research topic to the guardians of the data, but instead to appear open-minded and even somewhat naive. A male sociologist described how he generally presented himself to guardians:

> I explain who I am and what I am doing and seek to indicate that I am not completely naive or ignorant to what they are doing. I try to maintain the role of a competent, intelligent *student* as opposed to being a numbskull or a smart-ass. I try to approach the field reasonably blank, in that I have some background, but I'm not sure how things work in this particular setting.

A female sociologist similarly reflected about how she negotiated her role in a data setting to assure she received continued access from the judges and lawyers to observe courtroom activity:

> I could speak the court language. I didn't know too much, but I knew enough to legitimize myself. I had legitimized myself and they all assumed I was a young lawyer in training, because that seemed to be what I was doing there.

Academic researchers also expressed that funding or grant money, their affiliations with major universities, and the various ways they presented their studies facilitated their access to data and data sites. As one male social scientist studying juvenile police records stated:

> In the beginning, when you are dealing with police, it's the *presentation*, a certain amount of credibility and proof that you have the best interest of, if not the agency, the citizenry. You are not just going to go in there and write a paper and blow them off.

Many respondents explained that being able to inform guardians that their studies were funded by major granting agencies or institutions provided further legitimacy and credibility to their research. Punch (1986) described how this may be due to researchers being seen by gatekeepers as "extensions of their political sponsors within the setting" (p. 22). A male sociologist stated that on one occasion he felt the only reason he had successfully gained access to police department records was due to the fact that he could declare his research was funded by the Illinois Criminal Justice Information Authority, an independent state agency that provides criminal justice grant administration. Similarly, one female criminologist explained:

> You need institutional affiliation, and credentials were important—credentials from your university and other agencies and legitimate documents stating this. I had full grant approval. I had this certificate stating I was a student of [the university] and a letter of recommendation from the faculty there.

Other researchers seemed to agree. A male sociologist stated:

> A letter explaining what you are up to is important, but not just any letter. It has to have legitimacy and credibility, in that it needs to come from the university, and needs to come from a certain person at the university, someone with clout. Someone who is saying "this is a legitimate study and we support it."

Further, a female criminologist expressed her view:

> I think it helps just coming from a university. [Gatekeepers] feel glad that someone has recognized their expertise and the institution validates things for them.

Interviewees related they often had to present their research as "mutually profitable" or "worthwhile" to the guardians of the data and subjects to gain continued access to a data site. The researchers explained they also had to convince the gatekeepers of the importance of their research and justifications for requiring access to data requested. Several interviewees stated they did this by producing an ongoing product, and sharing drafts and preliminary results. A male sociologist expressed how he presented his research to gatekeepers of school data: "I try to convince people that it is an honor to be associated with my research and to be one of the sites selected. I discuss how the study will benefit *them*." Another male sociologist stated similarly:

> Make them believe that this is honestly and sincerely a mutually profitable transaction. To that end, I've indicated I'm more than happy to send them articles or copies of whatever I've prepared.

Some of the academic researchers suggested other techniques they utilized occasionally to facilitate their access to data sites, such as paying subjects money or providing gifts for their information, or citing various acts [i.e., the Freedom of Information Act (1975)], which may ensure successful access to some agency records. A female researcher noted how one of her colleagues researching in a school district had bought each of the elementary school children small trinkets in order to get them to willingly participate in her survey research. A male sociologist reflected his personal techniques to gain access to gang members:

> We are essentially providing them a service. We have paid them $25.00 for a two-hour interview, but we really help them get jobs, go to court with them, or we've counseled them.

Essentially, the academic researchers interviewed reported several similar procedures and practices they have utilized in order to facilitate their access to data and data sites. Each also found it necessary to use these various techniques to overcome hurdles that hinder, delay, or impede access to data or settings.

BARRIERS INVOLVED IN ACCESSING DATA

Academic researchers described four major types of barriers that affected their access to data and data sites: gatekeepers, institutional barriers, organizational hindrances, and personal obstacles. Each of the academic researchers interviewed explained that they found the various gatekeepers of data and data settings to be significant hurdles necessary to overcome in order to gain access to data. These guardians seek to protect information and have regularly imposed guidelines and restrictions on the researchers in order to assure the anonymity and confidentiality of the informants, subjects, and themselves (Babbie, 1992; Bower & de Gasparis, 1978; Hagan, 1993; Punch, 1986; Westin & Baker, 1972). Interviewees often referred to the gatekeepers' impositions as "extreme" and "products of paranoia," but admitted they were necessary for a society to provide and allow free access of sensitive or private information. A male sociologist explained further:

> The most difficult part of gathering data in this field is getting access through the justice system. A lot of trust is involved. I think the police are particularly suspicious that whatever it is you collect will be used against them.

A male criminologist attempting to access police records disclosed he actually "took the data anyway" when its guardians refused access, but reported he used the findings positively. The majority of the researchers, however, discussed the practices and procedures they used to comply with and submit to the gatekeepers' commands for anonymity and confidentiality, such as obtaining informed consent of the subjects, utilizing anonymous collection of data, signing waivers, or having questions available for the gatekeepers in advance of the data collection. Interviewees reported they must convince the guardians of their intentions to assure confidentiality and anonymity, regardless of how it may influence their research goals. A male sociologist stated:

> I develop gradually, over a period of several phone calls, a research relationship of which I manage to convince them that I am involved in research and I will honor their confidentiality. That I will respect things that they ask me or tell me.

One male sociologist studying urban gangs recalled his efforts to honor the anonymity of his subjects:

> Many years ago we got subpoenas from the Senate subcommittee to turn over the data [names of subjects and their criminal behavior] we were collecting. They wanted to use the data to put people away. We told them we would cut out the identifying information from the research automatically.

According to the academic researchers interviewed, gatekeepers seemed to fear most that the researchers would report negative findings to the media and "burn" or "blast" the agencies if they allow access to their information. Many interviewees reported that when they first entered a data site, they often were mistaken for journalists or reporters and, therefore, found it necessary to convince gatekeepers of their research intentions. A female criminologist stated she often knew someone from the agency, before requesting access to their data, who could "vouch" for her credibility to provide assurance that she wasn't "some kind of professor in this ivory tower that was going to exploit someone." A male sociologist advised:

> What those researchers starting out have to understand is that these are difficult issues to people inside the agencies. The media takes things and blows them out of shape . . . People are very concerned about, in particular, those who aren't accountable to them in any way, and this is problematic.

Another male criminologist described his similar view:

> Whenever possible, developing personal relationships [with gatekeepers] becomes crucial. People will give you data if they like you. Have a mutually supportive relationship and they will put their guard down against their biggest fear—that academics will bite them, in that we are like reporters, we have tenure, so we don't care about other people losing their jobs.

Interviewees also described how certain gatekeepers and respondents in the agencies or settings have delayed or impeded their access to the data due to their perceived incompetence, unfriendliness, or irresponsibility. An anthropologist recalled some of her experiences while conducting fieldwork in a foreign community:

> I occasionally ran into the passive-aggressive librarian, and the problem was only overcome by the help of the locals. Eventually she got a phone call that she was going to stop doing this. I knew a more important government official that was going to make sure I got access.

The same researcher recalled a similar situation when she encountered a registrar who wanted to charge her $10.00 per search for the court records. The anthropologist explained that she called the chief magistrate and he "took care" of the problem. Further, a male sociologist described the delays that occurred when he accessed data from his respondents, male prostitutes:

> The male prostitutes were undependable. I couldn't count on them to show up, being sober, to be responsive. It took 28 months to interview 28 people. It was like getting blood out of a turnip.

The academic researchers interviewed discussed several other barriers that delayed or impeded their access to data and data fields for their studies. Institutional barriers, as described by the interviewees, consisted of bureaucratic "red tape" or runarounds researchers encountered from agencies, bureaucracies, the government, their own academic institutions, and other regulatory systems. These obstacles included the confidentiality restrictions imposed by guardians in institutional review boards at universities, various governmental privacy acts, and the anonymity or confidentiality-based restrictions imposed at the data sites by agencies' gatekeepers and administrators. Many researchers cited these hurdles as the most time-consuming and difficult to overcome. This was often due to the sensitive nature of the data they wished to access and the gatekeepers' or guardians' fears that access, if allowed, might be too intrusive, uncover negative findings, or violate subjects' rights to privacy. A male social scientist stated his views:

> It is very time-consuming to get access to a bureaucracy. It takes an awful lot of time to get any kind of decision out of a bureaucracy. It's not their

> priority to give [this researcher] information. What they are doing is making sure their butts are covered. If it's one thing I learned by working with agencies, it's "CYA—cover your ass."

A male sociologist observing junior high school students further explained some gatekeepers' fears:

> School boards are swinging back to the right. They do not want their children's privacy jeopardized . . . in every case, the principals want parental consent. They see [research] as an intrusion by liberal academics, and principals also have to worry about the image of their school.

Therefore, in order to successfully access data and data settings, researchers are forced to comply with gatekeepers' restrictions, agencies' rules, and governmental or institutional regulations and statutes through various practices or techniques. A female criminologist surveying elementary school students discussed her efforts to overcome the restrictions imposed on her by her university's Institutional Review Board (IRB):

> Anytime you deal with a school system, you deal with a protected population. I went to survey the schools and got a low response rate the first time, because the IRB wanted consent forms. I went back to the IRB to see if I could get around them. It was very difficult. I had to get my chairperson to petition the IRB. They finally agreed on implied consent of the students and that way I got a better response rate.

Other researchers recalled similar situations when forced to abide by the regulations imposed on them by their universities' institutional review boards. A male sociologist stated his views:

> I know the rules, I mean, I served on the IRB. In many cases they are trying to rewrite the research proposals and imagine every little thing that could go wrong. I get very frustrated with [the IRB] and I'm one of the people that comply with the rules . . . It's particularly frustrating for students to work with the IRB, because students are often only working on a project for a few months or a year and don't have time to get jerked around.

Each of the academic researchers interviewed also presented several organizational barriers that have hindered or impeded their access to data and data sites. These obstacles seem to be created by the conditions at each specific data setting, field, or site. For example, interviewees discussed the organizational barriers involved with "fitting in" with the people or employees of the agencies or data fields, and "going around their schedules" while accessing data. Researchers repeatedly mentioned how "busy" their subjects were and how the intrusiveness of their research could potentially, but understandably, affect their access to data. A female anthropologist stated that during one previous study, her only problem with accessing interview data from lawyers was the fact that they were always so busy, although willing to speak with her. One female criminologist recalled:

> My dissertation data was at a maximum security prison and my advisor was the director of research at that facility. I was immediately able to come into the setting, but I still had to get along with people and not do things that would upset them. I had to obey all the rules that come in a maximum security organization. You have to present yourself in a professional manner and fit into the routine.

Researchers noted that their research could potentially disrupt the research setting, and discussed how intrusive and interfering data collection could be when accessing information from school children and in educational settings. For example, a female criminologist stated, "You have to have support from the teachers because you may have to interfere with instructional time." Another male sociologist similarly explained, "If researchers came into the schools for every little issue, there wouldn't be any time left to teach!"

The academic researchers also discussed the organizational barriers that revolved around the internal or external politics of the data sites they attempted to access data from. Previously, Gordon and Heinz (1979) found that many bureaucratic agencies often claimed they felt politically threatened (externally) at the time of the request for access and, therefore, denied or delayed the access of data (pp. 200–207, 280). The researchers interviewed described similar experiences. Political issues within the agencies stemmed from such situations as media attacks, criminal or other investigations, the hiring, firing, and promotions of employees within the organizations, and others. On several occasions, these political wars were so influential and powerful, they obstructed the researchers' access to the data. Most attempts were successful only because the researchers utilized the various practices discussed earlier to overcome the political obstacles. A male criminologist remembered his efforts to access police department records:

> I wanted to do some research in the [city] Police Department so I wrote a letter to the Chief and didn't get a response. So, I wrote another letter and I got a negative response. This was because there was a Presidential Commission looking at police agencies . . . they had the expectation that they would be treated in some degree with confidentiality and anonymity, but there was an article written that stated that this and that thing was done in [the city]. So they were not really willing to work with new people at that time.

A criminologist recalled his similar experience when attempting to access police data:

> When we made a request to the [city] police department, they said that we could not come in and do this. And it came down and became evident why this was so: the police department was then in the midst of a struggle with the people in the legislature who were battling in court over monetary issues.

Another female sociologist encountered the same problems:

> Around juvenile court I kept hearing "Greylord" [an infamous scandal involving the bribery of county judges]. Someone did tell me that I couldn't get into [agency X], but the [agency Y] office is dying for someone to look at their files. But [agency X] is under public scrutiny . . . it's just quirky. This is to me, paranoia. A lot of it is how you introduce yourself. Don't use the wrong name or nobody will talk to you.

This same sociologist, however, did recall a study where she utilized her networking skills in order overcome a political hurdle in a courtroom setting:

> Some [gatekeepers] were cold and some were nice. People kept assuming that I was a journalist and they were having internal political problems. I couldn't originally get into [city], because the head deputy I had talked to had been punished, and he thought I was sent from downtown to watch him. I needed to get permission from on high. My brother-in-law's sister had been a secretary in the district attorney's office for years and years, and she told me who to call. I called him, and he had a daughter who went to [the researcher's university] and we chatted and he said I could go anywhere I want.

Interviewees also presented organizational barriers that dealt with the conditions of the data accessed. They discussed lost and missing records, the absence of information in files, incomplete and inaccurate data, and disorganized and unkempt files, mainly when accessing police, court, and prison records. As a result, and in order to assure the quality, accuracy, and validity of their data, the researchers had to gain access to data from several different sources and crossreference data. These practices added to the time needed to conduct research and access data.

In addition to the three types of barriers presented, the interviewees discussed personal obstacles they found necessary to overcome to access data and data sites. These hindrances dealt with the inner and private constraints experienced personally by each researcher. The majority of this sample reported that the most significant obstacle to accessing data was the tremendous amount of time it took to gain approval from their Institutional Review Boards and then to gain access through gatekeepers. Researchers implied they felt pressured and experienced stress while gaining access to data. This was not only because "data ages so quickly," as a female criminologist stated, but also because accessing the data adds to the time taken away from other affairs in their lives. A male sociologist explained:

> What inhibits research? Families. We have a lot of people that do their thing, get tenure, and kick back. The successful people I know really put in the hours for their research.

Another male sociologist agreed:

> A barrier that comes up is trying to manage several things at one time. When you are trying to do research, teach, and do committee work, it's really hard to keep things going. And some people are better at doing it then others. I take pride in what I do, but I do have a life outside of my work.

Other personal barriers that hindered their successful research included inadequate research training and a lack of mentoring for their studies. Furthermore, most of the interviewees expressed that their abilities to gain access to data successfully came with much time and experience as they became "seasoned veterans" in their fields of research.

CHANGES IN ACCESSING DATA

The academic researchers were asked if their attempts at gaining access to data and data sites have changed as they have matured as researchers and what they might do differently next time. In general, interviewees report that as they became more seasoned researchers, they recognized "stumbling blocks" more quickly and, therefore, are more patient, careful, open-minded, and allow for more time to gain access to data.

They also presented several techniques and practices they have acquired and will implement in future studies, such as negotiating their research roles by appearing more naive and less coercive to gatekeepers, or advertising in newspapers to secure subjects. Most interviewees stated they would use more personal contacts and connections, and apply for additional funding. Several members of the sample also reported that they now do more "homework" and "groundwork" before attempting to gain access to data; they learn more about the environment in which they wish to do research.

A few of the interviewees also reflected that they may utilize the advances made in computer software and Internet communications to facilitate their future access to data. Essentially, each of the academic researchers interviewed stated that they would and have changed their practices and procedures for gaining access to data and data sites to overcome previous problems they encountered. These changes seemed to be made regardless of the fact that the interviewees' past experiences when gaining access to data have primarily been successful.

CONCLUSIONS

The purpose of this study was to understand how academic researchers in criminal justice and related fields gain access to data and data sites for their studies. Nineteen academic researchers from four Illinois universities were interviewed to examine the procedures and practices they utilize to facilitate research and to overcome problems they encountered. General accessing issues, different techniques to gain access, and future research strategies were discussed.

Results revealed all the academic researchers first needed permission from a gatekeeper, and often their subjects, to gain access to data or data fields. This required them to learn about the field or setting, to identify gatekeepers, and to utilize various techniques to gain permission. Interviewees discussed how they negotiated their personal roles, used their networking skills, and presented themselves and their studies professionally and prestigiously to convince gatekeepers and informants of their credibility and legitimacy. They also made assurances of confidentiality and anonymity.

This research also examined the barriers researchers face and the procedures utilized to gain access to data. Four main types of the obstacles have been examined. Wary gatekeepers were seen by the researchers as significant hurdles due to the restrictions they imposed on the researchers and their fears of exposure of negative results. Interviewees discussed institutional barriers, such as various bureaucratic "red tape," privacy acts, and confidentiality-based rules, that delayed or impeded their access to data. Organizational obstacles were presented that revolved around the personnel and politics of the data sites, the condition of the data, and the intrusiveness of the researchers' data collection and procedures. The personal obstacles described by the interviewees included time constraints and the lack of training. This study also briefly presented the changes in procedures the researchers anticipate they will make in the future.

Although the researchers came from various educational institutions, disciplinary backgrounds, and research specialties, essentially all the interviewees reported similar practices and problems encountered when accessing data and data sites for their studies. Each of the academic researchers interviewed reported methods they have changed, or would change, in gaining access in future studies. Notably, however, in very few instances did researchers report they have failed to achieve access to the data desired. Academic researchers have learned from experience as they have matured in their fields and have acquired the skills to do what it takes to gain access to data and data sites successfully, regardless of the significant time and effort involved. As one male sociologist stated, "It's a hassle to get good data, and expensive, and troublesome, and it's a lot of dirty, hard work."

The results of this study should be beneficial to academic researchers in all fields of research, particularly to those approaching their first field experience. The study provided techniques, such as role negotiation, to facilitate access and overcome common barriers, such as organizational obstacles, that many researchers may encounter, as discussed by previous researchers (Gordon & Heinz, 1979; Patton, 1990; Punch, 1986; Wilson & Smith, 1983). This research also provided other procedures utilized to gain access to data, as related by academic researchers themselves. Therefore, academic researchers should be both forewarned of the barriers to accessing data for research, and encouraged by the fact that through persistence and proper techniques, access to data and data sites can be achieved. Essentially, the present study provided an improved understanding of how academic researchers gain access to data for their research endeavors, which may allow future researchers to address such situations and facilitate access to data.

Conclusions derived from this study are limited as a result of the sampling methods utilized to access the 19 academic researchers from four Illinois universities. Specifically, the sample was formed through my own local and personal contacts, as well as recommendations from these respondents. Further, the sample only included researchers working in academic settings. The student status of my position and research imposed time constraints on the persons who could be interviewed. Consequently, if the study had been conducted with a larger and more diverse sample, in an extended geographical area, and using a random sample, the data may have yielded different results.

Researchers must keep in mind that they may have been denied access to data that, if collected, would have materially changed their results. In fact, it may well be that this study is limited to only that information that I was able to obtain from respondents. For example, the one researcher who denied me access may have had important information for this study. Therefore, access to data is essential in the pursuit of knowledge in the fields of criminal justice and related social science areas (David, 1980). However, a balance needs to be maintained between the privacy of information and accessibility of data for research purposes.

REFERENCES

Attorney General's Advocacy Institute, Office of Legal Education. (1989, September). *The freedom of information act for attorneys and access professionals.* Washington, DC: U.S. Department of Justice.

Babbie, E. (1992). *The practice of social research.* Belmont, CA: Wadsworth.

Boruch, R.F., & Cecil, J.S. (1979). *Assuring confidentiality of social research data.* Philadelphia, PA: University of Pennsylvania Press.

Bower, R.T., & de Gasparis, P. (1978). *Ethics in social research: Protecting the interests of human subjects.* New York: Praeger.

Briggs, C.L. (1986). *Learning how to ask: A sociolinguistic appraisal of the role of the interview in social science research.* New York: Cambridge University Press.

Bureau of Justice Statistics. (1980). *An analysis of privacy issues: Privacy and security of criminal history information.* Washington, DC: U.S. Department of Justice.

———. (1981). *Privacy and security of criminal history information: Guide to record review and challenge*. Washington, DC: U.S. Department of Justice.

Charmaz, K. (1983). Grounded theory method: An explication and interpretation. In R.E. Emerson (Ed.), *Contemporary Field Research*, pp. 109–126. Boston: Little, Brown.

David, M.H. (1980). Access to data: The frustration and utopia of the researcher. *Review of Public Data Use*, *8*(4), 327–337.

Department of Communications, Department of Justice. (1972). *Privacy and computers*. Ottawa: Information Canada.

Duncan, G.T., Jabine, T.B., & de Wolf, V.A. (Eds.). (1993). *Private lives and public policies: Confidentiality and accessibility of government statistics*. Committee on National Statistics, Panel on Confidentiality and Data Access. Washington DC: National Research Council.

Emerson, R.M. (1983). *Contemporary field research*. Boston: Little, Brown.

Gordon, A.C., & Heinz, J.P. (1979). *Public access to information*. New Jersey: Transaction Books.

Hagan, F.E. (1993). *Research methods in criminal justice and criminology*. (3rd. ed.). New York: Macmillan.

Juvenile records and record-keeping systems. (1988). Washington, DC: U.S. Department of Justice, Bureau of Justice Statistics/SEARCH Group, Inc.

Maltz, M.D. (1976). Privacy, criminal records, and information systems. In S. Brounstein & M. Kamrass (Eds.), *Operations research in law enforcement, justice, and social security*, pp. 247–261. Lexington, MA: Lexington Books.

O'Brien, D.M. (1981). *The public's right to know: The Supreme Court and the first amendment*. New York: Praeger.

Office of Justice Programs, Bureau of Justice Statistics. (1991). *Assessing completeness and accuracy of criminal history record systems: Audit guide*. Washington, DC: SEARCH/The National Consortium for Justice Information and Statistics.

———. (1991). *Statutes requiring the use of criminal history record information*. Washington, DC: SEARCH Group, Inc.

———. (1992). *Criminal history record information: Compendium of state privacy and security legislation*. Washington, DC: SEARCH/The National Consortium for Justice Information and Statistics.

Patton, M.Q. (1990). *Qualitative evaluation and research methods*. (2nd. ed.) Thousand Oaks, CA: Sage.

Punch, M. (1986). The politics and ethics of fieldwork. In *Sage University series on qualitative research methods, vol. 3*. Thousand Oaks, CA: Sage.

Sanjek, R. (Ed.). (1990). *Fieldnotes: The makings of anthropology*. New York: Cornell University Press.

Weiss, R.S. (1994). *Learning from strangers: The art and method of qualitative interview studies*. New York: Macmillan.

Westin, A.F., & Baker, M.A. (1972). *Data banks in a free society: Computers, record-keeping, and privacy*. New York: Quadrangle Books.

Wilson, O.H., & Smith, W.J. (1983). *Access to tax records for statistical purposes*. Alexandria, VA: American Statistical Association.